LIVING FAITH

LIVING FAITH

Belief and Doubt in a Perilous World

Jacques Ellul

Translated by Peter Heinegg

WIPF & STOCK · Eugene, Oregon

Wipf and Stock Publishers
199 W 8th Ave, Suite 3
Eugene, OR 97401

Living Faith
Belief and Doubt in a Perilous World
By Ellul, Jacques and Gill, David W.
Copyright©1983 Les Editions de la Table Ronde
ISBN 13: 978-1-60608-979-8
Publication date 6/15/2012
Previously published by Harper and Row, 1983

JACQUES ELLUL LEGACY SERIES FOREWORD

Jacques Ellul was born (January 6, 1912), died (May 19, 1994), and lived most of his years, in Bordeaux, near the Atlantic Coast of southwest France. In a fascinating life that included participation in the Resistance to Nazi Germany and the collaborating Vichy regime, his primary institutional connections were (1) the University of Bordeaux, where he served from 1946 to 1980 as Professor of the History and Sociology of Institutions in the Faculty of Law and Economic Sciences and held a chair in the Institute for Political Studies, and (2) the Reformed Church of France, the heirs of the Huguenots. In addition to his academic work in history and sociology leading to the doctorate, Ellul was a well-educated theologian and biblical scholar, having completed the whole seminary curriculum except the final capstone exercise with the Strasbourg faculty (displaced to southern France during the Occupation). For more than forty years Ellul served not just the University as a distinguished professor but also the Reformed Church, not just on various committees and commissions but, most significantly, in the local parishes, among the people, as a teacher, preacher, worship leader, and pastor/mentor.

Jacques Ellul's first published book (other than his academic theses) appeared in 1946: The Theological Foundation of Law (French edition 1946, English translation 1960). His most durable little classic on Christian faith and discipleship in the modern world, Presence of the Kingdom, appeared in 1948 in French and was his first book to appear in English (1951). It has remained in print to the present. Ellul's best known and most influential book has been The Technological Society (French 1954, English 1964). This sociological and historical study of the nature and broad-ranging impact of technique/technology on human life has sold well over 100,000 copies. All told, Ellul published fifty books in his life time, thirty of which were translated into English, but less than a half-dozen of which (in English) have remained in print in recent years. These numbers need to be qualified slightly by the observation that sometimes, some multivolume works were bound together in France but published separately in English, or vice versa. A few Ellul manuscripts have been published since his death in 1994. Some collections of Ellul articles have been published in recent years as new "books" by Ellul.

For at least two big reasons, Wipf & Stock's commitment to publishing the work of Jacques Ellul in English translation is to be enthusiastically welcomed. First, if not the most important 20th century critic and analyst of the impact of technology on human existence, Ellul is certainly near the top of any top-ten list along with Heidegger, Grant, Borgmann, Mumford, McLuhan, Postman, Mitcham and whoever your favorites are.

Ellul started writing about technique/technology as a general phenomenon and in its profound impacts on politics, the state, economics, communications, art, religion, warfare and the other domains of life as early as the 1930s. His most famous book The Technological Society (1954; English 1964), praised by author Aldous Huxley for "making the case I tried to make in Brave New World, remains in print even today. Technological Society was followed by The Technological System and then The Technological Bluff, but even these three big volumes barely open the Ellulian analysis that includes such studies as The Political Illusion, Propaganda: The Formation of Men's Attitudes, Autopsy of Revolution, The Humiliation of the Word, The New Demons, and Betrayal of the West. The sheer scope of Ellul's critical perspective earns him a loud and well-deserved "Bravo" from those of us who think about these issues.

Along with the breadth of Ellul's critique of technological civilization, though, is its remarkable depth. Unlike many writers in our myopic age, Ellul was a first-rate historian. His five-volume Histoire des Institutions, long a standard textbook series in France, is exhibit one. But in virtually all of his works Ellul does not just describe what is; he explores what was, and how that helps us understand not only what is but what could be. And while he is a historian of the west, first of all, his knowledge of our civilization antecedents in Egypt, the Arab world, Asia, and Africa adds richness to the texture of his critique that is rarely found in others.

Is technology any less a driver of 21st century human existence than it was in the 20th century? Hardly. Our era of the internet, social media, advanced robotics and biotechnology begs for the kind of historically-anchored depth analysis that Ellul's works empower.

The second great reason for Ellul's ongoing importance is his radical theological and ethical perspective. At first, students of Ellul's sociological critique of technique may set aside his biblical and theological writings as the pious asides of a traditional believer. But nothing could be further from the truth. If his sociological critique is critically important in today's discussions, it is absolutely the same for the critical importance of his theological perspective. In the presence of the sterility and impotence of much of the theological left and the idolatry and betrayal of much of the theological right, Ellul introduces a cross-cutting, third way that is deeply grounded in and creatively inspired by the Word in Jesus Christ and Scripture. His theology, biblical exposition, and ethics all breathe the fire of the prophets and the enthusiasm of the evangelists. He unmasks the "new demons" that have taken over our sacred thrones in a post-Christian world. He overturns the money-changers' tables in today's temples. He challenges all traditional, self-justifying exploitations of scripture.

Some references in Ellul's theological writings are to events and leaders of the late 20th century which have receded from our view.

But the problems he addresses are precisely the same: conformity to the world, uncritical embrace of means and methods that enslave us, and the demise of authentic faith and hope. In an era in which many Christian voices challenge us just to sprint harder to keep up with the latest fad or tool, this radical biblical teaching is a soul-strengthening diet.

So two contributions: the sociological critique of technology and the biblical theological account of radical discipleship in the world. What has to be said at the end is that the dialectic which Ellul establishes between the two is the dialectic of life and freedom. These are not to be thought of as parallel lines that never meet. They meet, as Ellul often said, not in an intellectual resolution but in an existential resolution. In other words, it is in our daily life that the sobering insight of the technological critique and the bold call to radical faith and hope can be lived out in a life of freedom and relationship. For facilitating and enabling this renewed hearing of the Bordeaux herald of the way, the truth, and the life, all of us can be most grateful to Wipf & Stock Publishers.

David W. Gill, Ph.D.
President, International Jacques Ellul Society
Professor of Ethics, Gordon-Conwell Theological Seminary
South Hamilton, Massachusetts
May 2011

For my grandchildren,
Wim and Eric,
Mikal, Tikwa, Joanne,
and Raphael;
one day, perhaps,
they will encounter Jesus Christ
in this book,
in fellowship with their
grandfather.

Contents

Author's Note

This book—essay, meditation, act of commitment—is neither an autonomous work nor a creation *ex nihilo*. It comes from a certain environment, with roots of its own, which I must inform readers about right from the start. It has deep and distant roots, by which it is nourished in the ever fertile soil of Søren Kierkegaard and Karl Barth; other classic theologians are of less consequence here. But the book also has more immediate roots. It makes reference to three works I consider fundamental, three works which, although they come from totally different directions, I believe converge perfectly. They are, in chronological order: Ronze's trilogy, *L'Homme de quantité* (1976), *L'Homme de foi* (1977), *L'Homme de Dieu* (1978); Jean Sulivan's latest book, the overwhelming *L'Exode* (1979); and the brilliant synthesis by Bernard Charbonneau, *Je fus—Essai sur la liberté* (1980). These are my three modern sources. I have not yet slaked my thirst in them.

INTRODUCTION

by David W. Gill
Associate Professor of Christian Ethics
New College Berkeley

You hold in your hands a bombshell. *Living Faith* is not another "nice" description of "simple Christian faith." Nor, despite its size, is it an exhaustive, definitive encyclopedia on the topic of faith. Rather, this is the message of a modern-day prophet standing on the edge of both society and church. *Living Faith* is no less than a massive, fiery challenge to all who have ears to hear, to all who are willing to rethink the meaning of faith.

Jacques Ellul, recently retired from his post as Professor of the History and Sociology of Institutions at the University of Bordeaux in France, continues his lifelong quest to describe the reality of our society and the truth of the Word of God. Half of his forty books have probed the nature of politics and Technique ("raving rationalism") in our era. The other half wrestle with Scripture, theology, and ethics. Neither of these two tasks is carried out without relation to the other, however, Ellul's study of faith is carried out in full engagement with the politicized, technicized milieu in which it must exist.

Ellul is convinced that the Pauline "virtues" of faith, hope, and love provide the best summary of the Christian life as it is offered in biblical revelation, and thus his consideration of faith is intended to be taken as part of a threefold study. He has written on *Hope in Time of Abandonment*, and a companion volume on the ethical implications of hope has been published as *The Ethics of Freedom*. Ellul is currently finishing his study of *The Ethics of Holiness*, an ethics implied by faith. The study of love and its "ethics of relationship" remains on his agenda.

Ellul wrote on hope and freedom first, because he believes these are the greatest needs in our hopeless era; and the present volume frequently recalls themes from those earlier works. But it remains true that, biblically, faith is the most prominent. For every reference to hope, the Bible has six references to faith. For every reference to love there are two references to faith. "In the Gospel is revealed a righteousness that is by faith from first to last" (Rom. 1:17, NIV). "When the Son of Man comes, will he find faith on the earth?" (Luke 18:8). "Without faith it is impossible to please God" (Heb. 11:6). "With faith all things are possible" (Mark 9:23). From the perspective of the biblical canon alone, we do well to consider and reconsider the meaning of faith.

Hope, for Ellul, is seizing God's future. It is the transfer of loyalty and citizenship from the present age to the coming Kingdom of God. The ethics of hope is an eschatological ethics wherein good and evil are defined by God's final judgment, now revealed in the Bible. God responds to our movement of hope by granting us freedom in relation to the present age. Thus we have an ethics of freedom. Faith, then, arises from hearing the Word of God in Jesus Christ. It binds us to Jesus Christ and separates us from our milieu and from other competing gods. God responds to this faith by making us holy, sanctified, different—the salt of the earth, the light of the world, sheep among wolves. Love, however, thrusts us back into the world, back into relationship with our neighbors. The ethics of love is the ethics of the renewed and restored relationship. Love cannot be truly Christian unless it is part of this dialectic with faith. Separation and relationship go

together, and both are incorporated in the gift of freedom.
Thus Ellul's consideration of faith grows out of a robust biblical formulation and is intended not to stand on its own but
to be taken as part of the threefold pattern described above.

If the Bible itself impels Ellul to the study of faith, it is
equally true that the character of our age and its perils urges
this study, for two reasons. First, the world is in a very sorry
condition. In Part 3 of this volume, Ellul describes in lurid
colors the horrors, planned and unplanned, that beset the
world. Political strife, wars, the threat of nuclear catastrophe,
ecological disasters, poverty, hunger, repression, meaning-
lessness, and anxiety—the catalog is awesome. We need
"critical distance" and a "cosmic lever" to be budged from
this sad situation and avert our self-made doom. Recalling
this catalog of horrors is an important exercise, for we have
become so numb that more often than not we repress these
items from our consciousness. Ellul helps us to face up to
reality.

Second, despite the vast amount of recent, self-indulgent
"testimony" literature, as well as more serious studies of
faith, there is great confusion over what faith is, and what it
is not. The dialog between Monos and Una in Part 1 is an
extended demonstration of the confusion about faith and belief in the modern world. This confusion hardly helps to al-
leviate the impending disasters. Do we search for precise,
restrictive definitions of faith and then despair of what we
find (Monos)? Or do we accept more eclectic definitions and
verge on naiveté (Una)? The message of Part 1 is that clarity
is absent on the present scene; we are often left to muddle
through with our unanswered questions.

As in his work on hope (and much of his other work), Ellul
adopts the stance and the style of the prophet. He stands
"over against" the world and the Church (or at least the
theologians). Like Søren Kierkegaard (whom Ellul cites as

the best teacher on this subject), Ellul often displays uncon-
cealed anger and sarcasm. His disappointment over the absence of true faith (as earlier over the absence of hope) borders
on depression. Then suddenly hope appears. Faith is possible
after all. This is an intensely personal record of one modern
intellectual's struggle with faith. Ellul lays down a decisive
challenge to his readers to rethink the meaning of faith—and
not just in abstract intellectual categories. He drives us toward
concreteness and the presence of authentic faith in the midst
of the real world.

Sandwiched between the dialog of Monos and Una on the
meaning of faith in Part 1, and the extended reflection on the
nature of the modern world in Part 3, Ellul provides his own
critical understanding of faith in Part 2. For the sake of study
he stipulates definitions of belief and faith to describe what he
sees as two very different phenomena. Following Ludwig
Feuerbach, Karl Marx, and Karl Barth, Ellul argues that
there is a thoroughly human phenomenon which he here calls
belief. This is fundamental to the phenomenon of religion.
The New Demons is worth consulting for further study of the
sacred, myth, and religion. Belief, in Ellul's sense, is a general phenomenon of human experience. It is irrational or non-
rational at its origins, but it is necessary to supply answers to
our questions about human existence. It joins together communities and provides a basis for social groups. It tends to
combat and exclude doubt. Belief is fundamental not just in
traditional forms of religion but in today's "religions" of politics, science, and technique. Our intellectual presuppositions,
personal relations, and confidence are based on this kind of
belief structure. But, with Feuerbach, Ellul says we are
merely creating gods to answer our needs.

In contrast to belief, thus defined, is faith. Faith is specific,
rather than general. Its home is revelation rather than religion. It participates in God's questioning of us rather than

our own questioning. "Who do you say that I am?" "Whom do you seek?" "Where are you?" "What have you done to your brother?" These biblical questions get at the heart of faith's origin, which is God speaking to us. Faith, then, is hearing this God who addresses me. In this hearing we are separated, set apart by the Wholly Other God we now hear. The solitude of life in this world is broken by the voice of God. And it is in this break that the possibility of life, love, and hope can once again penetrate our existence. Our world is closed in upon itself in a vicious cycle of forces out of control. The Word of God breaks through this bondage and despair with a promise embedded in the threat, "Yet forty days and Ninevah will be destroyed." Ultimately the salvation of Ninevah is possible, but only through the faith that comes by hearing. With that faith, all things become possible again.

It is important to read Ellul with full appreciation of his genre, which is prophetic challenge, not systematic rigor. Readers will discover that Ellul occasionally outdoes himself with overstatement and heavy-handed criticism; not all the French thinkers with whom he is in direct dialog will be immediately recognizable to American readers; elements of his biblical exegesis can be challenged. Some readers will miss Ellul's claim that he is not advocating a resuscitated Protestant individualism in his call for individual faith. Others, in their attention to the despairing world situation he describes at length, will miss his profound hope.

Nevertheless, Ellul makes at least three contributions that should not be missed in this volume. First, he makes vast strides toward a better understanding of faith (especially given the confusion that prevails on the subject). Second, he continues his lifelong attempt to move beyond abstract orthodoxy to concrete engagement with the world. Faith is not merely a private movement, without regard to the world around us, but lives and moves and has its being in concrete encounter with God and then with our neighbor and the forces of society. Finally, Jacques Ellul continues to stress that he does not have the final word on either the world or the Word. His study of faith, like all of his work, constitutes an implicit challenge to go beyond the author, to think through the topic for oneself, to reflect more and better on the subject. Such a challenge, coming as it does from a wise old prophet, and on a subject as central as faith, can be ignored only at our peril.

David W. Gill
New College Berkeley

Jonah began to go into the city,
going a day's journey. And he
cried, "Yet forty days, and
Ninevah shall be overthrown!"
Jonah 3:4

PREFACE:
SOME QUESTIONS

Spiritual Fashions

Why bother adding to the virtual deluge of religious works being published these days? A large number of people, it seems, have written little pieces on their faith, their conversion, their dramatic return to religion, their idyllic experience with God and the angels. Some writers prefer to describe in detail their personal encounter with God, while others sketch splendid vistas of the new theologies. "The ultramarine skies fall beneath blows from a bludgeon." But that shade of ultramarine is the beyond, the other world, and we are bored silly with so many revelations. Since the publication of that beautiful, extremely beautiful book (I was going to add "prophetic," but let us refrain from such facile piety), *La Foi d'un incroyant* (*The Faith of an Unbeliever*) by F. Jeanson, the way has been opened to all sorts of shoddy mystico-romantic stuff: "The Unbelief of a Christian," "God Is Dead but I Have Seen Him," "The Revolution Is the Resurrection," "God Acts in History Through the Proletariat" (or through

"Power" or "the Unconscious"); and there's always Freud—
or Marx or Nietzsche—to the rescue, not to mention
"Myth," "Structures," and "the Abyss." Gnoses of all sorts
now reappear: the mad attempt to recover the *ipsissima verba*
in the Gospel of Thomas, the claim that now at least we've
got hold of that enigmatic Jesus so distorted by Paul, and the
no less insane "scholarly" discovery that there has to be another dimension, something beyond everyday reality, for
science to continue. Teilhard de Chardin did a good job of
framing this latter issue and his prodigious success was a por-
tent of things to come, the situation we're now familiar with.

If you had seen as I did in my younger days the time when
Christians were aflutter with the belief that science, and in
particular Heisenberg's principle of indetermination, was finally coming to their aid, you would learn to take a sober
view of such things too. But that doesn't prevent people from
beginning the process all over again with new data, and the
"Excavations Confirm Bible" approach gets more popular all
the time. But let's not bait Christians; everyone these days is
caught up in the same giddy trend. Books on extraterrestrial
worlds and parapsychology, complete series of them, are sell-
ing like hotcakes. The whole business is hopelessly confused,
but no matter.

For those who have the right to speak out because they
have paid dearly for calling themselves Christians, because
they know the cost of talking about a truly demanding God—
what a carnival show, what a *commedia dell'arte* it seems,
these many thousands of people rushing forward to applaud
each new person who writes his or her story with blood,
sweat, and tears. Do you really think that this sudden rash of
charismatic outpourings, this explosion of religious passion in
broad daylight constitutes something new in our society?

On the contrary, it seems to me that there's a pattern here.
Our world, with its inflexibility, its rules, regulations, and

endless demands, our work, with its stringent methods, our inexorable sciences—all this cries out for a counterweight, whatever the cost. That counterweight is eroticism.* But eroticism can only invent, discover, or imagine so much. Then, inevitably, it vents itself in drugs, "artificial paradises," violence, and, of course—let's not forget that other card dealt it by society—religion. We've known them from the beginning, those three aces, eroticism, violence, drugs—all trumped by religion. Whether it's the executions of the martyrs or the blood shed by the Inquisition or the wars of religion; whether it's Bluebeard or Flaubert's Saint Anthony, group ecstasies or the religious drugs of the dean of Felice, we find our four-card hand at every turn in the road. Modern times have made no new discoveries. After the erotic delirium of the 1960s had run its course, the great resurgence of religious mysticism we're now witnessing simply had to come. Not that I equate the two. I merely note certain similarities from an empirical-scientific point of view. And I would think myself at fault if I denied the true mystic experiences or authentic faith of either group. But I'm familiar with the pitfalls here, perhaps because I have dealt with them before. Readers may rest assured that I am neither a skeptic nor an unbeliever nor given to subtle denigration of pure, unquestioning evangelical faith. But in matters so serious it's important, I think, to keep self-deception to a minimum, to delude ourselves as little as possible, to avoid the easy answers.

Serious matters? After all—or first of all—yes. In my attempts to clear up the confusion am I absolutely alone? Does anything make any sense? Is the past altogether lost, forever? Is there any reason to hope? What about Camus' question

---

*It is suspected that by "eroticism" Ellul means *perverted* eroticism in this particular discussion.—ED.

that keeps coming back to me: Who will forgive us? This is
not simply a matter for participants of Western culture as
shaped and misshaped by Christianity—we have heard these
questions or similar ones posed by all societies and all peoples, including the most scientific and rationalistic. And we
shall continue to hear them. To avoid illusions, it's not
enough to think that a lovely dream is better than reality, that
"a pleasant memory is truer than happiness." I love certainty,
the things in front of my nose, the things I can touch. I've
learned the hard way to distrust everything else.

But in this current welter of religious publication, on top of
which it seems pointless for me to throw another pound or so
of paper, I find two aspects surprising. To begin with, in
those spectacular conversions and spiritual sagas, the authors
expose themselves directly, display themselves, and blabber
what ought to be their most intimate secrets. We like this
inner drama; indeed we crave it. The masses need heroes; the
movies and television have manufactured them for us. The
ideal figure, the star, is, does, and lives what I would have so
longed to live, do, and be, but alas I'm only a shipping clerk,
a check-out girl in a supermarket. Still, we can dream. While
I watch the screen I live the hero's or heroine's life vicariously. And exactly the same thing happens in these personal religious dramas: *I* can't manage to believe, but that writer can,
the other one can. That person does what I don't, is what I'm
not—the guru, the mahatma, the ayatollah, the one who's
come face to face with God—think of it! And then, through
that person, I can have the same experience. How cruel to
have to say that whatever that person met, it wasn't God.
Because if God is God, then by definition you can't come face
to face with him. Whatever else is possible, that isn't. Of
course, my reasons for saying this are theological, that is,
"worthless." I don't deny that people claiming to have seen
God have had a spiritual experience and may be speaking in

good faith. I simply maintain that there's been a mistake, and that John of the Cross is right when he argues in *The Dark Night of the Soul* against the *famulus*, the supposed intimate of God.

But what really surprises me about this aspect, what absolutely astounds me, is that it's all running so smoothly. How amazing that the era of stiff-necked rationality has passed, that we should be abandoning ourselves to the wild emotion of all those spectacular romantic confessions, of all those spiritual stripteases laying bare what ought to be the most secret, the most chaste, the most unutterable region of the soul. Making love on stage strikes me as far less exhibitionistic than describing in detail one's encounter with the Almighty, throwing in for good measure all those magic words like "witnessing," "the truth," "the good news," and so forth. It's interesting to note that what excites people here is the phenomenon of conversion itself. No one cares in the least for the story of the person of great faith who for thirty or forty years has lived in the humble quest for God's truth and come to know what could be known about God—that's of no interest. But how thrilling when a non-Christian suddenly declares herself a believer, or the other way around, when a Christian heaps on the erstwhile object of his deepest personal certitude a mountain of leftist-revolutionary abuse. And, of course, there's always the piquant exchange of one faith for another, the Christian turning communist, or the communist Christian. There we have the quintessence, the ne plus ultra, of authenticity; there we have a true adventure at last. See, obviously our society is not so perverse after all! We are not held closed, straitjacketed, rigid, or frozen in place. We're in touch with the most unforeseen, the most burningly intense feature of humanity. Indeed.

As I see it, religious exhibitionism of whatever sort is suspect. And its audience is only sampling delicacies from what is now, we must admit, a groaning board. What is served up in the name of conversion is triviality and emptiness, which suits us very well. But it's interesting, no doubt about that, interesting and informative, novel, up to date, all things we surely want to encourage.

And the other thing that surprises me in all this is the boom in refurbished commonplaces, with people raving over them the way they raved over the first man on the moon. Look at Bernard-Henri Lévy discovering what writers have been tirelessly repeating, in more or less the same terms, for a little more than two thousand years: that Jerusalem and Athens are at odds. What a worn-out topic (how often Kierkegaard talked about it—and better than Lévy). Lévy appeals to the Law, but I doubt if there's a single rabbi who hasn't made a stronger case for it. He addresses the issue of the relationship between the most aggressive manifestations of modernity and the spiritual order, transcendental law, but in my opinion the last fifty years have seen hundreds of Christian intellectuals deal with the same concern. They have said more about it, gone more deeply into it, understood it more clearly than Lévy. They knew more about it and never made the sort of grotesque mistakes that this young man has —but no one is interested in them anymore. And just because Lévy's telegenic and knows how to clothe the worst platitudes in fine phrases, all of a sudden he's got a tremendous following. It's a simple matter of the bond uniting a public in need of something and an intellectual in search of stardom. Hence the tumultous reception for what turns out to be a vapid rehearsal of an old refrain.

The phenomenon is hardly unique—I'm thinking also of the prodigious success enjoyed by a book with nothing in it, *Hypotheses About Jesus* by Vittorio Messori. Four hundred thousand copies sold in three months . . . merely to tell us what everyone has known and acknowledged for ages.

Granted, the narrative is brisk and the plot reads like a detective story; but Messori's success substantiates my point that what counts in the first instance is "conversion," insofar as the author begins in a skeptical frame of mind. Then there's the style and method of presentation—a fashionable but irrelevant issue that brings us not a whit closer to the truth. What then are we to do in the great spiritual and religious hurly-burly of this age?[1]

Self-Critique

But then I ask myself, how can you not rejoice, you skeptic, you? Here is a truth you believe in, for which you've fought so long, and now all of a sudden it explodes, bursts forth, breaks through the limits on its way to acceptance by thousands of people who were living in hesitation, in doubt, and who now see their salvation in it, the answer they were

---

1. Jean Sulivan on the modern religious renewal: "With all due consideration, one might think that the church, striding cheerfully into the era of the spectacle, that is, into the functional mode of modern societies, has rediscovered some of its old vigor. The church is once again worthy of the media's attention. And the officials of the church have surrendered to the age with a shudder of delight. Each sociological, that is, quantitative, success has been celebrated with a lyrical debauch. . . . True, this need for excitement and applause is only human. But our movie star–politicians have been exploiting it for so long, they have done so much for the universal narcotizing of consciences that we ought to be on our guard. It's perfectly natural that information specialists should work this vein; they're simply reflecting the way things are. It's a matter of professionalism. The church is moving. It's true, their Excellencies are traveling on all the roads of the real world. . . . Things will be looking up for *almost* everybody. . . . The journalists are only doing their job. But how frivolous of the "masters" of the spiritual life to lose control and start talking about "miracles" and "resurrection." . . . If they are so gifted with the "will to believe," so apt to work themselves into a state, to mistake the circus for the Transfiguration, how can we help doubting what they believe?" (*L'Exode*, 1979).

waiting for. Can this new religious fervor be a sociological movement? Why not? After all, what's at stake here is personal faith, and all the groups in the movement obviously provide the individual with rich opportunities. This phenomenon is "sociological" since so many people are involved in it, but does size mean participants don't have access to the truth? Why should the truth have to be reserved to a small number? Is the Gospel elitist? Jesus declares that he is on the side of the humble, of the little children, of those with barely any intelligence, while the wise men of this world are to be excluded. Perhaps you haven't grasped the parable of the shepherds and the magi, even though you yourself once explained it. You were unhappy when you noted that the "masses" were strangers to the Gospel, were totally indifferent to the spiritual life and to salvation. And, see, now that a major spiritual trend is in the making, you get fussy and ask whether all this is right, legitimate, and so on. . . . Didn't you yourself try to reach those crowds? Haven't you sought to create strong, community-minded groups dedicated to the pursuit of truth? You have failed in that effort, in fact you have failed all across the board.

But shouldn't you rejoice, now that you see your old message accepted, heeded, honored as true? And those communities you dreamed of, those centers of resistance to society's faceless anonymity, hoping to prepare the world of tomorrow —some of them now exist, solid and likely to last. Why then this reticence, this criticism? It doesn't matter who the spokesperson is who preaches the Gospel. In any case it's not you or your friends; all of you are out of the running. Which is as it should be. Did you also fail to grasp those words you've quoted so often, "I planted, Apollos watered, but God gave the growth" (1 Cor. 3:6). Paul and Apollos don't count, as you well know. The essential thing is the message transmitted; it has to be gotten across. And to go back to your two examples, do you think that what Bernard-Henri Lévy says is false? You know it isn't. Is what Vittorio Messori says false? You know how much you agree with him, how much you enjoyed reading his book. Very well then, why not let others cheer him? And if Lévy has gotten Parisian intellectuals whom you never reached to discuss the Bible, why this bitterness? And, once again, why this distrust of large numbers? You'll probably say that you're wary of the motives involved, that this new vogue looks inauspicious to you, that popular crazes are a shabby business, that all this recent talk about religion is just not serious. Could be, could be, but haven't you yourself always taught the opposite? Haven't you constantly reminded others of Christ's command not to judge—then who are you to judge the faith of these people?

How can you deny the authenticity of those stirrings in the heart and mind that plumbs the depths of human beings? And don't you have to judge yourself first of all—where are your works so that I can know what kind of faith moves you? And, still more, how many times have you taught that there was no fathoming the reasons behind a conversion? That's none of our business. Some people convert because they're afraid of death, because they're in terrible pain and looking for consolation, or simply going along with a trend, or out of simple gratitude for the help given them by a neighbor, or because they have no idea which way to turn, feel weak and lost, need shelter and assistance, can't manage to find something philosophically sound to hold onto, can't find any kind of certitude whatsoever except in religion; others convert out of joy and gratitude for an unexpected blessing. . . . Must we reject the sincerity—more than sincerity, the truth of such faith—just because it grows out of concrete motives? Are there any who don't have some kind of ulterior motive, who are pure enough to forget themselves completely and to believe simply because God is God? You've often said yourself that it's God after all who guides us along whatever path we take, that in the final analysis the only thing that matters is the dazzling victory of faith. You said that this victory was the key to understanding the mysterious ways leading up to it, and that we didn't have to rate people's intentions to assure ourselves that their faith was genuine. Once again God is the only judge of that. You don't know, for instance, whether the fear someone felt might have been engendered by God himself, to get that person to confront the crucial decision. . . . You know perfectly well that no faith is pure, including your own. God is the one who sanctifies it. No work, no prayer of yours is worthy of God, because it is he who makes them worthy in the first place. And it is because he listens that your words have any meaning at all.

So why get up in arms over this religious movement, which sprang up without any help from you? There's no sense in proclaiming, "But I've already said that a hundred times, and nobody listened to me." "We piped to you, and you did not dance; we wailed, and you did not mourn" (Matt. 11:17)—don't you recall that simple, unmistakable passage—"To what shall I compare this generation? It is like children . . . calling to their playmates . . ." (Matt. 11:16). See, we did what we could to make them dance or weep; they didn't react. And now someone comes along, the Son of man, and the children have taken to listening, to dancing, to weeping. . . . The others are unhappy. . . . Frankly, isn't that your reaction? You've worked so hard, and it all went for nothing. And now other people come and succeed where you failed. . . . Isn't it sheer jealousy on your part? And this jealousy isn't from God; there's nothing holy about it. God will decide if your work has been in vain. There's another point you've made many times: we should be detached from our works; they don't belong to us anyway; let the Lord dispose of them. So practice what you preach.

Beside, now that you're about to write this book, aren't

you going to add to the very spate of publishing that you've criticized? You're going to act just like the others and, still more, you're going to profit from that sociological movement you treat so severely. If you were above reproach, you would turn away from all this, figuring that either the battle has already been won and so there is no need for you to join in, or that the whole thing is warped, that this whole recent business of religion is a gross error, and in that case there is likewise nothing for you to do. You just said that these days people feel a need for a literary hero, that they're living their faith vicariously. But isn't that exactly what you're getting involved in now, and aren't you too about to put on a rather shabby performance?

But, let's get serious. You've accused what might be in each case an authentic longing of being a mere fashionable trend. Yet you know how anxiety-ridden the world is; so, instead of seeking out the fragile glories of the purist, can't you pay attention to the ordinary folk living in that world and help them to unravel the tangled skein of seductions they're enmeshed in, help them to escape the spider's web of possibly empty beliefs, to discover where to go and what to do? It's not a question of absolute pronouncements, "This is true," "That's false," but of a humble word or two that might prevent them from getting caught up in some crazy venture. And don't use "criticism" as a means of driving them to the limit of complete despair, in other words, of death. For intellectuals can toy with these matters and not be affected, but others, for whom words don't come easily, take words all the more seriously and literally. Someday, thanks to words, they could become the equivalent of the heartlessly cruel SS men or Jews burned to ashes, could become suicidal motorcyclists or incurable drug addicts—or people walled up in eternal, impenetrable silence because neither spouse nor child nor friend can make out a thing they say. So you shall have to weigh your words carefully here.

PART ONE

MONOS AND UNA:
A CONVERSATION

1

Anxiety

Monos: Let's look into this, Una. What is the most obvious and the most recondite element about the human condition to emerge from the ads, the paperbacks, the TV dramas, the items served up by the news media? . . . Watch the faces in the crowd on the street, at the end of a public meeting, in the bars and restaurants in the evening, or at factory gates when the day shift ends. Looking beyond their attractiveness or excitement or fatigue, we don't find it hard to discern a sort of common denominator, an essence always the same whether in young or old, student or worker, conservative or liberal. Everywhere we meet a kind of basic fear, an anxiety, properly speaking, over this world, over the people in it, over this era, over the groups that make up society. Anxiety has been the great motor propelling society in the twentieth century and all previous cultures. We can hear the anxious call of the young people with whom we've had contact and we know that their recourse to drugs is at the same time this same cry, as well as a chance to escape for a few hours from that endless constriction of the throat, that nameless, quite literally nameless and unnameable, tension that has no origin, cause, or end.

I don't know whether humans are, in and of themselves,

creatures of anxiety and have been since the beginning, but I do know that today, here and now, in the Western world and spreading to all other cultures, anxiety holds in its clutches those who have the least reason to feel anxious. And the more happiness increases, it seems, the more people are full of dread and call themselves unhappy. The more security they have, the more they fear the morrow, are apprehensive of the slightest violence, and live in a state of permanent precariousness. The more they consume, the more they tremble at the thought of want. The easier their work gets, the more they complain of deadly tedium. The more reasons they have to play and enjoy themselves, the more they get bored and go off in search of some inexpressible novelty. The more they know, the more they discover a forbiddingly unknown universe. Everything threatens and overwhelms them; they can no longer put up any resistance. They are weak as they were never weak before, lacking both reason and conscience. In a fundamental contradiction, nobody knows what anxiety is and everybody's living it. Thus we have antagonism within the self, "I die of thirst at the fountain's edge . . . ," and everyone experiences the obverse of reality. "Well received, dismissed by all." People feel they have to flee, travel beyond this place, go to a faraway world where they can find a way to escape, to get out of themselves.

Despite their profound analyses and anthropological sciences, people in our time are constantly misjudging their situation, except on one point—the fact that they are unhappy and living a life of inarticulate anxiety. "That's the way you can tell how much people exaggerate when they say that they're retreating or say that they're advancing, or that they have no room at all in their giddy heads either for a grand refusal or for a positive observance. But you also know that they're not exaggerating—when they say that they're naked, that they're trembling, that they're unhappy, that they're all these things, staggered by death and shivering from the cold. . . ." And it's the same anxiety that now besets our world, both in the rich countries, which crumble under the slightest pressure and are haunted by the demons of history, and in the starving countries, the Third World, where all the demons of prehistory once again raise their heads. There we see developing a whole complex of anxieties combining the ancestral fears of malign powers with the bewilderment that accompanies loss of identity and with all our modern phobias. The terror of famine joins forces with the fear of a nuclear holocaust; the resources of the sea die off for reasons that could only have come about through the malicious intervention of spirits together with the sickness that comes from them; from lethal pollution. We witness the complete confusion of good and evil in an inextricable tangle that we have no idea what to do with. We have become convinced that the labyrinth of fear we wander in has no exit whatsoever—the fear of nuclear weapons or the fear of subterranean dangers, the fear of want, the fear of the invisible menace that is all the more frightening because we know that humankind produced it but no longer has it under control.

And we shake our heads, sagely repeating that we have played the sorcerer's apprentice. We refer to the old legend because we're trying to reestablish a connection with something familiar. We like to think that what's happening to us is nothing new, that it has a prior history—as in the tale of the sorcerer's apprentice. And we modestly try to cover up the fact of our forgetting the formula that's supposed to stop the water or the broom. But in saying this we confess our total impotence. And since knowledge is impotent, one must turn to belief—there's no other way. Scientifically minded atheists refuse to accept this and are still triumphantly exclaiming, "Eureka, the future is ours." But in the depths of their hearts they know that all the sciences are involved in belief too, even mathematics; they know that we can't master anything and that the prophetic words of Ecclesiastes, "He who increases knowledge increases sorrow" (1:18), have come true. But they can't admit it—that would mean losing the air of quiet self-assurance they exude and reverting to the belief they spurn.

Thus, contrary to any reasonable expectation, people continue to maintain that science will solve all our problems. The point is not to deny the incredible expansion of scientific knowledge and experiment, but simply to realize that the more science advances, the further the limits of the cosmos (macro- and micro-) recede, and the dimensions of the unknown—and perhaps unknowable—increase proportionately. The world, the many different worlds, governed by a variety of laws are proving to be more and more complex, more and more difficult to grasp, and impossible to imagine. Contrary to the expectations of nineteenth-century science, we have not reached the limits of reality or of the knowable. We've gotten into a game where we'll never find out more than a tiny number of the rules and objects, a game whose patterns change constantly as we go along, so that we no longer truly know if what we've attained is in the least way real or whether all our knowledge might not simply be the product of the rules we laid down to guide our own thinking.

The public, of course, has scarcely any notion of the uncertainty scientists experience at the very moment of their greatest triumphs. And, of course, we catch nothing but distant echoes of those tremendous scientific debates that are so far beyond us. What the public does see clearly is the helpless inability of politicians to control events, of economists to resolve economic crises, of technicians to handle the smallest technical accidents (ten months to stop the flow of oil from a well at Ixtoc, the impossibility of refloating the *Tanio*). What would happen if we had a real catastrophe? People see the failure of knowledge clearly and under such circumstances turn toward belief.

One needs a kind and helpful god, unless one prefers to offer sacrifices to win the silence of a cruel and fearful god, to calm his wrath and avert his vengeance. Since our anxiety comes from every direction, and in the first instance from within ourselves, from the depths of the unconscious (whose existence we have learned to fear but not to control), that anxiety makes us die of a fear we won't acknowledge. But it really exists—must we put on a show and pretend it doesn't? Must we pretend metropolitan dwellers don't barricade themselves in their apartments every evening for fear of some unintelligible aggression, or that the members of motorcycle gangs aren't fleeing their own fear by hitting the throttle—and sometimes committing acts of aggression that they too find unintelligible? How can we refuse the help proffered by belief, since nothing can cure our ills anymore?

The correlation between anxiety and the absence of belief, as our daily lives make plain, is incontestable. Western society has given up on providing its members with a global vision, a final purpose, a direction, and it no longer has any clear sense of identity. It is, to be sure, a tolerant society, but precisely to the extent that it has lost its identity and no longer knows what to make of itself. People go about like wanderers in the dark without a light to orient themselves by. There is no frame of reference, and this generates anxiety. The weaker a group's identity becomes, the more the people in that group lose their individual identities (even when they're based on opposition to the larger society), and the greater grow the diffuse fears of unknown dangers. The malaise afflicting our time, here in the West, is bound up with the loss of identity (i.e., of a belief system) among adolescents and its degeneration among adults.

What we are looking at is a world in search of faith. And it doesn't matter whether that faith be a symptom of neurosis or a reflection of the truth, whether it expresses the weakness of humankind or their many-sided splendor, as long as it gives them a place of refuge. Would you refuse a life preserver to a drowning person under the pretext that it wasn't the most up-to-date model or that it was manufactured by capitalist industry, the product of proletarian exploitation, or some other reason like that? Our world is looking for a faith, for something that will enable it to overcome its faintness of heart, its anxiety, and the countless books on this question no doubt reflect our situation. We haven't found a belief that satisfies; we still don't have a feeling of victorious conviction. But it's quite clear that our attempts to find it are too serious to be simply a matter of fashion. On the contrary, we find ourselves at the heart of the problem troubling us all, individually and corporately. We're at what could be both the source of a renewed understanding to help us grasp what is happening to us and of the courage to enter the combat from which humankind may perhaps emerge with the victory. But we need this courage; we must drive anxiety away. And the psychoanalysts won't be of any help here, at least not for *this* anxiety. We have to overcome our fear, but it's so widespread and so solidly based on the facts that only a spiritual tidal wave can prevail against it.

2

The Man Who
Was Right

Una: So then, Ludwig Feuerbach was right. Everything you've just explained to me—and I don't deny any of it—enters into his profound analysis of religion. Remember his argument: when humans created the gods, they were attempting, first of all, to calm their primordial fears, to reassure themselves by getting some sort of purchase on the unknown. They couldn't do anything by themselves about a storm, but if the storm was caused by a deity—closely resembling a human person—then it was the expression of anger, and anger is something we know how to deal with. In the face of a powerful adversary they could kneel down and show how feeble they were, a reflex action comparable to the way a puppy turns over on its back when it faces a threatening adult dog. They could confess their faults and thus escape or at least attenuate their punishment, while the adversary they acknowledged as supreme judge quenched its need for vengeance and gave proof of its magnanimity. Finally, they could offer a sacrifice and by this offering and the implicit vow not to repeat the sin they could break down the anger syndrome and mollify the one who was about to strike them (the blow aimed at them strikes the sacrificial victim dead). So there is something they could do. They could feel reassured because when the god's wrath was calmed the storm too would abate. And if that didn't work, it meant they'd taken the wrong route and would have to redouble their religious creativity to calm the god whom they simultaneously knew and didn't know.

In any case people came up with the means of resolving their problem.

Monos: But science maintains this means is false. . . .

Una: It probably is, but in olden times, before science, it had its uses; it was the only thing humankind had at their disposal to surmount their intrinsic weaknesses; it gave them the courage to be.

Monos: I can see this, but nowadays how could we be satisfied with religion's crude metaphors?

Una: Well, Feuerbach is even more on target when he tells us that the gods people invented served as an easy (not always that easy) explanation of the incomprehensible realm beyond human ken. Humans, those restless parasites, those intolerable predators, wished to seek out and get to the bottom of what they couldn't understand. And so, rather than remain in the amorphous mire of sensations, reflexes, impulses, intuitions, and mimesis, they have built themselves a world that makes sense, with hierarchies, interconnections, meanings, limits, lines of force, taboos, and imperatives, all of them false but extremely useful for survival. The surprising thing about this is that although this complex is illusory, mythical, hallucinatory, imaginary, and, let us repeat, false, it has permitted, in fact has positively promoted, effective action, adaptive behavior, and organizations in congruence with reality, however falsely interpreted and represented.

Monos: Let's stop at Feuerbach and his descendants. It's quite certain that people used to attribute to the gods whatever they failed to understand. And, as you were saying just now, we're tempted nowadays to follow the same procedure. But we're quite aware of its limitations. As soon as the real, that is, scientific, explanation of anything appears, the tremendous silhouette of the Divine Explainer disappears into the mist. Medicine has put to flight not only magic and its spirits and demons but Aesculapius too. After the age of religion comes the age of science. Auguste Comte was right as well as Feuerbach.

Una: But, Monos, don't forget that Comte himself ended in a burst of the greatest religious insanity.

Monos: Don't interrupt me, Una. You can reply in a minute. Back in the years when people were heralding the death of God, God was irreverently called the stopgap of our knowledge. As knowledge increases, the gap grows smaller. There isn't much space to fill in now, and so the "God of the gaps" loses his usefulness, his importance. We turn away from him, having seen the accomplishments of modern humankind. It's not irrelevant to point out that we speak of the *miracles* of science. This means not only that science does things that the ordinary person doesn't understand, but more, that we attribute to science what once was part of the divine order. In other words the domain where we need God is constantly shrinking.

It makes no sense to have God intervene in some process that has already been completely explained and whose results are precisely what was to be expected from the process itself. Nowadays it's pointless to repeat, except out of slightly hypocritical humility, the famous words of Ambroise Paré, "Je le pansay, Dieu le guarist" ("I dressed his wound, God healed him"). God has nothing to do with the case anymore. The remedies taken, the operation performed have achieved exactly what we anticipated. Our response today to this situation would more likely be that of La Fontaine's ironic fable of the wagoner stuck in the mud. When the man invokes Jupiter, the god does nothing more than give him the necessary technical advice. The wagoner simply performs a few human acts, and then with a little crack of the whip the wagon is off. The moral of the story, "Heaven helps those who help themselves," is a skeptical one, since in the fable Heaven, strictly speaking, did nothing. In his astonishment the wagoner credits Jupiter with what was actually the fruit of his own labor. La Fontaine's fable, in fact, means: do whatever is technically necessary and you'll succeed; it's useless to call upon Jupiter.

This is a far cry—indeed, it's completely removed—from the gospel parable of the loaves and fishes, where the disciples bring Jesus five loaves and two fish (the small amount people can contribute) and Jesus provides inexhaustible nourishment for five thousand. Humanity's minuscule effort is indispensable for God's great miracle, but that remains a great miracle, and we remain minuscule. Which is just what Ambroise Paré said. But we've changed all that—La Fontaine is the true modern. And the true miracle takes place without any help or intervention from God. Open-heart surgery is a miracle, and walking on the moon is a miracle, but there was no need for God to manifest his presence in either. The only domain he has left is that of chance, of unforeseen accidents. When an operation fails, there was an imponderable factor frustrating the expected result. In other words this God is nothing more than the God of obstacles, failures, and bad risks. The real expression should be: "I dressed his wound, and God prevented him from getting better." Are we dealing with an evil God, then? A jealous God who makes human power come to grief, the God of roadblocks and catastrophes? For the moment let's not go so far. But you can see that in the end that's what we'll be left with. And you can understand, if you extrapolate from Feuerbach's prophetic remarks, why people are abandoning the classical forms of religious life.

Feuerbach also puts us on the track of the evil God when he explains that people project into the realm of the absolute their attachments, their values, their perception of the good. They long for justice, goodness, purity, solidarity, and freedom. They recognize that they don't possess them, or only in very small amounts, and that they're not materializing, except fragmentarily, in society at large. Must people despair then? Must they think that these ideals are unobtainable, that they can never be realized? If they do, it becomes very easy to transfer them to an eternal Being, beyond the finitude of time and space, who can represent unconditional justice and goodness. This is an easy way to get oneself a perfect, unchangeable model, but it's not without its dangers. Critics have pointed out two consequences in particular: on the one hand, in comparison with that Absolute the things we see around us are contemptible, without value or interest. Why practice a little justice when we can see the model of absolute justice shining in the distance? We can spare ourselves the trouble of being personally just since it amounts to such a trifle. And this first consequence is confirmed by the second: the believer's posture of folded hands and averted eyes—since the sum of all justice is in God, since God himself *is* justice, will he not give it to us? All we need do is pray and await his good pleasure. And while we wait let us do nothing. Let us renounce both the best part of ourselves, the most important thing in our lives, and the action necessary to bring it to fruition. Let us wait for God to take care of everything. Projecting all goodness on God makes him a sort of vampire of humanity (in the Romantic era vampires were quite fashionable and Marx made frequent use of this comparison). Religion, as dissected by Feuerbach, is a self-referential system.

Circumstances have changed in our time; the means, and perhaps the psychology, have been modified, but the process by which humans fashion gods, adore and serve them, is still the same. Feuerbach's discovery was the work of a genius, and it effectively took belief apart. Nonetheless we should not forget that Feuerbach was also trying to save Christianity from the debacle that he saw brewing with the advent of the sciences. But in Christianity there's not just one basic structure or impulse, but two: faith and love. We've shown that the whole realm of faith and belief lies in ruins, that Feuerbach's explanation is definitive. Once it has been applied to the false reasons people have for believing, nothing is left; belief has been truly destroyed. But what about love? Here we stand on much more solid ground: the Christian teaching on love of one's neighbor can't be attacked from a scientific standpoint. It remains the key to human relations, to the possibility of life for society as a whole (on which, moreover, the development of science depends).

It is here that Christianity has shown the true path for human life to follow. But it does no good at all to believe in God so as to love one's neighbor. Within Christianity we must distinguish between the part that goes back to the dawn of humanity, belief based on fear, values raised to absolutes, humans despoiled to God's advantage—all of which is just a useless atavism—and the part that contains permanent truth, that makes people more human, the love of humanity. After all, isn't this what we've found with the death-of-God theology, which shows how useless the biblical God is for the practice of adult Christianity? And haven't we found this as well with horizontal theology (the theology that concerns humans in the world), as opposed to vertical theology (the theology that concerns the individual's relationship to God)?

Now we see clearly that Christ dwells in each of the "little ones," the poor, the humble, who are our brothers and sisters (those others, the rich, the powerful, the proud are the only ones who aren't our brothers and sisters), and nowhere else. What good would it do for Christ to be seated up there at the right hand of God? What does "up there" mean, anyway, or "right hand," when we speak of "God"? How simple-minded these images are, just like the language of religion (always a rich source of instruction). One hears Christians calling their God "the Lord," but in our day who would ever think of declaring anyone a lord? It's a medieval custom, and it plainly stamps the belief it comes out of as medieval too.

For a while people tried to prove that Christianity implied the presence of Christ between a person and his or her neighbor, and that love was impossible except by his mediation. We have put that fantasm to flight. We have learned from our experience with the priest-workers that the only worthwhile thing to do is to enter into the other person's way of life and thus to make love possible. And so the mists of faith vanished away, leaving us the splendor of brotherhood and justice, sought for and won by the community. And if you want God, God is here, not somewhere else, in the humanity of Jesus, the model of love, who is the Christ because he puts that love into practice, and who is present in the least of his brethren because love is there. Thus the death-of-God theology and horizontal theology express the ultimate truth of Christianity for our time. As for belief, it's fine for weak-minded individuals, as Montaigne so rightly said: "Perhaps it is not without reason that we attribute facility in belief and conviction to simplicity and ignorance; for it seems to me I once learned that belief was a sort of impression made on our mind, and that the softer and less resistant the mind, the easier it was to imprint something on it."[2]

Isn't that crystal clear? What could you say in reply?

---

2. *The Complete Essays of Montaigne,* trans. Donald M. Frame (Stanford, CA: Stanford University Press, 1965), p. 132 (*Essays,* I, xxvii).

3

Belief Is Everywhere

Una: "For our time"? For today? Do you really believe that, Monos? I would be inclined to say, "for yesterday." These theologies enjoy only short-lived triumphs; they strike me as fading away as quickly as they flared up. They're a handful of resinous wood chips that catch fire at once and give off thick black smoke, but they go out in an instant. Left to burn out on a smooth stretch of sand, they leave nothing behind. . . . All I see here are a group of latecomers affirming those rather stale truths whose origin you've reminded us of. They're a war party off to conquer a new form of expression for Christianity, but first they slackened their pace and then they went astray. The prophets had spoken a little too soon. Remember, Feuerbach, then Comte and Marx gave Christianity barely a generation to outlive itself and finally disappear. Marx announced that Christianity would disintegrate by the end of the nineteenth century at the latest. Many of us thought differently, but the end of the nineteenth and the first half of the twentieth century did seem disastrous for all beliefs. People made desperate efforts either to penetrate the working-class world or to shore up the institutional church or to reformulate theology, and all the while the mass exodus of lay people (and after 1960 of priests) from the church created the impression among those who stayed that the world was coming to an end.

But the tide has turned. I don't know for how long, but as things stand now, I feel rather strongly that this is not a transient phase, that a renewal has occurred. But I can't vouch for it, and in any case I don't care all that much. And I won't make myself ridiculous by saying I told you so. I'd prefer that you consider the situation from any other angle. Have you ever thought that belief is everywhere? Let's not talk about any specific belief determined by any specific God. Just try to imagine a coherent pattern of relations with every simple belief excluded; try to conceive of a science without belief at its core.

When Kurt Gödel raised his now famous questions about the validity of mathematical demonstration, he overturned everyone's notions of scientific certainty. When Kuhn proposed his theory of the role played by paradigms in the development of science, he upset the tranquil confidence of people who thought that scientific discoveries simply accumulated one after another, demonstrated, proven, guaranteed. Science rests on a number of presuppositions held to be absolutely correct (held to be, that is, believed). But as scientists find themselves limited—of necessity—to their field of specialization, they're obliged to believe what the other specialists tell them. And even within a given specialty, scientists are not going to waste their time by redoing everyone else's experiments and demonstrations. They consider them solid fact, that is, they believe in them—an arrangement, by the way, that makes possible some stunning hoaxes. Recall the altogether fascinating case of Schubert and Derr, important biologists known all over the world,[3] who announced in 1978, on the basis

3. *Nature*, no. 281, 1979; *New Scientist*, no. 84, 1979; *La Recherche*, no. 106. See also Blanc, Chaponthier, and Danchin, "Les fraudes scientifiques," *La Recherche*, no. 113, 1980.

of years of research and experimentation, that they had discovered an effective remedy for workers poisoned by contact with toxic metals (plutonium or cadmium). Their discovery was so significant that seven research teams were set up in different parts of the world to carry on their efforts and draw all the possible conclusions. And then a year later at a conference in Tokyo the two men declared that all that new research was pointless, that the results they had provided the other scientists with earlier had no meaning because it had all been made up. There had never been a single bit of hard evidence in their announced findings: people had simply believed them.

But, granted that this is an extreme example, belief is an enormous factor in all areas of science. Take the elementary fact that in physics, biology, and astronomy you have to learn to observe, that is, to see *what has to be seen.* You are told that a given vague and unspecified form or shadow or variation in density means such and such, and so, because of the confidence you have in your instructor henceforth you effectively "see" in the microscope or telescope what has been previously agreed on. This is, admittedly, not an arbitrary convention, but it "holds" only until it's been falsified.

The same thing happens when one relies on the experimental or scientific method as rigorously exact: it doesn't give rise to any absolute realities. Take the simple problem of determining which variables in any experiment are truly significant. This is the key to the whole operation, but haphazard choice always plays a major part in it. One has to "bet," that is, believe that the ones one has chosen are "truly significant."

Monos: But isn't this choice gratuitous?

Una: I see the point, and I agree, but do you think that beliefs are gratuitous and simply absurd? In our recent exchange we showed that believing is a quite reasonable mode

of action. P. Bourdieu is entirely correct in reminding us
(others have said it before him) that there are systems that
run completely "on belief," and that there's not one system,
not even the economy, that doesn't owe to belief at least part
of its ability to function.[4]

So now we consider belief and science far from occupying
two exclusive domains: the first has deeply penetrated the
second, which decidedly rests on the foundation of a body of
commonly accepted beliefs. We know now that pure rationalism just does not exist (rationalism necessarily begins with
faith in reason). We used to say that the world of belief is
artificial and based on arbitrary images. Fine, but then what
should we say now about the world of science, which is no
less artificial, insofar as the images it gives us (of matter, for
instance) don't correspond, strictly speaking, to anything?
Remember, Monos, those beautiful drawings and sculpted
models of the atom and its nucleus of electrons, neutrons,
and protons—simple people might think that "it's really just
like that," only not so big. In exactly the same way simple-
minded Greeks might have thought that the majestic Athena
standing in front of the Parthenon wasn't a symbol but a
precise replica of the celestial Athena. Scientific representation is purely symbolic, and we trust those who make use of
it to give us an idea of reality, which can't be represented.
But this is every bit as arbitrary and artificial as the statues of
the gods.

And what should we say about the habitual acts of faith in
our everyday relationships. Fortunately, when I go to the
butcher's, I have confidence in him . . .

Monos: But that's confidence, Una, not . . .

Una: What, don't you know that confidence and faith have
the same root? To confide in or trust someone is to believe in

4. Interview, *La Recherche*, no. 112, 1980.

him or her; *confidere* is related to *fides*, "faith." And *fides* means having confidence in someone and at the same time believing his or her word. So, fortunately, when I go to the butcher shop, I believe that he's not going to give me poisoned meat. I don't even consider the possibility. All our relationships are rooted in that faith, that belief in the honor, the word of another person. Without it life would become utterly impossible. And one of the dramas of our time arises from the fact that, thanks to half-baked, misunderstood notions of psychoanalysis, people withhold confidence from others, refuse to believe their word. People look for a speaker's hidden meaning; they search out what he or she *didn't* say; they decode meanings that the other person never intended but that the structures of discourse, cleverly manipulated, put in his or her mouth. This is the era of suspicion, something I've sufficiently discussed elsewhere (along with other writers), and any society suffering from it has a mortal illness. Not to believe the Other, simply and straightforwardly, is exiling oneself from life. Ultimately, it's a disease that quickly degenerates into a persecution complex. Unending interpretation of discourse, as opposed to belief in another's words, destroys the one who practices it. It's a form of madness, disguised as lucidity.

And I'd go so far as to say that wherever faith and confidence break down, human beings become the permanent prisoners of madness. Some people are scandalized that lunatics are imprisoned, but they're already locked up inside themselves, because they no longer believe that those around them are capable of being truthful, good, and loving. All human relationships are modeled on that of a man and woman who love, and for that reason believe in, one another. As soon as one stops believing in the fidelity, good faith, or honesty of the other, life for the couple turns into hell. And no proof or demonstration has ever succeeded in replacing confidence and belief. And no investigation or rational thought has ever managed to quiet suspicion or heal the rift between enemies. Only faith can bridge that sort of gap. Without belief we live in the bone-dry, withering atmosphere of reason, of evidence (which is never strong enough). And, whatever the greatness of science, no one has ever been able to live in that harsh, austere climate, in the rarefied air of abstract experience and anonymous codes. From the most casual conversation to the most intimate relationship, everything depends upon that confidence-faith that gives rest to the soul and joy in the presence of others.[5] A relationship with another person does not become a Sartrean hell unless one person turns a palaeographer's or entomologist's eye on the other person, who is now nothing more than an old parchment to be deciphered or an insect to be placed in a complex taxonomy. And despite all your efforts, Monos, I really don't think you'll ever win us over to that madness in the name of pure, exclusive reason.

5. Castelli, *L'Enquête quotidienne*, 1972.

4

From Belief to Exclusion

Monos: You're jumbling things together, dear Una. It's too easy to confuse faith and confidence, despite their etymologies. Believing in a truth and having confidence in a person are two very different things, almost unconnected I would say.

Una: Do you think so? Is there a truth existing independently of humans that isn't represented by some person or other? And don't you transfer the confidence you have (or don't have) in that person to the truth he or she conveys?

Monos: What strikes me as intolerable is the blind faith that stirs up passion. You were speaking of love. Well, the Greeks were right to make Cupid a blind god. Love is blinded—and blinding.

Una: Tell me, Monos, do you really believe that? The famous dilemma has yet to be resolved: we can't know someone we love, because we can't be objective about that person. But on the contrary we know the beloved as nobody else can, because love is the road to knowledge. . . .

Monos: But I don't want to talk about love. I want to talk about belief. Can't you see how belief imprisons us within ourselves, walls us up, fences us in? We believe, and from that moment on we can no longer accept any other belief. We can no longer relate to anyone unless they share the same belief. When we believe, we think we have the truth under lock and key. Look around you, reflect on history: has anyone been more exclusive, more intolerant, more of a persecutor than the person who believes? Scholars know that the truth they're inching toward is fragile and provisional. Skeptics are capable of lending a favorable ear to any statement: after all, it might contain its portion of wisdom. But believers, imprisoned in certitude, reject in advance anything that might call that certitude into question. They immediately enter the lists to convince their interlocutors, to win them over and convert them.

Don't forget that believers are necessarily the ones who invent the maxim that the end justifies the means. Their belief in an unshakable truth is so strong, so overwhelming that they approve any method whatsoever to persuade others and to thus thrust them into the believers' paradise. And if this belief is related to some kind of religious truth, then the situation gets even worse, because a person's concrete, practical life counts for nothing in comparison with eternal salvation. I'll spare you the presumptuous declarations and ignorant oversimplifications of those who proclaim that only faith kills.[6] They obviously don't know what they're talking about, never having lived in the world of faith. They merely seize hold of a few random historical commonplaces to find exceptions to the rule. Their frivolousness in handling these issues is sometimes criminal. Nonetheless their challenge to belief is on target.

There's no point, I suppose, in bringing up the Inquisition or Charlemagne's baptizing of the Saxons. They're insignifi-

6. Bernard Houdin, *La Foi qui tue*, 1980.

cant; the key here is the wars of religion—all of them. As long as war is waged for economic reasons, to occupy a territory, to get control of resources, it can be kept within limits. It makes no sense to devastate the country you want to annex or to massacre the population to the last individual when all you want is their wealth. Everything changes, changes radically, the moment war becomes a matter of Glory, Truth, or Justice, that is, when you mix values with violence, claiming to put the latter to work for the former. Glory is in itself a religious concept, something you believe in: in manifesting martial prowess military leaders become demigods. They do more than conquer the enemy; they reveal themselves to be of a different species from ordinary mortals; they arouse religious fervor. This is particularly evident in primitive practices where the conquering leader devours the heart or liver of his enemy, thereby appropriating his strength; or when, in accordance with the grisly Aztec custom, the cacique or enemy chieftain is carved into pieces while still alive, care being had to keep his skin completely intact so that it can be filled up with air and made into a marvelous drum.

Whenever belief, whether religious, magical, political, or rational, gets mixed up in war, war becomes ruthless. Death is no longer death but either the opening of the glorious gates of paradise to welcome the heroes or the hurling of the defeated enemies into the eternal flames. Such enemies are no longer fellow human beings defending themselves but the incarnation of evil, of falsehood, the quintessence of everything that must be cast out to finally achieve true humanity. And whether it's the holy war waged by the Hebrews upon entering the Promised Land, a combat that would end in the *herem*, or the jihad waged by the Arabs after their conversion to Islam, which can only end with the extermination of the infidels, or the wars of religion between Protestants and Catholics, or the conquest of America, which was a war of religion too . . . everywhere, time after time, religious beliefs lead to atrocities because the exclusive possessors of truth can't tolerate the persistent survival of "error," that is, any other truth than their own.

The classic religions don't wage major wars anymore, but that doesn't help much. And colonialist aggression, driven by pure economic interest, pales by comparison with the new holy war waged by communism against capitalism. Here once again it's a matter of religion, but compounded when on top of ordinary religion we get nationalistic or, by a perverse twist, "patriotic" religion. When one is added to the other, the way is open once again to catastrophe. Nazism, a religion par excellence, showed just how far belief in a charismatic leader could go, while communism, another religion par excellence, shows how far belief in the truth of a doctrine can go.

You were telling me just now—and apparently with relish —that the modern world is a world in search of a faith. That makes me shudder. . . . That reminds me, old as I am, of 1937. . . . In those days we witnessed the explosion of the Nazi madness, and communism too had turned into the frigid kind of delirium we're familiar with. Some French politician (Édouard Daladier or Paul Reynaud, Pierre Cot, or perhaps Guy Chambre) delivered a long speech to explain that France's weakness was its lack of idealism. What the young people of France needed was an ideal to mobilize them. France needed to rediscover a cause, a passion, a burning enthusiasm—what he meant by that, of course, was an activist ideology, reasons for getting oneself killed, blind beliefs to justify the plunge into dictatorship and war.

"Youth must have an ideal"—that meant, we have to have a way to motivate those young people to risk getting themselves killed. . . . People cannot rest in the place where belief leads them once they have gotten hold of the truth; they have

to get others to share it. Belief is always accompanied by atrocities. The others are no longer human beings—they are first
of all scapegoats. When they are thrust forth from our midst,
then and only then shall we be pure. Kill the Jews. Kill the
Nazis. Kill the bourgeois. Kill the communists, and we'll finally enter the world of utter clarity, of purity, of justice;
peace will finally be possible. Because it's clear to believers,
animated as ever by the purest of intentions, that they're not
the ones who disturb public order and prevent people from
recognizing and understanding each other; they're not the
ones who start wars—never. Catharsis completes belief. Believers project all the evil onto others, and find purification
for themselves in this way, purification and justification, provided that the scapegoats are driven out of the camp, cast out
into the desert, into the malevolent shadows where they belong, no longer human beings in any sense. When you look at
all this, you can see why the unbeliever has always distrusted
the believer, however much the latter may protest. Here is a
curious item: in a country as dechristianized as France a short
while ago one might have read an astonishing (at first blush)
declaration by the president of the Atheists Liaison Commit-
tee: "For all the permissiveness of our society it's very hard
being an unbeliever."

Una: How remarkable that for the believer the difficult
thing in our society is precisely to declare oneself a believer!

Monos: This is undoubtedly because minorities that overturn fixed habits exasperate the authorities. Freethinkers who
dare to question the multiform taboos of the sacred are
looked upon as pariahs. . . . The atheists remain different,
they're truly the "others." . . . "As an atheist I demand simply my indefeasible right to present, explain, and defend the
freedom of unbelief."[7] These words unquestionably reflect

7. Caillavet, *Le Monde*, 8 April 1980.

the feelings of unbelievers, skeptics, and even liberals. Time after time we've seen so-called liberal academics in this fear-stricken attitude, understandably enough, since they're menaced by the beliefs of both Right and Left, and they have a great sense of isolation.

Obviously there are no real threats to French society now (1980), but we have learned how readily people will hurl themselves, body and soul, headlong into the rapture of belief. And if Pascal could say that he was only ready to believe in those truths whose witnesses were willing to die for them, we, alas, have learned two altogether different lessons. The first is that getting oneself killed for lies and errors doesn't make them true. Nazis and communists sacrificed themselves heroically. And, second, we see that the truths that carry the day are the ones in the name of which the believers kill the "others." So we've arrived at a point exactly opposite from the one you wanted to prove to me, my dear Una. You built your argument on the universality of belief, on the impossibility of not believing. You thought everything was based on people's beliefs. But that same proof now backfires on you, because all it positively demonstrates is that belief belongs to the order of necessity. Perhaps it's necessary to people, perhaps people can do nothing without it. But in that case it's the opposite of freedom, which is just what I was telling you. The believer is a slave. And because belief is necessity, an expression of ineluctable forces, people must get rid of it, if they want to be free.

5

The Most Uncertain, The Most Improbable . . .

Una: Alas, Monos, how well I know everything you've been telling me—just as well as you. And it causes me more grief, perhaps, than it does you, because it denies the very core of my life. But what a strange, incoherent line of argument. How can you fail to see that there's a basic contradiction between belief and absolute certitude? If I stretch out my hand and take hold of a flower in the vase on my table, I have no need to believe anything. Belief is directed only toward uncertain, fragile, improbable things. If I believe, that's because I have no proof, no assurance, no guarantee that what I believe will come about—far from it. As for probable things, I've no need to believe in them. Only the improbable, the incommensurable calls forth my belief. I might be wise to pay no heed to this since it lies beyond my reach, but isn't that precisely what has always driven humanity—the idea of going beyond? Of heading into the unknown, to a place where no one has staked a claim before, of continually moving westward to find the land where the sun sets, to ride forever across the steppes of central Asia or the waves of the Atlantic.

I believe because otherwise I get nowhere. Belief has no

other content, purpose, or presence. "Blessed are those who have not seen and yet believe" (John 21:29). There's the heart of our problem. Being a believer doesn't mean that one is entrenched in a fortress and overpowers one's adversaries from behind its walls. It means rather to be put in the most vulnerable of situations, to hang in the most delicate equilibrium, to expose oneself to assault from all sides. Otherwise I have no need to believe. Evidence or reality is enough; my believing adds nothing. But it's true that this position is so uncomfortable that it may not be possible to maintain it very long.

My interpretation of the historical phenomena you mentioned is also different from yours: it's not the mere fact of believing in a certain truth that leads to intolerance; it's the fragility of belief that causes people to be dismayed and to try to fill up the gaping hole in existence. I know deep down that what I believe is uncertain, fragile, unstable, that that belief can change at the slightest pressure, that I have no proof and no certainty, that I'm defenseless, and at the same time I know existentially that this belief is a vital necessity for me, that it's the vital center of my life, which will be threatened if I lose it. For this reason, or rather on account of this situation, I throw up fortifications around my belief, I make it rigid and exclusive, thinking to provide myself with more guarantees and security, in hopes of protecting and strengthening my belief. In the extreme case I rule out all criticism, I exclude all other kinds of belief, and I banish the people who maintain them. Beyond that I build myself a rampart of dogmas and institutions, a sort of outwork to defend the core of my belief (whose vulnerability makes this kind of carapace inevitable).

Look how it's always the most empty and aberrant beliefs that are the most violent and exclusive. A sect is always more closed and intransigent than a church. Consider the ferocity of Nazism: didn't it come from the fact that deep down they knew it was totally absurd to believe in that nonsense about Aryan racial purity, about the divine character of a man incarnating the entire *Volk?* The strength of this belief came not from itself or from its truth but from its very absurdity—which had to be made believable, whatever the cost. The same thing goes for Stalinism. The communist begins to rage the moment one calls into question the "scientific" nature of Marxist-Leninist doctrine.

If you doubt that all believers want, regardless of the price (to others), to uphold the truthfulness of *their* faith, then observe the behavior of people whose belief, for one reason or another, has been destroyed. Look at those ex-priests and ex-ministers who've rejected their faith, those ex-communists (it's not enough to be thrown out of the Party, you have to lose faith in it): see how disoriented they are. They can't get used to living without belief. And yet these are no feeble, dim-witted creatures. In general they're valuable men and women, but now that their beliefs have been shattered they wander about aimlessly, with no frame of reference, restless, deeply wounded, plunging into amorality, as wretched, sometimes, as the dog that crawls off into the shadows to lick its wound over and over again. These are not exceptional cases.

In the days when, facing a powerful church or a universal Party, a lonely individual arose to proclaim his or her loss of faith, when the apostate was banished and found him- or herself all alone, the situation was a terrible one. But nowadays the number of ex-priests and ex-Party members is legion and yet, when they get together, they feel perfectly miserable. So you see why believers close themselves up like a clenched fist, ready to strike out at whatever challenges them. It's a sort of vital reflex. Belief always rests on the most uncertain, the most improbable of foundations, but if it didn't, it would be experimental or rational certitude and not belief. It would be shielded by objective proofs, whereas now it's extremely weak, having only conviction, believers' personal certitude to defend it. And hence they have to maintain their position with rocklike rigidity.

But at this point a thought gives me pause: this is the way it has to be; it couldn't be otherwise, because the faith that possesses me is faith in this world, a belief in temporal things, in a given political success, a given social truth. I have no other guarantee than this external certitude, which amounts to the force exerted by society and the world. And this faith in the world (a "horizontal" faith, as Christians would say) will necessarily take on all the characteristics of what goes on in that world. It will be surrounded by violence, because everything, positively everything, in modern societies is based on violence. It will be exclusive and radical, because, as with everything else that makes up our world, it's clear that all blows to the body of its truth are fatal. It will be treated as unique and all of a piece, because as soon as one begins to criticize it, to cut into it, it crumbles into dust. This, I think, is the heart of the matter: criticism devastates it; it leaves *nothing* behind. The moment one finds oneself on the level of concrete existence in this world, at the place where something can vanish, that is, die or change, there are no more ashes and before long no memories either. "Who's Hitler?" You see, then, why this combat is so fierce. In this world it's all or nothing. The liberal's position is, strictly speaking, untenable, and hence it can't be held for long.

On the other hand, I don't see any reason why that sort of behavior should occur when belief relates to a transcendent Being who lies beyond our grasp. Believers should be asking themselves: of what consequence are criticism, verbal assaults, the rational or scientific destruction of my faith or my church? If in any case God is God, he can't be touched by any of this. And just as I have no power to defend him and can't

make a fool of myself by becoming the advocate or champion
of him (who alone is God), so I can look serenely on impotent
acts of aggression, which can at most destroy a few errors
about God. It seems to me that this would be the only normal
attitude.

Nothing is more dangerous, more closed off than a faith
bound up with something in this world (be it the Neighbor,
the Poor, Goodness, Truth, etc.), while nothing is more
open, more calm, less aggressive than a faith aimed at the
Transcendent. But you were quite right, Monos, when you
pointed out just now that the two positions are fundamentally
alike. The only explanation I can think of for this is that faith
in the Transcendent is nothing of the sort. If it is, then it's
just a manner of speaking, a way of hiding our powerlessness
and our incapacity to recognize that there's something that
doesn't depend on us.

Christians behave in all things as if the God whom they
proclaim had no active reality outside of themselves, their
church, and their dogmas. In other words, in throwing up
fortifications around their faith they attest to the fact that
they believe in nothing except this world. The enormous institutional machinery of churches, councils, ecumenical or
otherwise, the enormous intellectual apparatus of totalitarian
theological systems, the arsenal of apologetic or missionary
weapons, the moral or disciplinary codes, all the liturgies,
catechisms, and exclusionist confessions of faith—all that is
merely a device to reduce the Transcendent to our own dimensions. But since belief always remains an affirmation of
the most uncertain and improbable reality—and belief in the
Transcendent more so than any other kind—if I put the free
and sovereign God in parentheses, then in all respects my
faith must henceforth be more threatening, violent, and authoritarian than any other kind. If I really believed in it, I
could enter upon a life of freedom, flexibility, and humanity;

I could expose myself without fear to the sharpest critical thrusts, while the inaccessible object of my faith would never come up in that worthless debate. . . .

6

Solutions and the Real World

Monos: But it's not just religious belief in itself that strikes me as frightening, ominous, and destructive. What disturbs me as much as anything else is the effect of belief when it imposes itself on the real world. Consider, Una, how far beliefs have gone toward denaturing our relationship with reality, with the real world around us. Instead of simply trying to understand, to analyze, look how believers set up their assumptions as established fact. Now I'm not attacking your Christianity. But what of Buddhism or Islam and their flight from the real world? When we're led to believe that reality doesn't exist, that the world we live in is an illusion pure and simple, that time and space are meaningless accidents, and that nothing exists except as conjured up by our deluded senses, the conclusions one comes to are quite dramatic.

Some people take these ideas for wisdom, but if they were, the logic of such wisdom would call for absolute nonintervention. After all, why try to change the flickering images from the magic lantern of the universe? Steppenwolf is right. Even more, we have to press on and give up the business of maintaining this illusion. Why take part in time at all, in the duration of that phantomlike absence? Very well, but then stop eating. Kill yourself. If everything is an illusion, even death, the only consistent stance is complete detachment. But, other than the Buddha, who has gone that far? And even he didn't commit suicide.

Again, logic demands that one cease to have any more children—they will only chase after illusion and perpetuate it. What we see, however, in the Eastern and Middle Eastern countries is exactly the opposite: a deluge of children. It's the limit of inconsistency. I know, I know there are other religious factors behind this burst of fertility, but that only shows the incoherence of belief. And, worse yet, I see those who have acquired supreme wisdom thanks to their conviction that all is illusion, and what use do they put that wisdom to? To exercising their powers. How strange: the fakir trains himself to endure suffering. Why? To perform miracles (as Westerners view it). Why do that? We're constantly told that precisely because everything is illusory one can achieve perfect mastery of one's body, one can control time and space. But what's the good of that? As far as miracles go, I realize that it's our Western mentality which interprets them as manifestations of power because we're obsessed with it. Nevertheless, it's still a matter of doing remarkable deeds by methods unknown to us. But, once again, what does that mean if everything is illusory? Why take the trouble of going through a long ascesis, of mastering oneself, of altering time and space? It's all inconsistent, on the order of the Cathars, who ought not to have had any children, whereas their families were as large as ever.

In the final analysis these extreme beliefs are true only for a tiny number of people, a handful of groups capable of following them to the limit. But the danger begins when that sort of belief, thoroughly adulterated and largely forgotten save for a few scattered fragments, is widespread among a people ready to abandon itself to its religious instincts. The latter, as I see it, link up with Freud's death instinct (whether he's right or wrong in everything he says about it, I think it unquestionably exists) and lead humanity into a pattern of behavior absurdly out of line with reality.

And at the other end of the spectrum of faith, look at Islam, for which the real world is ultimately a place of invasion, conquest, and domination. I'm not talking here about the Islam of the mystics and sages, but the no less real Islam that played such a crucial part in world history, with its emirs and heads of state, its rulers of land and sea, its fanatical masses (the adjective is banal but accurate) for whom the real world had no other purpose than to be filled by Islam, to be its container, to be shaped and directed by it, to *submit*. Despite Averroes and all the Muslim philosophers you might quote against me, that's the only conception of reality in Islam. How could you find a belief in anything more fragile and uncertain? Belief in Islam always equals the helmeted warrior, the knight in chain mail, or the Palestinian clenching a hand grenade. The real world is nothing but Islamic territory and has no meaning but the one conferred upon it by conquest.

Contrast that attitude toward reality with the scientific method. Science's first concern is to self-effacingly respect whatever it examines, while belief necessarily leads to domination and self-aggrandizement. And when believers get hold of the work done by scientists, disaster is just around the corner. What believers expect from science, in the end, is the answer to a number of concrete questions. They want a solution—and nothing is more dangerous than people convinced they have it. Solutions of that sort are always a matter of belief. Science and reason can provide solutions only when there's a problem framed in strictly scientific terms. Let me hark back to a distinction—a crucial one, I think—drawn by

Henri de Jouvenal: there is no *solution* in the real sense of the word, except when the statement of the question is comparable to that of a mathematical "problem." But things never work that way in reality (in the usual sense of economic, political human reality), which can never be reduced to a series of neatly defined problems, where all the data can be fixed and determined. There's always the element of chance, always vagueness and uncertainty, and finally there are far too many aspects to be fit into any equation.

But believers are convinced that solutions are everywhere. They believe in them, and they pour abuse on people who don't offer one. It's a peculiar accusation, but we've heard it often enough. In 1968 when student demonstrations broke out everywhere in France, the great cry of condemnation of the participants was: "They don't even know what they want. When you ask them what kind of society they're looking for, all you get is confused stuttering or useless general ideas. They're wholly negative and destructive. They have no plan; they propose no solutions." We hear this same speech periodically today, sometimes aimed at young people when they happen to challenge the adult world (a rare event these days) or else at the leftists: "Look at them, they're assassins. They want to destroy society, but what for? They have no idea. They have no solution for the difficulties we're in now." Same thing with the ecologists. "They don't want to have anything to do with nuclear power. They talk about alternate energy sources, but everybody knows they would barely provide ten percent of what we need. They've got no solution to the energy crisis, but they don't want any more pollution. They're just idealists."

What an odd reversal. It's the young, the leftists, the ecologists who seem to be dangerous idealists, devotees of irrational ideas, whereas their accusers are the realists, whose feet are firmly planted on the ground and who are not swept away by passionate belief. Well, in my view it's just the other way around. It's the leftists, ecologists, Third-World residents, and feminists who are the realists, who see reality as it is, who detect the dangers menacing us and bring them to light, who call our attention to new features of age-old questions. Their accusers are dangerous idealists and fantasts, because they believe (but that's all it is, an idle belief) they have solutions —which are nothing of the sort.

Before accusing those sometimes vacillating movements of lacking a program, we ought to begin by asking whether we, the adults, the old-timers, have had real solutions over the last half century to the problematic situations that have sprung up. Did we come up with answers? Evidently not, which is just what the young are accusing us of. Well, that being the case, how could we have the gall to demand that such movements, now groping their way forward, have ready at hand something that we ourselves couldn't find after a thousand studies and every kind of scientific, philosophical, and humanistic research?

Unfortunately, after all these twists and turns what should we run into again but belief, because while we have no true, precise answer to our problems, we all *believe* we do. Each of the political parties has its own, as do the bureaucrats, intellectuals, and technicians. We all believe we possess the secret of the just society and the solution to our crises. But I would argue that this faith in solutions is among the most baneful anywhere. It leads us from errors to lies, from directives to dictatorships. It's a mistake to think you can have a solution when there isn't even a problem in the sense explained above. Take city planners: they raised the issue of the ideal human habitat, but this isn't a "problem." It can't be reduced to a specific number of clear, exact, and limited data. As soon as you formulate it as a problem, you do find a solution (since you set it up that way), but when you move on to practical application, the result is *always* a human disaster. To date no city planner has discovered how to make people as comfortable in a planner's "creative environment" as they are in their homes.

Things get done as circumstances permit, by action and reaction, with the slow evolutionary movement of life itself. Of course, you can speed up that vital rhythm and get hens to lay two eggs every day for a year, after which they croak. You can turn out marketable chicken in a month and veal in six, but it's garbage. Things have a rhythm of their own, and if you want them done well, you have to respect it, without imposing solutions from outside. Our solutions are always responding to problems on the periphery of the truth. The world of living, human things comes about by risk-filled choices of people with a stake in it, through successive decisions made by these people. Such decisions may seem to take strange paths, but their slowness is needed for maturation. And all this has to be made up step by step as you go along without any preconceived ideas except the ones from past experience whose lesson has been learned.

Hence to believe, to have the conviction that you have "the solution," is always the radical opposite of the principles that make for life and for livability. And what makes matters considerably worse is the fact that because believers are by definition convinced that their system is the only answer to the difficulty facing us, they inevitably try to put it into practice. Scientists, sticking to their prudent, rational method, which is always overshadowed by doubt and rests entirely on precise, objective foundations, can stay tolerant and maintain their distance from things, but not those who believe in the Solution. They will necessarily end by wanting to force it on people, since their credulous folly assures them that it will redound to the welfare and salvation of everyone. Thus belief corrupts thinking. Believing that one has the solution to political or economic problems is one of the catastrophes afflicting our society. The proliferation of planning in all realms of modern life is, like our passion for forecasts, a fatal disease. In this sense our society is worse than those where people lived in a religious universe, because those societies knew doubt and uncertainty, while believers in scientific and technological solutions are the merciless executioners of our world, untouched by scruples or remorse.

7

Veiled Reality

Una: I couldn't agree more with your reading of the danger you rightly denounce as coming from the curious practical application of belief in true solutions. But I'm greatly troubled by your own certitude when it comes to the real world. You're afraid of belief being imposed upon reality, but you seem to me quite positive about the existence of that reality.

What is real? What is reality? We've gotten beyond the naive notion that whatever our eyes can see and our hands can grasp must be real. We know that reality is a construct. You know as well as I that a fact, or what we call a fact, is always synthetic. We never get to know a thing as it is in itself—assuming that it actually exists. A fact is a set of interpretations of signs decoded for us by our cultural milieu. We read reality by means of a cipher or key that we learned along with nursery rhymes and the drawings and cutouts we were made to do in kindergarten. Forms, colors, and words are all learned; it's our culture that has us grasp, assemble, and interpret what we will subsequently call the real world. The latter, then, only exists against the background, not of knowledge (in the strict sense) but of slightly random beliefs. Those whose belief is richer and fuller will be better able to interpret a reality more charged with meaning for them.

Surely you know that some scientists have gone so far as to say that the real world is simply that entity which, thanks to our most advanced measuring devices, we may suppose exists. But you have to begin by believing in the accuracy equipment. I might say that believing is reaching out one's hand toward reality, not only toward truth but reality. Reaching out one's hand like a beggar, pleading for a parcel of reality, seeking the limits of the real, a hand that should neither be too greedy nor clutch one particular feature of the real world. . . .

Believing is stretching out my hand toward a world whose presence I have trust in, without being able to prove it or affirm it, stretching out my hand to welcome nature as well as another person, and thereby to free myself from unbearable uncertainty about a world that means nothing to me and a neighbor whom I'll never reach. Believing is abolishing the distance between Achilles and the tortoise.

How could you get along without a decisive affirmation of the real world? And as soon as you pronounce the word "reality," your affirmation becomes belief. We've learned nowadays that the truly basic element in the universe, its creative, innovative force is disorder or noise (in communication systems) or turbulence, whatever resists precise formulation, whatever doesn't follow established laws. The keys to science are no longer order and regularity but turmoil and unexpectedness, between "the mirror and the smoke." I know, of course, that this exasperates certain scientists, but they strike me as behind the times.

So now we have a universe in motion, largely unforeseeable, which has a present identity and future prospects only because it includes a permanent potential for disorder. So tell me, how can you come to terms with a universe like that without some sort of belief? You have to hold on to the conviction that through all the *dis*order order is being built up, that the mouth will not devour itself, that the turbulence will not end up being a fragment of chaos but the possibility of life. . . . You have to have the certitude without which science would be unthinkable—and through it you discover the close connection between the positive and the negative, the source and resource of the same reality that you contrast with belief.

We now know that things are not so simple, that nothing fits the overly clear categories of the old interpretations. I much prefer the prudent approach of modern scientists who respect the fullness of human beings in their multiple and contradictory dimensions. Think for example of the "veiled reality" that Bernard d'Espagnat addresses so carefully in his indispensable book, *The Search for Reality*.[8] D'Espagnat shows how wrong physicists and positivists are when they claim that it's meaningless to discuss things we can know nothing about. What's truly meaningless is that sort of reductionism. Contemporary physicists are obliged to recognize that scientific descriptions are often metaphorical, even mythical. And the theorem of nonseparability, which is one of the central issues debated by scientists today, brings us right back to a veiled reality. Physicists are forced to acknowledge this or else they must keep silent about almost everything since they know they're unqualified to speak with certainty about the real world. They're resigned to dealing exclusively with measurements. D'Espagnat shows why, if science is to remain a live possibility and not to collapse into reductionism, we have to bet on a "qualified realism," that is, a realism not naively physical, but irreproachable nonetheless, so that the world around us becomes a comprehensible reality. It's an admirable book, Monos, and you ought to read it. It points out that the most rigorous scientific thinkers of our day have abandoned the stress on

8. Bernard d'Espagnat, *A la recherche du réel*, 1979.

clear and simple thinking that reigned supreme a century ago, and that knowledge of reality presupposes a fundamental act of faith. There was a time when one could separate the subjective and objective dimension as you do, but no longer.

Don't you see, Monos, that it's just too easy (and makes too little practical sense) to disjoin these two domains, consigning objectivity to science and subjectivity to belief? One could settle—barely—for such an arrangement in the nineteenth century. But unless belief is mere infantile stammering, can we accept this division of knowledge today? Beyond that, isn't it clear that if you deliberately renounce objective descriptions of the way we know God, you make it impossible to say anything at all about otherness?[9]

---

9. On these two points see the remarkable essay by André Dumas, *Nommer Dieu*, 1980.

8

Believing in Death

Monos: But, Una, isn't the weakness of belief due precisely to the immense diversity of its applications? My reason can apply itself, can get involved in only a small number of forms, which are limited by certain specific conditions. On the other hand I see belief everywhere, as you do, but that's just what makes me suspect it. One can believe everything, which proves nothing. One can believe whatever one wishes, which implies indifference. But what a strange passionate kind of indifference this belief is! Take another look at the contemporary passion for destruction, for everything destroyed and dismembered: doesn't this triumphant derision make you suffer? Aren't you pained by the massacre of things, by the way people admire ruins rather than the peaceful harmonies of an eighteenth-century facade or a full life? The madness of the bacchantes, like the cultural revolution in China, spares nothing. Both are models of belief, which these days seems to me to be steering ever more directly toward death, nothingness, the void, instead of toward the gentle lure of a real, freely chosen good. When you think how people admire the destruction of language, how they prefer mumbling to proper speech . . .

If so many young men and women commit suicide today,

it's not simply because of social trauma and discouragement
—it's a somber passion for nothingness. We're familiar with
this, to some extent, from the Romantic era, but then it was
a matter of a small group of bourgeois intellectuals, whereas
nothingness is now becoming the object of a collective fascination. Is this a premonition that some massive holocaust is
on the way? Isn't it rather the dark side of belief, always so
ambiguous and dangerous with its lack of coherence and concrete foundations? Look at the man whom some propose as a
model and contemporary hero—Yukio Mishima. Blessed
with so many gifts, leading a life "full of brilliant deeds, of
travels, works, and proud display," he committed ritual suicide in 1970, thus ending his combat against the mediocrity
of our time and the abandonment of ancient values. This fascination with death must prove something, but what? Perhaps that the ancient heroic values persist and that the only
way to bear witness to them is by following them through the
act of hara-kiri. Yet what folly to hope to base one's life on
the denial of life—which is often enough the fate of believers.
Look at Henri de Montherlant, that extreme instance of the
will to live, or Ernest Hemingway: the vital urge they felt to
test their own identity and effective presence finally resolved
itself in suicide. Belief seems to be singularly rich in suicidal
tendencies these days.

Una: Yes, but in earlier days . . .

Monos: Well, I don't know about that. The only period I'm
familiar with is our own, and all throughout it wherever belief
has had free play, we've seen the negation of humanity and
the undertow pulling it out into the unnamable, in the literal
sense of the word. I'm frightened by this wave of nihilism,
even though it doesn't necessarily lead to physical suicide.
I'm alarmed by this submissive willingness to let oneself be
carried along by the lethal flood waters of the crowd, of a
system, a whole society, or a maelstrom of images and

sounds; to conform, collapse, find one's identity by losing oneself, to be other than oneself by being nothing at all. But if you want to enter into this ludicrous spectacle, you have to believe in collective survival, in the appearance of distraction, work, and relationships—but only the appearance of them, the mere façade. Yet this would be intolerable unless one believed in a possible escape into annihilation.

What disturbs me, then, in the proliferation of belief is seeing how well it fits in with all the forms of destruction, collective or individual, impassioned or apparently rational. It seems in fact to carry the germs of all of them. Belief has no critical standards. It's the most childish and dangerous kind of behavior because nothing can stop it; it can't be reasoned with or contradicted. It overwhelms the minds of philosophers, leading them to postulate a solid foundation in the void or the universal dominion of absurdity. It's all simply a matter of belief—but once you go in that door living becomes problematic.

I'm thinking, for example, of that brilliant and deceptive experiment that sent intellectuals into such ecstasy, the new pedagogy of Summerhill: no more rules, no more norms, no more duties, no more taboos, no more discipline—a marvelously exciting program in a society so burdensome and constricting. But it's a great mistake not to see the depth of a child's need for guidelines, models, and norms. These shouldn't be rigid, of course; they have to be breakable, because breaking rules is a fundamental part of our existence—without it the child remains a child forever. But it's wrong to *believe* (and you can't *know* when there's no scientific fact or hard reality here) that children are happy when they can continually roam aimlessly about and do anything they wish. In this situation, children get terribly anxious, because they have no fixed point to orient themselves by. They play but they don't become properly integrated. They do what they feel like at any given moment, but they don't enjoy it since they haven't earned their playtime. They're always unsettled and end up sinking into boredom unrelieved by the diversity of "anything you like." They can never be self-assured without suggestions, without a framework to fit things into, just as they need role models if they are to grow up at all.

It's no accident that so many children raised according to the Summerhill method later on in adult life joined the army or the police. Once having reached maturity they chose jobs with a maximum of constraint where they found the strict rules they had missed in their youth. The founder himself was no different in this regard: in his childhood A. S. Neill had been hemmed in by all sorts of harsh regulations, which he overcame to make something of himself. I don't condemn the man personally; he came by his success honestly. But once again we see someone *believing* he's got a universal solution: if I was unhappy during my childhood on account of the obligations and restrictions I had to endure, let's get rid of them all and make children happy. Neill failed to see that if he hadn't had to struggle against those rules, his growth would have been permanently stunted, however cheerful he might appear to be. "Freedom" that consists in complete exemption from obedience is every bit as traumatizing and confusing as massive, insurmountable constraint. Beliefs such as Neill's are based on false ideas about people and on other beliefs, especially that of the natural goodness of human beings which says leave them alone and everything will be fine. This shows how belief removes us from real life, how it warps and distorts our existence in this world, how readily we throw up rickety scaffoldings under that belief, each part supported ever so tenuously by the one beneath it.

Nevertheless, when I say that belief carries us away from reality, that's not quite true. At the root of every belief there always lies a tiny bit of reality, but through a terrifying process the act of believing adds on to reality things that weren't there to begin with and thus falsifies the human position in the cosmic territory that should have been their home. People believe; they believe in everything. It's belief that makes money so powerful and produces the disasters that come in the wake of our economic obsessions and of the twin monstrosities, capitalism and communism. If money had never gotten beyond the level of an instrument pure and simple, without being swathed in illusion and blown out of all proportion; if it had remained just a concrete useful object, without all the ideological freight and hypnotic fascination it now has, it would have no power over humanity and would not pervert it the way it does. But we had to add on the belief that money lets us do everything, that everything has a price tag, that thanks to money all power is in our hands. It's belief that has cast a halo around this new god of mortals, this new god who brought on the injustices and massacres of the modern world.

And I would say the same for political power. It's a weird alchemy that transforms the banal power of organizing, managing, and ordering into a sublime function that concentrates within itself all powers and armaments, all rights and abuses, with the consent of the oppressed—because they believe. They believe in that omnipotence; they meekly stretch out their necks and submit to the yoke. Belief gives birth to passivity; it engenders a kind of surreal world which is the sine qua non of alienation. The person placed squarely in front of reality, who looks it straight in the eye, can fight oppression and move on to freedom. But in order to do that, one must begin by destroying myths and beliefs.

Ah, the anarchists were right to trace all forms of alienation back to belief in God. Put that aside, and the only things left to struggle against are realities—which we're quite capable of handling. If we stop believing in the State, we can disobey;

and if we do it as a body the State, for all its arms and laws,
no longer has any effective power. Thus all the evil of society
comes from our belief in it. I am most certainly not the first
one to say this, but we have to become aware that the situation is in its most radical manifestation nowadays—we can see
the phenomena of belief steadily increasing along with dangers of every sort, the dangers of the growth of technology,
the dangers of the spread of power. . . . And the connection
between belief and these modern perils is no accident.

You know, Una, that I'm not talking about exceptional
cases, the mass delirium of Hitlerism, say. I'm referring to
what is now everyone's lot: it's becoming more and more perilous to live in a world where totally fictitious beliefs are
pinned to real things, to dangerous and oppressive things that
have to be faced head-on (that is, without those beliefs) if we
are to overcome them. Which is precisely what the weaver of
illusions does his best to prevent, so as to safeguard his own
power. He makes you believe in a surreal world, and why
not? It's extremely useful. It's extremely useful, for instance,
to make us believe that humanity is naturally good. This is
another example of how subtly beliefs are intertwined. It's
not just that a surreal dimension makes us accept the real
one; there are also, to complement that, consoling beliefs that
lead us to accept the side of reality we ought to be fighting.
Because, after all, if by chance humans were evil, if by chance
humans were children and by no means adults, if by chance
at their very core there was hatred, the death wish, covetous-
ness, the love of power, conquest, and domination, a fero-
cious lone-wolfishness, if by chance that was the case, how
could we accept the unlimited growth of the means of aggression and destruction? Would you give hand grenades
to three-year-old children? Of course not. But if someone
managed to convince you that these children were extraordinary beings, reasonable, self-controlled, interested only in

goodness, and capable of weighing the consequences of their acts, then why would you refuse them the grenades? You would be working with the assurance that they wouldn't set them off accidentally, unknowingly, or to hurt their little comrades.

It is this absurd belief in the merits of humanity that brings on the destruction of morality. What we see today (and the liberated children of Summerhill foreshadowed this) strikes me as profoundly disturbing. All ethical systems are either in ruins or empty—empty when they come down to the mere repetition of ancient and obviously outdated rules, when, for example, socialist regimes show no ethical creativity whatsoever. With regard to work, sexuality, marriage, obedience to authority, civic and military duty, they bury one up to the ears in the worst sort of bourgeois morality. Socialism has produced nothing by way of constructive innovation in this area; it has simply repeated the past, which proves just how passé and sterile it is.

But what do we see on the other side: a facile moral nihilism mistaken for freedom, when it's actually a tissue of incoherence, absurdity, and weakness. With mocking irony thousands of novels and plays savage the morality of days gone by; they attack our grandparents' or our greatgrandparents' taboos, the rules nobody gives a thought to anymore. Critics fall into each other's arms, congratulating themselves on their great courage in slaying skeletons, in triumphing over phantoms that cast no shadow, that exist only in the minds of those who wish to put them to flight, thereby earning for themselves a round of applause.

And so, destructive beliefs do in beliefs that are already dead. We see here, in this hallucinatory game of mirrors, how the phenomenon of belief serves to avoid real confrontations, bloody battles with hard reality, with society as it is today rather than as it was yesterday or the day before. You'll never convince me, Una, that there's any positive value in belief. I've seen the lot, and I've found them all to be empty, hollow, and noxious. I've seen all sorts of deceit, illusion, and evasion disguised as conquest; I've seen deeply distressed men and women refusing to acknowledge their own identity. That's what believing is, that and nothing more. To my mind all beliefs are empty, but people never grow up; they keep on evading reality, though for different and contradictory purposes. And belief keeps on giving birth to new beliefs or counterbeliefs—here at least there is nothing new under the sun. . . .

9

Losing Oneself to Find Oneself

Una: Come now, Monos, stop trying to frighten us with your gallery of monsters. What it comes down to is that you have neither pity nor love. Believing isn't what you say it is; it's not *just* that at any rate, though I admit there's some truth in what you say. There is, quite evidently, no infallible criterion for choosing the content and object of one's belief. One can, undeniably, have faith in any kind of folly. One can transform reality so as not to see it or to use it in a passionate delirium—but what does that prove? That belief brings about a state of frenzy or infantilism? The opposite is true, if we can take it for granted that nothing is possible, for better or for worse, without belief, that belief is where our freedom of choice and hence our responsibility is actualized.

If you restrict yourself to the level of the real world, measured in strictly scientific terms, if you adapt and conform to it (and what could justify nonconformity?), then you're determined by the facts as you've ascertained them. If you restrict yourself to the level of logic, of pure rationality (that tempting refuge from everything irrational), then you're likewise determined by the laws of logic and reason's imperative. The only way to escape determinism is through the imagination, through myth and the return to origins, but none of these three approaches is possible, or rather none can be taken seriously, without belief, just as belief finds its roots in all three.[10]

We were saying that it looked very much as if belief was a necessity of human life. It's always been that way. If you want to thwart destiny, to escape from fate, you have to believe. But, of course, destiny too plays its tricks, just as reason and history do, and it can turn belief into slavery or a death sentence. But that's only one possibility. But in that very fact of possibility itself is where we find our responsibility mingling with unusual opportunities for renewal, thanks to the explosion and implosion of imagination. If one single reality convinces me of the potential for human freedom, it is that very dimension ingrained in humankind itself—namely belief. But everything depends upon what or whom one believes. Where to place one's trust? You attacked, and rightly so, naive belief in human goodness, but belief in the basic viciousness of humanity strikes me as equally disastrous.

Monos: Can we let that assertion stand for the moment? I plan to return to it later.

Una: Consider the importance of believing in the miracle of a human race unique of its kind in the whole galactic universe. Now that we no longer believe in God, we moderns, in order to assuage our loneliness, have solemnly begun to imagine that there might be life, even intelligent life, somewhere beyond this earth. Some claim to have received messages from extraterrestrial beings, and for a while a number of scientists worked frenetically to interpret certain radio-astronomical data as signals. Which only shows how credulous experts can be—and how little science and reason protect us from illusions. Naturally people have tried, ever since

10. Laplantine, *Les Trois Voix de l'imaginaire*, 1972.

Galileo, to draw on such idle, far-fetched ideas for every conceivable sort of argument against God and still more against Jesus Christ. In the face of the enormous mass of galaxies in an expanding universe about whose origins we are completely in the dark, we wonder why a God should take any interest in our little bit of the cosmos, in this insignificant microplanet lost in the infinite reaches of space. And against the background of millions of nonhuman but intelligent life forms that may be scattered throughout the universe, what are we to make of the story of a God supposedly incarnate in human flesh? What a lot of childishness.

Actually, if you're looking for childishness, there's no better example than this line of reasoning. More and more scientists are beginning to think that we are alone in the universe after all, because if the distance between our planet and the sun had varied ever so slightly, no life of any sort would have arisen here: a change of plus or minus one percent and there would be no such thing as intelligence as we know it. Hence the likelihood is extremely small that the right conditions for the emergence of life and intelligence exist anywhere else. Shades of the ancient legend that God chose the earth on which to plant a unique garden and to bring forth the unique phenomena of life and mind. . . .

This is all a matter of belief, of course, but if we do believe in that uniqueness, it ought to give rise to a special degree of prudence and responsibility. If the act of creation spawning intelligent life really did take place, it would behoove us to preserve it lest the cosmos once again become empty space and the galaxies mere blind mechanisms on which no one would ever again cast a contemplative glance. Today scientific probability links up with the inspired belief of the first ages of humanity. Early humans stood up—and discovered that they were unique. They named everything in relation to themselves; they even saw God as human. Primitive anthropomorphism? Elementary anthropocentrism? The sort of thing that once we were adults, of legal age, vaccinated (against belief), we reject with a little smile of condescension and scorn? And whither have we been led by our pride over having discovered that we are one of the products of chance and necessity, that humans are a sheer accident of no importance? Where indeed if not to the verge of possible universal extermination.

The rejection of belief—because in our towering superiority we have entered the kingdom of reason—has brought on the pitiless age of contempt and mass murder. The primitives who waged war for their beliefs had, to an overwhelming extent, a very lofty notion of the adversaries they were obliged to kill. One sacrificed a prisoner captured in battle to the heavenly or infernal gods so that that person could carry a message to them and because he or she was admirably suited to be offered as a supreme sacrifice to the gods. Nowadays, out of the conviction that we are nothing but ordinary inhabitants of the universe, having lost faith in the dazzling miracle of the birth of humanity, we begin by degrading, by spiritually, ethically, and psychically destroying the masses whom we wish to slaughter. We have freed ourselves from higher modes of belief in order to abandon ourselves to the orgiastic extirpation of what is most human in people. Such is progress. We must recover our belief in that miracle; we must tremble once more with fear and respect before the unique mystery and recover the sacred terror, the taboos that made human life an act of wonder. We must rediscover faith in a beauty formed with us in mind. The stars are not blind heavenly bodies when—and because—we look at them. The poets are right, not the mathematicians. The stars send us signs charged with meaning, just like the ocean, like the explosion of plant life in spring.

If we still had the fundamental confidence that everything

was made for us and is directed to us, that we are the caretakers of reality, we should then be a great deal more prudent and modest. Look at the old myth of Genesis—I know you don't believe in it, of course, but you can look at it anyway—nowhere does it say that God appoints the Adamic couple the absolute, unlimited, arbitrary masters of the earth or the garden, that destiny requires them to exploit it to death. On the contrary, they are placed at the summit of creation so that it may be respected. They are its guardians; that is, they must safeguard it and keep it beautiful and well, in accordance with God's plan. Humankind is responsible for—that is, they will have to answer to God for—what happens on earth. And God can always ask them: what have you done with the world's beauty, its harmony, its perfection?

Human beings are the stewards of the world out of love, for the sake of love. If God tells them to "rule over" it (that phrase so often invoked as a license to exploit, gouge out profits, and separate humanity from nature), this comes *immediately* after the proclamation that man and woman together are the image of God. The image of God is Love; there is no other. And that means that people ought to rule over creation in exactly the same way that God himself does, that is, not by violence or constraint or technology but by love. Love is the only driving force behind this myth. And people are called to manage the world in and through love. But once people no longer believe in the unity of the world, once the earth we inhabit is a bit of wreckage wandering in space and we ourselves the uncertain product of chemical combinations, how could you expect there to be any respect, any limits? It's enough to be powerful, to accumulate resources, and to make money at every step. The death of the old childhood beliefs has also been the death knell of the world we find ourselves in.

And yet the moment our obsession with output and con-

sumption loosens its hold on us, how can we not be stunned
by the harmoniousness of this world, by the correspondence
between beauty and the perpetuation of the species? A banal
notion, to be sure, but the blossoms come before the fruit.
And why did those flowers have to be so beautiful? Oddly
enough, there seems never to have been a human society that
wasn't struck with wonder at the grace of animals and the
beauty of flowers.

There's a curious symmetry present here, as if some deep
instinct kept people attuned to those promised graces, which
are not, it turns out, gratuitous. Flowers have to expend their
fragrance lavishly to attract bees. Beauty is indispensable for
reproduction, for the survival of the species, whence the
beauty of woman and of man, which flourishes at the time of
the birth of love, with a view to the love of birth. All this
might have been made a simple mechanism, a kind of clock-
work or biological data-processing, but it wasn't in the least.
Instead we were given the added dimension of grace, the order of pleasure, beauty, and spontaneous generosity. And all
this for us, bound up with humanity's faith that it *was* all
done for us. There can be neither grace nor pleasure if no one
is there to experience them.

People were not deceived in their belief. They began to lose
their bearings and go astray when they thought they were
*un*deceived. But look at all the consequences of their being
"disabused." Monos, you said you deplored the way ethics
vanished with the onset of the absurd belief in natural human
goodness. I would add that ethics began to disappear with the
breakdown of belief in humankind's unique role and responsibility. But if you dissociate yourself with all belief, how can
you hope to lay the foundations for any sort of morality? How
will you wind up with anything except rigid injunctions, external constraints, and "social control"? I know, I know this
approach is unfashionable. I'm aware of all the efforts to base

a morality on science, to preclude obligations and sanctions, to treat it as the direct expression of human nature. But these are intellectual games. No moral system of this type will ever get beyond a narrow circle of specialists. There is no morality if it's not held in common, if it's not spontaneously accepted by everyone in concert, so that those who infringe upon it know they are doing "evil," that they have made themselves outcasts. The goodness of humanity? No morality can grow out of that soil, only rampant evil. You yourself said so, and observation supports you.

Well then, starting with—at the very least—belief in human uniqueness, we have to find our way back to a morality that boldly distinguishes good from evil. Its definition of them will, certainly, differ from those of past centuries and other cultures, but these concepts are indispensable for creating one's identity and guiding one's steps. I believe in the possibility of an ethics of the individual, of freedom, of choice, of responsibility, an ethics of everyday life, conquering the present instead of constantly fleeing to an idealized elsewhere, to a scientific or apocalyptic future, a refuge consisting in antiquated political and ideological rites—those astonishing mummified remains piously handed down from one generation of sages, savants, and politicians to another as emblems of truth. Think of Lenin's tomb or the sarcophagus of Saint Ambrose. But mummies are the wrong place to look for the living source of morality, without which we shall go rocketing down the road to suicide. We are responsible, each one of us has to believe in and accept his or her own responsibility for this indispensable discovery, which won't be handed to us by some genius or society as a whole but will come from the belief that humans are unique, that the individual is the locus of all creation—the only locus. Now it's quite true that this creation implies first of all the unsparing destruction of whatever enslaves us. One must lose oneself to find oneself. We have to lose ourselves as a society that aspires to swallow up everything and shatters and breaks into pieces by trying to do just that. We must lose ourselves as men and women who mistake ourselves for something we are not—the beginning and end of everything—and as a result who wander about in aimless disorientation.

If the beginning and the end are in *us*, then we don't have the slightest chance of rebuilding the morality without which this world, this specific late-twentieth-century world, Western and Third or Fourth, is headed toward suicide. I'm speaking in the most basic terms possible. There is no other choice before us but suicide—or the reinvention, both individual and communal, of the ethics of responsibility. Once that happens—but not before and nowhere else—everything will become possible once more. And how can we achieve this without starting to believe? No part of the past or the future, neither science nor technology nor the revolution, contains anything that can help us to live, that can assure our life. We need to believe exactly like the Magi, bearers of Science, Power, and Gold, who simply *believed* that the Star was the only sign worthy of acceptance, and who undertook that absurd journey to the Star which we in turn must also undertake. But it wasn't then (and isn't now) a question of any old journey and any old star. We mustn't be misled. . . .

10

From Satan to Eros

Monos: Your appeal is moving, Una, but who would pay any attention to it? What group, what class, what elite, what church, what party would be prepared nowadays to go on such a march into the wilderness? But wait, we're always marching into uncharted areas. We never stop forging ahead, even on the moon, and, thanks to our technical mastery, we're moving at a speed greater than ever before.

Una: But what's our destination, Monos?

Monos: Ah, then, you mean you want to enlist us for a campaign essentially *different* from all those waged for the last two hundred years. What folly, what an ironic dream! How do you intend to get them moving, this human race you believe in, when they're completely self-involved but on the other hand they no more believe in themselves than in absolute evil?

Consider the strange paradox of our age. People undoubtedly no longer believe in your star-signs, or any other signs indicating the presence of transcendence in this world, but they gladly welcome other forces, forces they won't really call demonic, in which they have total and exclusive faith. Words like "the devil" and "Satan" provoke laughter today, but they're nonetheless seductive. If you want to know the bedrock faith of our time, it's belief in the devil. Look at the success of the "horror films," which are actually about the devil. We can grimace at the idea of them in a lofty intellectual manner, but *Rosemary's Baby* remains the key to our dreams. Of course, we no longer believe in medieval demonology but rather in a much worse and more elusive variety, one where the devil—an unnamed devil whom we nonetheless believe and revere—does his work in our own human functions. Remember, the devil is the one who divides, the divider.

And what world was ever more torn than ours, more divided in all its parts? We see division everywhere—generations, families, nations against each other, Islam against Islam, imperialism against imperialism, communism against communism. Countries split; the oldest, most habitual ties tear apart. Marriage fades like a shadow. The umbilical cord no longer binds the fetus to its mother, who now wishes only to get rid of it. In this time of malediction there is division everywhere. And this is not a division arising out of some majestic dialectical order but division as incoherence, as absurdity, division by the radical disappearance of every kind of love except eroticism, the division of ridicule, of the mask, of the spectacle.

Whom are you trying to call, Una, to recruit for your journey to the Star? In its practical behavior humanity has shown that it no longer has any cult or belief or Lord but one, and that is the *diabolos*, the devil. We can see this in everything it does. We thought we were free of the old mythologies, but once again we find something more cunning than we are. The devil has veiled his face, but all those now passionately engaged in the ruthless holy wars we mentioned before ought to realize that the belief driving them on comes from the mysterious devil of conflicts and estrangement. Wherever we see a lethal rupture shattering the bond of mutual love, whenever the finger of vengeful accusation points, exposing its target to collective hatred, at that moment Satan and the devil possess those hearts and move those hands.

And then consider how the monster of accusation triumphs in this world, declaring that now it's the victims who must not only admit their guilt but bring charges against themselves as well. Satan is so perfectly concealed here that the line between prosecution and defense is blurred. He deftly leads victims to play Satan against themselves, so he need not even be there to accomplish his task. Jean-Paul Sartre was right: there's no more "eye" in our tombs to watch us. The mere fact of being looked at by another is enough to put us on trial. But now I am invited *to be* that Other who tears me to pieces and proves my guilt. "Hell is other people," but, thanks to the subtle devices of auto-criticism, that is, of auto-accusation, the Other is myself.

Psychoanalysis too has been known to play this game. What a strange sort of crisscrossing and intermingling of forces. You look at yourself, you talk to yourself, you descend into the darkest and most unknown depths of yourself, you go back to the roots of your childhood, and thus, they tell you, you have the possibility of a fresh start, of liberation. But that's exactly what you're promised by the tender-hearted commissar in charge of your self-criticism: once you have scrutinized every element of your life, once you've subjected it to the searchlight of theory, once you've discerned the point where you started to wander off course, to leave the path of doctrinal purity and correctness, once you've said out loud, in the presence of that discreet, secret witness, all the things that made you a wretched sinner against the Party line, then you'll be delivered; you'll feel the burden lifted that wrung your heart and twisted the expression on your face; you'll be a new person.

And in both cases it'll be the role of Satan you have been

asked to play, to be for yourself, with *exactly* the same promise that the old Serpent has been making since the beginning:
"If you accuse your other self, you shall be as a god. As free
as a god and knowing all things." Ours is a marvelous epoch:
after so many complicated shortcuts and beneath so many
masks we find once more the most ancient of myths. But
we're totally ignorant of this, so we press forward, blind believers, on roads that are not ours, that are not even human.
And after purifying ourselves by self-condemnation, by becoming Satan to ourselves, we don't stop being Satan, the
accuser. Listen to any piece of news, look at any spectacle put
on by this hallucinating world, and what do you get but a web
of accusations?

There are no better accusers than those who have been
Satan to themselves. There are no better commissars than
those who have staged their own self-critiques. And the kindly psychiatrists (but no, they don't have to be kindly) who
have only one objective (but no, they don't have to have an
objective), namely to cure the patient, must themselves have
undergone psychoanalysis. Once you begin, there can be no
end. Satan's triumph is not the banal Dance of the Damned,
the childish images of Romantic vampires, which are all mere
literary amusement. Satan's real triumph is the general accusation of all against all. We are living through a gigantic trial
where each of us plays the fiery prosecutor, deliriously excit-
ed to be the Explainer and Redresser of Wrongs. Every time
we accuse another (the fascist or the communist or the Jew or
the immigrant or the young person . . .) we simultaneously
set ourselves free and assure ourselves of our own righteousness. We've found our scapegoat. And indeed we spend our
time looking for scapegoats, to place our hand on their heads
and so disburden ourselves of all our faults, and then to send
them off into the wilderness to become the prey of wiverns,

of incubi and succubi, of the phantoms that represent our own hatreds expelled at last.

We have to admit that through the extraordinary successes won by science and our intelligence, through our beliefs both implicit and explicit, Satan has been gaining ground literally everywhere—without existing per se. All we need do is be ourselves and believe in ourselves—and then the serpent coils. After this phase of swelling accusation the end result can only be seclusion in the self, the self-sufficient, self-satisfied personality, content to contemplate itself, a Narcissus who will not drown himself because he is already dead, assassinated by his own accusation.

Yet he must go on living after all. How poverty stricken is modern perverted eroticism! It presents us with the surprising absurdity—which is only one of many—of self-realization through eros. It points to the Marquis de Sade as the Great Emancipator, the heroic example of a kind of transcendence (of humankind? of self?), which cannot express or complete itself in the act of sex. Reread de Sade carefully and you'll see—and this is no superficial moralizing—that every one of his adventures ends in an impasse, an impossibility. And what about the Other, what have you done with him or her in *your* perverse erotic adventure? I'm quite amused by the hectoring attitude displayed by the proud inventors of the new sexual freedom. "You've made women into a object," they cry (that much I agree with). "Now she's going to liberate herself through eroticism; she'll finally become herself. . . ." But perverted eroticism always means solitary pleasure, and so how can we fail to see that anyone we use is never anything more than an object to consummate our pleasure? In perverted eroticism the Other is never anything more than a slightly improved instrument for masturbation.

Eroticism so-called today is imprisonment in the self, nothing else and nothing more, while as for that object, you're prepared to throw it aside, since once again it bears what could be your mark of infamy, except that, fortunately, you've managed to project it onto him or her. You've fallen back upon yourself, stiffened your defenses against the look of another. At the same time you make use of the Other to shield yourself from all accusations and to satisfy your passion of Narcissus, the living corpse.

So there we are. There we have the fundamental belief of every man and woman in our age of reason and progress. And do you dare to speak of this peculiar species with love and tenderness, do you dare believe in it? Yes, you dare to talk about believing in the uniqueness of this accidental species, which has no ultimate goal now except to kill itself. You're giving in to clichés, Una, and to your own kindheartedness. You want to hope where there's no hope left.

It's true, you could reply that I myself am giving in—to the credo of the people who believe in nothingness, after I myself rejected them. It's true that, with the world as it is and people become the *diabolos* and shaitan of themselves, I can scarcely believe in anything *but* evil. If I were a Christian, I would believe in something like original sin or in a wicked God. . . . And, by the way, if I did, I'd share that belief with millions of others. Christianity, it seems to me, has been swamped by its belief in original sin, which is surely nothing more than belief. If you examine closely that fine account in Genesis of the break between God and humankind, you'll note that it has nothing to do with sin. It was only later that the interpeters and *their* interpreters read that "sin" into the text; the text says nothing about any "original sin," which is merely a reassuring, simple-minded explanation of the presence of evil in the world. To come up with that formula they had to turn the story into something other than what it professes to be, to take it as an explanatory fact instead of as a myth designating

God, not people. This elaboration of the concept of original sin shows humanity's obsession with itself, the only thing of interest on its horizon, whereas the biblical text thrusts that passion aside to point to God.

But, when all is said and done, belief in original sin fits quite neatly into the pattern I've been trying to describe to you. Original sin is worse, if possible, than the Greek *ananke* (unrighteousness), because it cancels all human potential. It's in no sense an outside force that dominates and crushes human beings. If it were, then at least there'd be the possibility, the chance, the hope that humanity would find a cleft in the wall. But no, with this dogma evil is now rooted in the heart of being. Whatever people may do, they are trapped in evil. Whatever they create, however lofty or beautiful, carries the germs of death, ruin, and disaster because it comes from them. Think of it, generations and generations, an entire culture, persuaded of that, living with that hopeless belief.

Una: Not quite, Monos. Don't forget Jesus Christ. . . .

Monos: I said hopeless, and I mean it. People have not remembered Jesus, but the absolute perversion of what he stood for, a distortion so total that they've actually made themselves guilty of the death of God himself. Do you realize the effect that could have? How can we be surprised when, starting out with belief in original sin, people have wound up throwing the door wide open to the devil, to Satan, to eros, and that these have possessed their souls? What *is* surprising, if you take the trouble to read it, is that this unique narrative from Genesis plays such a small part in the Hebrew Bible. It tells the story, and then there's a fadeout, and all the action occurs somewhere else. Throughout the long procession of prophets and kings, of judges and laws, of patriarchs and sages, the text no longer deals with sin or absolute evil or an inherited calamity. . . . The story of what was later dubbed the Fall is an isolated event in that thousand-year record of "revelations." Yet the Fall became the central feature in the somber creed of the Dark Ages. We don't talk about original sin any more, but it has been so deeply branded into the soul of the West that every one of our thoughts and gestures bears its mark. There's belief for you: belief in evil, which is itself that evil and from which all other evils flow. . . .

11

Pardon and Forgetfulness

Una: Monos, my inseparable comrade, this is neither the time nor the place to try to elucidate the hideous nonsense that has turned love into self-hatred and grace into unending accusation. But before it even arises, can't you accept the other dimension of belief? Don't you have to believe before you can forgive? The only course you're willing to consider is the outright rejection of the world because you want to reject belief, yet it's not simply belief you're rejecting—it's everything human. And what else could we build our life on, if not forgiveness? I'll never forget the anguished question with which Camus ends one of his splendid books: "Who will forgive us?"

Don't you know, can't you feel that what people need more than anything else is forgiveness? People go on talking about various needs, "natural" or "artificial" needs, "subjective" or "objective" needs, aesthetic needs, the need for food or for comfort, the need for meaning or for drugs. But before anything else people feel an anxious need for pardon in the deepest part of themselves. Don't tell me, with your civilized scorn, that this need for pardon is a product solely of Judeo-Christian culture. Travel around the world and everywhere you go you'll find sacrifices, rites, taboos, offerings. It matters little to whom they're made or for what explicit purpose (for rain or victory, the death of enemies or success in the hunt). We have here the most basic expression of the need to be accepted. But this means at a more profound level to be pardoned, pardoned by the Unknown, the Ineffable, for what we are even more than for what we have done, pardoned by our fellows, our neighbors, our children, our friends, and pardoned by ourselves.

This is true even if the feeling is vague and inarticulate. I may have nothing to reproach myself for; and yet my whole being needs to be affirmed in its essence, that is, to be forgiven for existing, not for some fantasized guilt. This is all the more true if you're right in saying that people have become the *diabolos* and shaitan to themselves. Because in that case they can never grant themselves forgiveness on their own, can never absolve themselves and move joyfully ahead, dressed in gleaming silk and white linen. *Someone* has to pardon them. Can't you sense this, Monos, in the lucidity of your despair? Isn't it the absence of forgiveness that makes you talk on and on?

And if there is no God to turn to in whose name pardon may be given, the desire for pardon gets directed toward the Other, whose response is more necessary to me than my daily bread. And this is not a question of absurd scruples, or a delicate soul, or the bourgeois luxury of spiritual cares. We know that the most hardened criminals are at bottom racked with the anxiety that no one will accept them. Surely such things as mass political rallies, frenetic rock concerts, ritual dances by so-called primitives, shamanism, divine possession, and so forth, manifest our irrepressible need to be purified, justified, cleansed, in a word forgiven. Whether we're trying to drive out demons or to locate the source of evil in the enemy, such ceremonies are all designed to wipe out the evil in ourselves—though we may not even know that we're stricken with it—to prove, in effect, that we are forgiven. . . .

But if we insist on placing ourselves at the center of the picture, how are we to forgive and be forgiven without belief? Even the political commissars who sentence people to death or to the gulag, the high priests of modern times, the eternal successors of Fouquier-Tinville (who wanted to make the Republic pure and undefiled, to remove every possible corrupting influence), even they can act only because of a cluster of beliefs. These alone permit them to declare millions of innocent victims guilty and then have them executed, without being mere assassins in their own eyes. They act to win collective pardon and purification for the regime, while they themselves, the exterminating angels, are pardoned for their injustice by the blissful destiny of the humanity that will emerge from all those executions. Without forgiveness life is impossible. Without belief forgiveness is unacceptable. The very examples you gave only strengthen my conviction. You've continually likened humanity to its demons, but you were perfectly aware that there too it was a matter of belief—and deep down didn't you long for some kind of saving exorcism?

I'm altogether convinced that people have always been possessed by powers beyond their control. Yesterday it was the demons of the forest, nocturnal devils, phantoms returning from the past; today it's money or politics or technological excess. But we'll never find our way to deliverance simply by going back to "right reason" or the clarity of some philosophical system, or by plunging into the darkness of the unconscious and exploring the furthest subterranean recesses where iconoclastic festivals go on. You know as well as I do that these psychoanalytical rites, these flashes of hermeneutics only worsen the state of possession. . . . And when that soul was neatly swept, was clean and empty at last, seven demons rushed in to take the place of the one who had been driven out. . . .

What we need here is something more, and at the same time much less. We need exorcism, not the medieval kind with ritual recitation and solemn gestures, not a magical operation, but the exorcism of forgiveness, which obliterates evil and completely convinces the person forgiven that this obliteration has indeed occurred. And all your demons can do nothing about this forgiveness. The one thing that Mephistopheles can't do, in fact, is forgive. But how can you put this exorcism into practice without belief? "But this kind [of demon] never comes out except by prayer and fasting" (Matt. 17:21x), which are both necessarily expressions of faith.

You've aptly described the breakdown in human relations and the syndrome of accusation, yet how can they be surmounted, unless we begin by believing in others? Unless we believe, even when they lie to us, that there is also truth in what they say, that even when they hate us they have within them the potential for something else—provided that we take the first step by trusting them. Unless we believe that even if they deceive us, we must look for the spark of truth in them until we find it, that even if they tell us that they're good people when we know very well they aren't, we can understand that they're expressing a hope, not stating a fact. If they tell us that they're people without pity, we must find the cleft in the rock whence a few drops can always trickle. It's not a question of playing the simpleton, the credulous booby in the presence of the Other.

No, Monos, we have to be extremely lucid, we have to hear what they're saying—which is a lot of fancy nonsense. We can see through it all, and we may perhaps take an ironic pleasure in it, but the point is not to let this show. The only way out of the situation is for us to trust them, despite everything we know, to trust that something else may come out of this. We're not to believe *in* them as one believes *in* God, but we believe the best *of* them because they're never what they say they are, or what they aim at being. The mere fact that someone has trusted them always changes them to some extent, gets under their skin, even if they wink an eye when we're not looking and say, "I've got them." So what. You have to understand, Monos, that this is the only road open to all of us, to the whole human race, unless the evil powers are exorcised—forgiven and then forgotten.

Some empty, superficial people will argue, "If we can't forgive, let's at least forget." Or then, quite the contrary, at some ceremony commemorating the slaughters of the past, one might hear, "We're willing to forgive, but forget? Never!" What paltry rhetoric, at once so obvious and so hollow. What is forgetting without forgiveness but the ashes of time covering the corrosion that eats away at the metal beneath the painted surface until there is nothing left? And what kind of pardon is it that can't wipe away the memory of the wrong we have suffered? What sort of friendship or reconciliation can send down roots when the fact of the denial of justice is always being evoked afresh by these artificial ceremonies of "remembering"? Remembering what? The evil done by others? Perpetual vendetta? If there is forgiveness, our memories are blotted out. And hence there is more mercy in the heart of the individual than in the memories of society or its information systems.

Forgiving and forgetting go together, so long as they're solid and not a form of shadowy self-deception. They are the reciprocal conditions of possibility for our life together. Without them we have nothing to look forward to but destruction (and this is why the computerized memory bank strikes me as so menacing: flawless, incapable of forgetting or forgiving . . . coldly technical manipulation). But they must have a solid foundation on—need I say it?—belief, not on some arrogant, exacting mode of knowledge, on a science case-hardened in its own certainties, which will never forgive, that is, will never leave the guilty in peace (and everyone is guilty) but continue to arouse the raging Furies every time. Only a humble act of faith in the untapped possibilities of the person who has deceived us can both give our life a deliberate freedom and at the same time put his or her life at a crossroads, constantly open to the choice of a different self.

12

What I Believe

Monos: Isn't it remarkable, Una, how much ground we've covered? Every turn in the road has revealed new aspects of belief, opened up clearings in a very dense forest, only to show all the more pointedly the ambiguous nature of belief. It's both everything and nothing. It applies to everything, that is, to anything at all. It plays a tremendous role in history but it melts away into thin air the moment you expose it to the harsh light of analysis. Which makes me wonder—and worry—at the strange thumping success enjoyed by so many books on "What I Believe." What are we to make of such declarations? It seems to me that their popularity represents a major social trend that can only be explained by the deficiency or craziness of belief in our society—craziness in the sense that one speaks of a compass gone crazy.

What a place for me to be—plunged into a world of grimacing faces, like that of "Dulle Margriet" or the faces surrounding Jesus in Hieronymus Bosch. I find it simultaneously fascinating and horrible: walking through a mad universe, whose madness has some thoroughly agreeable features, I see myself in a room full of mirrors which is spinning round and round, or at the center of a giant kaleidoscope constantly turning and forming a thousand whimsical patterns. Where

could there be certitude in all this? Where, I anxiously wonder, can I find a frame of reference to orient me and tell me
where I am? How can I get anything really solid to hold on
to? And then, amidst this befuddlement, somebody comes
along proclaiming "What I Believe." Am I finally going to be
freed from my uncertainty? Someone is coming and will tell
me, at long last, what the truth is. We need people who bear
witness—to what exactly we don't know yet, but somebody
simply has to reassure me by testifying that there's something
permanent to believe in, that despite this world gone crazy
there's still a certitude I can lean on. Like children frightened
by the dark we cry out to one another, and hearing someone
tell me "I believe" sets my mind at rest and reassures me that
I too can go on.

Now if you take a good look at the situation, you'll see that
this is the limit of absurdity. Just consider the "What" in the
phrase "What I Believe"—it's grammatically neuter, which
ultimately robs belief of any, shall we say, existential import.
If we're talking about something neuter, how could I learn
anything from it? It's nothing more than an opinion, and I
have no use for opinions. We're dealing with an object, just
an object, of whatever sort, a doctrine, a science, ideas, a god
placed like a statue on a pedestal for me to bow down before,
a group, a class, a nation, a *Führer* or First Secretary, a gran-
diose work of my own contriving, a satellite or microprocessor, a history or vocation, even "humanity" itself. "What I
Believe" amounts to a little bric-a-brac, and nothing more.
The "What" can only designate something like a porcelain
vase, which I offer you as if it contained some marvelous
secret.

And after "What" we get the "I," the speaker. But why
should I care that so-and-so believes such-and-such? Perhaps
that interests the person who's speaking. I. Look at me. It
has to be said that the rage for the "What I Believe" genre

only echoes the passion for memoirs and intimate diaries, which are a subspecies of the novel. And the increasing popularity of the novel is a measure of the dwindling reality of human existence. The less you live, the more you read about other people. The less of a hero or heroine you are, the more you need to meet a hero or heroine. The less genuine sexual satisfaction you get, the more eroticism you have to look at or read about. The less your life is an adventure, the more you live out vicarious adventures. Through these vicarious experiences we feel that we're *not* nobodies, that we're *not* alone. Our life begins in the dream life we make up from other people's stories.

That allows us to handle without getting burned the explosively dangerous question, "What's it all worth, my life, my work, my loves, this civilization, this culture, this society, what's it all worth?" Luckily someone appears on the scene to tell me a little fairy tale—a novel. And then comes the more serious stuff: the great man recounts his life. He must have been something to become the supreme Writer, the Philosopher, the Marshall, the National Hero, the President, the Musician, the incarnate absolute that he is now. He must have got hold of the secret that I don't have. Perhaps when I turn the next page I'll catch a glimpse of what brought him greatness and success. Perhaps he'll give the recipe. Even if I'm doomed to disappointment I'll at least have rubbed my mind up against all that solid, recognized, indisputable greatness, and I'll have something to show for it.

Diaries do in fact provide us with an exemplary slice of real life, but we've made some progress recently beyond this area. We've gone beyond the interesting problem of André Gide's flannel underwear, or Jouhandeau's exemplary conjugal spats, or even the meditations and glorious utterances of Charles de Gaulle. Now we're reaching the core of true seriousness: somebody is talking to me about what he or she believes. As simple as that, but that's a lot. My life takes on his or her meaning . . . and see what happens to my truth . . . and just see what a positive, sensible interpretation I can now give the world. (But why do we never read these models as if they were written by Pirandello?)

What I believe. Let's pass over the slightly morbid curiosity that attracts such an eager audience for these exhibitions, pass over likewise the vulgar taste for imitation (to be modern one should say mimesis) that induces a writer to produce his or her own little opus. . . . Let's take a harder look at this. After all, if I want to be honest about it, what do I care about the beliefs of X or Y? What difference does it make, what guarantee do I have that Mr. S. or Mrs. G. believes this or that? . . .

Mr. R. believes such and such. . . . Well, good for him; it's his business, not mine. How could his belief (a mere belief) help me, given who I am and the way I am? So let him keep his belief and let me look for myself. . . . You don't think I'm serious? On the contrary, I'm dead serious, for myself first of all. And I know very well what I'm doing with this critique whose primary target is myself. Bringing somebody else a "What" makes no sense, handing out a "belief" makes no sense. The only thing left is the "I," and everything rests on that. I need an "I" whole and complete, but I've learned to be on my guard. This "I," whatever it is, is subject to so many variations and metamorphoses that its loud proclamation of belief may be a momentary thing with no future.

There have been quite a few intellectuals who insisted they believed something precisely because they didn't believe it, because a sort of visceral doubt drove them to bolster their courage by speaking out loud, to fight the doubt gnawing the vitals of their intelligence. So they provided themselves with guidance and reassurance in the shape of beliefs, which they hoped to turn into certitudes by getting others to share them.

It's not the subjective nature of the "I" that arouses my skepticism—like you I have never believed in objectivity—but the uncertainty of the "I" itself in an epoch like ours.

And these same intellectuals have done a rapid about-face and exchanged their belief for something totally opposite a few months if not a few days later. Oh I know, I know, some of them stood up and were counted for their beliefs, and I respect them for it. But if you look at the more important ones, what vacillation. Martin Heidegger was seduced by Nazism, an unpardonable crime as I see it. If that's the utmost in lucidity I can expect from such a philosopher, how can I trust him when we're dealing with realities a thousand times more complex than the blatant facts of Nazism and realities beside that I have no way of verifying? And Sartre is still worse: waltzing about in perpetual hesitation, the intellectual preaching commitment who in the final analysis never committed himself to anything (attending meetings, joining in protest marches, and signing petitions—all that hardly adds up to much of a commitment) and who over the course of time affirmed perfectly contradictory positions with unvarying candor and unequaled firmness. And in recent years we've seen some spectacular variations on this theme. . . .[11]

Among intellectuals we also note a fashion that is just as chic and alluring as that of the "What I Believe" books—the "What I No Longer Believe" genre. It's the reverse side of that former fascinating confession, but don't be mistaken, it's every bit as glorious, as tasteful and beneficial. An old-time Stalinist discovers with horror that . . . and ceases to be a communist; a Christian drops out because of his or her passion for the revolution or the poor or communism; and any number of others. And you still want me to ascribe any im-

---

11. Jacques Ellul, "De l'Inconséquence," in *Mélanges en honneur de De Rougemont*, 1978.

portance to all those "I"s who take themselves so seriously that they claim they can furnish all the guidelines and landmarks we need? They would be witnesses to a truth of which they know nothing. Thus, "What" doesn't interest me since I have no reason to go looking for an object. The "I" is simply a moving blip on a screen. As far as the "believing" goes, we've given it a thorough going-over. We know too much about belief by now to go on encumbering ourselves with it.

But at the same time I grant you, Una, that we're only too aware to what an extent we live on myth. Deprived of our myths we become like the blinded Oedipus: still a king but with no one except Antigone to guide our steps, incapable of making our way in a ruthless world to which our myths give meaning and hence a possibility of mastery. We're only too aware that we live by incessantly giving ourselves reasons to live, and whether they be brilliant or mediocre ones, they're never anything more than a walk in our own backyard, which we transform into a sublime adventure.

If that's the case, I might as well resign myself to the fact that I can't legislate belief out of existence. But it's also true that people act only for and through their legends, and this makes them terribly fragile and vulnerable because soon enough someone arrives on the scene to use those legends, myths, and their meanings, true or false, to control them. Antigone has changed into the sphinx. And today it's the sphinx who guides the blind Oedipus that all of us unwittingly are through the desert wastes of a land that once held life, of a city that once was human, but that we have laid in ruins. . . .

13

The Eternal Now
of Freedom

Una: Ah, Monos, your despair cuts me to the quick. This kind of skepticism strikes me as all the more overwhelming because I find your reasoning quite correct. But you too can see that it's nothing but *reasons*. You know the only thing I hold as truth is what I believe—now. This holds even for science. We've already said this: when science opens a door for me that up till now was closed, it's then that I'm convinced of its truth. And you know that that's how it goes in other areas of our experience. It's not demonstration or proof that do the job: we've entered an era when such things are undergoing the most profound scrutiny. Mathematicians nowadays go so far as to wonder what unshakable grounds, if any, they have to base their demonstrations on; they wonder what a demonstration is in the first place. And if it's true that the universe is one and inseparable, do we have the right to accept so casually, as we have thus far, the partial certitudes about reality supplied to us by physics? Think of the work of Karl Popper. Think of the dead-end logic (for that's what it is) that leads us to disallow as unscientific any statement that is not always open to falsification. Truth has withdrawn to the fortress of unverifiability.

What a strange coincidence that both theologians and atheists have taken the same route to the same conclusion: that the existence of God can't be positively proved or disproved. A fine discovery, you say; we've known it for ages. True enough, but what this means is that God doesn't belong to the scientific order, and so science has *nothing* to say about him. Science today no longer ridicules belief—and appears to me all the richer for it. We've learned that science, once so self-assured, is actually dependent upon its ideological, philosophical, and even religious context. Once it was the historians of science or the philosophers who called our attention to the role played by society's beliefs in the origins and development of science; now it's the scientists themselves.[12]

It's a grand opportunity for us, knowing as we do that everything isn't laid out in advance, that strict determinism has finally lost out, and that the universe remains open to chance, that is, accessible to our beliefs. You have to admire the richness of this idea: it brings disorder and disequilibrium into this world as an essential factor, as the source of order and potential life. How marvelous: the "noise" in information ultimately makes the information possible; turbulence is a constituent of all the phenomena of reality; the idea that order emerges—but only temporarily—through fluctuation; the notion of instability and complexity in kinetic theory; and the importance, now widely recognized, of "dissipative structures." ... How can we not rejoice when we're told that "Science (which was invented by humans in the first place) is once again finding the human's presence in the world problematic."[13] We have recovered the wholeness of

12. For example, *previously cited*, Bernard d'Espagnat, *A la recherche du réel;* Prigogine and Stengers, *La Nouvelle Alliance,* 1979.
13. Prigogine and Stengers, *La Nouvelle Alliance.*

humanity. Science is no longer a cold goddess with lifeless eyes and rigid structures. Everything is subject to entropy—*except* for information, into whose ashes we can always breathe new life. This is the starting point for efforts, which I for one warmly appreciate, at reaching a synthesis by that great human being and believer (in his case the two are inseparable), E. Morin.[14] But if I applaud such work, the fact is that after having once suffered as the helpless victims of nature, we then became victims of inflexible science, which turned out to be just another prison. We all felt trapped in that dungeon built by rationality, by science, both experimental and theoretical, with no way out.

But now the prison door has swung open, the sunlight floods in, and we see our place of captivity from a different angle. We used to be prisoners, but now we're once more free spirits capable of searching and experimenting beyond the old rigid norms. We believe in this kind of science! And what of our predecessors, whom we rightly criticize for falling into the trap of a narrow and overconfident sort of science, whom we reproach for having . . . believed too much (i.e., in scientism)—weren't they swayed by the same inspiration?

Once upon a time people were caught in the web of nature seen as fixed and unbending. Little by little they sank into the conviction of being prey to inexorable fate in every realm of life. The stars ineluctably determined the patterns of destiny, just as the slaves or the proletarians were doomed to their position at the bottom of society. Then suddenly the sciences appeared to liberate people from this destiny, the natural sciences that taught them to master reality. From then on the supreme thing was to use nature to dominate nature and transcend it. Medicine conquered disease, and Marxism taught

14. See all his current research, beginning with *Le Paradigme humain* and *La Méthode*.

slaves that history would inevitably set them free. How could they not *believe* in the science that opened the gates to freedom and pointed out the way? But that very same science was to become their new prison, and Marxism after Marx turned into a grim mechanism with no room for freedom. And then came a dramatic new revelation breaking the chains of the past: science became more fully itself by denying and renouncing what it had been before.

Yet this is not a retreat back toward natural destiny; it's the traveler's uncertainty over what road to take through a wilderness still bursting with promise, where we must enter bearing our own knowledge and hopes. And Marxism too has shaken up its once inflexible postulates. We're caught up once again in the fluid movement, the tides and undertow, of a society that may land us in any number of possibilities, none of which is given in advance. But why greet this new science so happily? Why does it speak so strongly to me, why does it stir me? Simply because, as I keep telling you, it opens a door in a closed universe. In all probability it's no more true, in the absolute sense, than yesterday's science. If we could see it from God's point of view, it would simply be a momentary episode in humankind's unending quest, not a truth to be added to older, more solidly established truths. I believe it's true at this moment, not for the simplistic reason that it supports one or another of my prior convictions, but because intellectually or materially I was in an impasse. I was imprisoned in a constricting ring of accepted truths. And then suddenly this new scientific research found a way for me to break out of it. Obviously I had no choice but to believe in the truth of such science.

Precisely the same rule holds for political prisoners, proletarians, slaves, and victims of colonialism: they will each cling enthusiastically to the movement that liberates them; they'll believe in its excellence, never suspecting that these liberators may be introducing a still worse form of slavery. But for the moment whom should they follow but those who have broken their chains?

This science is, for me, surrounded with seductive power; it becomes a kind of illumination. But I feel this light pouring over me much less from any exact reasons or proofs than from a splendid vista stretching out before me, a vast expanse to traverse and explore. And I rush off with everybody else. I believe that it *has* to be true because it gives me the potential for action and creativity. This illumination does far more than solve a specific problem; it affects me on a far deeper level, carrying me back to a state of certitude where I look upon my beliefs as true. And today it *is* true, objectively true, because I believe it. And I believe it because I have been touched in the depths of my existence by this illumination. People always put their faith in what they think must set them free. I mentioned earlier the case of prisoners (by which I meant true prisoners, not those who "worship their chains"), but the crucial point here is that the experience of liberation is not to be found in stability—in institutions, statutes, organizations, or repetitions.

Freedom exists only in the explosive instant of liberation. This is so in the life of the mind as well as in love and politics. Freedom comes in the fleeting instant when, perhaps after years of searching and struggling, suddenly the doors fly open. People confront their freedom in this momentary opening, this instant when they perceive the truth in a flash of genius, when their much hated master dies, when institutions break down completely, when the ecstatic joy of "everything is possible" is altogether real, when "everything is possible" has not yet been transformed into its ineluctable corollary, "then nothing is feasible." Thus the truth of science is tied to what I believe today—and it's no less true because I add on that "today." It's not an empty truth, because this is the way the cards are dealt to all of us when we play the intellectual-spiritual game of believing.

No responsible intellectual or scientist can continue to believe that someday everything will have been discovered and we can write "finis" in the book of knowledge. We're living in the relativism that was one of science's great triumphs. Perhaps that too will be rejected ten years from now. Nevertheless today we stand liberated from the heavy burden of positivism. Our mental evolution goes on under clearer skies, skies no longer darkened but bathed in light by the profound belief that springs from our humility.

14

The Last Word

Monos: My dear Una, I'm afraid that in all this you're lulling yourself into a false sense of security with mere eloquence. You discourse, admittedly, from the standpoint of what you believe, but it all adds up to words and nothing more. The picture experience paints for us is a far different one. We now know, alas, what such talk is worth, or rather we know that speech itself is not the key to what is being said: it's Heidegger's *das Mann* or some vast impersonal force that speaks through our mouths. And you, I fear, with your ingenuous faith and your defense of believing, may be slipping into that pervasive anonymity. You do the talking, but is what you say any different from what It says? Aren't the words the same? Don't they, coming from you, give the lie to belief once and for all?

Una: I get your point, Monos, but can you explain where what I say comes from? Is it simply a concatenation of rambling, incoherent words, a string of phonemes, or meaningless noise? Yet you understood quite well what I was saying; there was shared meaning, call it what you like, a metalanguage or whatever: I wasn't just talking, I said something, and my belief wasn't just a by-product.

Monos: Still, you're well aware that there's a bitter debate going on these days over this very question. We mistrust speech; every form of it is suspect. Belief has been harshly sifted by the sciences, and in the same way speech has been torn to pieces by hermeneutical systems until by now nothing is left. You'll never convince anyone, except for those you entrap or dazzle with your appeals—but can you seriously risk the lives of other people on such uncertain notions?

Una: But who's talking about uncertainty? Precisely the ones who have different beliefs, the ones whose supply of certitudes has, alas, been sharply reduced, or who drift along in the dilettantism of easy living, easy thinking, and easy talk. My purpose, however, is not to convince anyone of some idea or other, to persuade people to adopt some illusory or aleatory belief. If I speak, it's to share the most profoundly certain thing in my life—the surest, but also the freest, the most open and joyous. You tell me it's an illusion, but there's nothing illusory about living beyond the grip of anxiety and fear for the morrow. And I know that this state of freedom always comes from belief, from the act of believing, which connects us to something else or directs us to it.

Monos: For all that you can't turn my thoughts from the dangers of language—which you use so well. You can't erase from my mind the doubt—or judgment, in any case I agree completely with it—expressed by Roland Barthes when he said: "Speech, and *a fortiori* discourse, is not communication, as people are too fond of repeating; it's subjugation. All language is a generalized mode of ruling. Language, in the sense of all linguistic performances, is neither reactionary nor progressive; it's quite simply fascist, because fascism is not preventing others from speaking, it's obliging them to speak. . . ."

Una: Well, the eminent Mr. Barthes wasted a fine opportunity to spare the world a discourse, because when he delivered that one before his admirers at the Collège de France, what was he doing but communicating something to them? Precisely in view of his belief that language is fascist, in view of his analysis of linguistic performance, wasn't he literally performing for his audience: that is, not only putting them in a certain frame of mind, but also passing on to them a certain knowledge? And who was forcing him to speak? Obviously not language itself. It was simply a matter of ritual: the impact of society, his membership in the Parisian intelligentsia, his triumphal entrance into the Collège de France. *That* was fascist in his sense of the word. Roland Barthes had a strong belief in public honors.

Monos: You're very harsh, Una . . .

Una: I'm looking for authenticity, not conjuring tricks.

Monos: You're harsh, Una, but you can't stop doubt from creeping into our hearts and thoughts: it's there already. Both language and belief have lost their innocence, and we have to be on our guard, when we're dealing with them. Now Barthes, I'm telling you, helped to promote such vigilance even in his dilettantism, for playfulness, skepticism, and keeping one's distance are all good weapons against what will be unleashed against us. In these times when we see the brown plague of intolerance, nurtured by belief, springing into new life everywhere, when we watch the clashes between religions and the passionate conflicts of political parties, at the moment when a new holocaust is in the wings, how vitally important it is for us to keep cool heads, not to be carried away by words, by the power of language, the authority of beliefs, the seriousness of messages, the willful blindness of hearts . . .

Una: You speak well, Monos, and I'm with you, as you know, in your insistence on critical detachment and vigilance. But I can't yield to this disbelief in language, on which, in my view, everything depends. And I prefer Freud to Barthes when he writes, "Wherever someone speaks, it's daylight." That may have been the most profound thing he ever said.

The relationship between language and light is an essential one. As soon as language becomes possible, the closed petals of roses open up, the fist unclenches, once glance seeks out another, you discover that you're not alone, and that someone has something to say to you, to you and no one else, someone for whom, from now on, you count. And daylight begins with language. The words spoken have to be true, of course; they have to carry one's entire being with them. When they do, we achieve discourse. "In the beginning was the Word. And the Word was with God, and the Word was God. . . . In him was life, and the life was the light of men" (John 1:1, 4).

It's daylight, Monos, and we have to move ahead.

PART TWO

BELIEF AND FAITH

15

Traditional Misunderstandings

Out of the single verb "to believe" come noun forms for two radically antithetical actions: belief and faith. However, when I wish to use a verb form to give expression to my faith, I still have to use "to believe," unless I happen to use an even worse formula, "to have faith." Up to this point we have discussed the general theme of "believing" and the differences of opinion, the hostile and incompatible positions on the subject of belief all arose, in the final analysis, from the confusion of belief and faith. Sometimes the two characters in the dialogue were really talking about beliefs; sometimes Una was talking about faith.

Now I should like to make it clear that in opposing faith and belief, I am not referring to autonomous objects, to real, specific, independent entities. That goes without saying. Distinguishing between these two terms is simply a matter of convenience. The choice of these two words is arbitrary, every bit as arbitrary as the choice of the two words *espoir* (hope, in the sense of what one hopes for or places one's hope in) and *espérance* (hope, in the sense of the habit or tendency to hope or to expect) to designate what are in effect two ways of being. *L'espoir* is not a real concept any more than *l'espé-rance* is, but I had to have two words to give as examples of two contrary spiritual realities. The same is true of belief and faith.

Of necessity I shall be speaking about the faith that concerns me personally, that is, faith in Jesus Christ. In other words I use the term faith to indicate the revelatory order of Jesus Christ, while by belief I mean all the other attitudes referring to a religious or irrational dimension, to a world of non-Christian lived experience. Note that in making use of these definitions I am by no means claiming that the Christian faith is intrinsically superior, nor do I have any intention of devaluing in the least other religions or beliefs. But if I readily admit that the Christian faith is one species of belief among many, I'm also obliged to acknowledge that it possesses some highly singular features that make it radically different from other beliefs. To be sure, a non-Christian might say the same thing; that is, Muslims or Buddhists can vouch for the fact that their faith is extraordinarily different from other beliefs. I agree completely. It has to be stressed that neither sociology nor the history of religion give a true accounting of these specific differences. Such disciplines merely study various religions, ignoring the aspects that make them special and unique.

In aspiring to scientific precision the history and sociology of religion are always radically reductionist: they end up eliminating from their field of inquiry its one incomparable feature, namely faith. They think they are accounting for faith merely by cataloguing differences. This effort is something like assembling a mosaic, and it's not without interest. But unfortunately it's relatively useless both for persons who know the crucial constitutive factor of their faith from within as well as for outsiders, because it shows the latter the phenomenon from a false angle. But outsiders don't know this, and they're content with such superficial comparisons, believing that, thanks to the scientific mentality, they're above those vain superstitions or else making connections (e.g., calling Judaism, Christianity, and Islam "religions of the Book") that are never more than fortuitous and peripheral.

Thus to my mind all these "religions" contain more than just religion. There is in each case a unique relationship to what we may call God or an aspect of God. In affirming the special character of Christianity I am not casting the others into the "exterior darkness." But I *am* a Christian, and not by accident. This is a question of choice, a double decision—on God's part and on mine—not of birth and cultural environment. So I have to bear witness to the specificity, the unique and irreplaceable character of Christian faith, which is on the one hand totally different from what people lump together under the heading of "religion" and on the other has nothing in common with the category of faith, as far as I can make it out, in other spiritual movements. Hence I prefer to use as contrary the pair of terms: religion and Christian faith. I understand "religion" in the general sense used by historians and sociologists, which seizes on real elements, but only the most external and visible ones, in the various kinds of belief. To avoid any misunderstanding I would like to shed light on what is singular and particular to Christian faith.

From the first we have seen how impossible it is to liken any given belief to faith in the God of the Bible, who bears no resemblance to the God of the philosophers and savants. Pascal was right: God cannot be reduced to any action, intervention, or knowledge deriving from our own heads. God is not endowed with all the qualities that theologians have ascribed to him—prescience, eternity, omnipotence, and so forth. All that sounds fine, and from an intellectual point of view it's perfectly all right; but it has nothing to do with what God reveals about himself in the Bible. When it's said that God

suffers, that he searches for humanity, that he gives himself a
name that must not be pronounced, we are witnessing a fla-
grant contradiction between the text and the concepts superimposed on it. God is designated by the way he enters into
human company and acts in concert with them, but we are
never told what he is like "in himself." God is never described by means of philosophical concepts, which the Bible
never uses anyway.

It's all very well to proclaim that God is eternal, but strictly
speaking we don't know what the term means. We can talk
about God as all-powerful, but even if we figure mathemati-
cally the amount of energy released in the "Big Bang," we
still have nothing to measure that "all-powerful" with. In that
case we might as well keep silent rather than talk without
having anything to say and, still more, rather than say things
that will inevitably be wrong, the sort of things that make up
Christian "religion" as taught in the catechism and learned by
believers.

Throughout the length and breadth of the biblical text the
first thing that seems beyond question is the presence of a
God who is at the same time a father—not just a creator but
a Father. And if Jesus teaches us to call him My Father,
that's no novelty, because the God of Israel is also a Father
and the God of the Fathers, which implies an intimacy
beyond that of his role as Creator. God *is* Creator (though it's
worthwhile recalling that this concept occupies a lesser place
in the Bible than later theology claimed for it), but Creator as
Father, and he is always renewing his fatherhood through
creation.

Second, he is the God of the Word and the covenant, that
is, the God of pardon, reconciliation, and concord (heart to
heart), *not* the God of wrath, vengeance, and grim and un-
pitying justice. All the texts in the Bible that announce God's
wrath are accompanied each and every time by words of par-

don or the promise of life. All the texts announcing that implacable justice will be done are accompanied each and every time by the proclamation that mercy surpasses justice. It is an impious lie to separate these two opposing aspects. This lie has been spread as much by theologians (I'm thinking of that long and pitiless line of preachers excoriating sin and calling down fire from heaven) as by anti-Christians who have distorted the God of revelation, covering his face with the mask of a thundering Jove, making him a God of war, of the "celestial hosts," and ultimately of hatred. Now, just as we must not separate justice and mercy, we must remember that forgiveness, mercy, reconciliation, and the covenant always come *afterward*, that is, they represent *the last word*. From the biblical point of view there is nothing beyond the love of God—the God who reveals himself as love. His "justice" is part of his love. Once that is understood, everything changes, for we are no longer judged. "The life of faith is undoubtedly something like living on trial before God, but before a God who's alive, not dead, disappeared, or inflexible."[15]

Another unquestionable feature of God shown to us by the Bible is his role as the Liberator, which is how he first reveals himself to Israel. Here too you must know from what standpoint the ensemble of texts is being interpreted. You can't do this by splitting them up and placing yourself within the text itself; you have to have a "point of view." Now the Bible provides us with such a point of view, on the one hand by making the first act of the God who reveals himself to Israel the act of the God who frees his people from slavery, on the other hand by steadily affirming the promise of a definitive liberation that transcends the human condition. For Christians this has already been accomplished in Jesus Christ, who conquered death, the final slavery, the final power of destiny.

15. Dumas, *Nommer Dieu*.

There is no welter of possible interpretations here: the biblical perspective tells the one to follow. So much so that we have to read the Law,[16] the commandments, and the words of Jesus from the vantage point created by that fundamental revelation of liberation and the covenant. And when we do, God ceases to be a sort of dictator who lays down a constricting law, a crushing bundle of obligations, and becomes instead one who will finally say in the person of Jesus, "My yoke is easy, and my burden is light" (Matt. 11:30).

I maintain that here we have not gone out on a limb with personal interpretations[17] —"You've chosen your approach, but it's only one of many. . . ." I believe instead that if you take the text as a whole, you can have no other revelation about that God: it surely tells us nothing of his Essence, his *ipseitas,* his dimensions, his universal will, and so forth (and on all such matters the only possible theology is negative theology). We know nothing about God until we hear the revelation about him that begins with his entrance into human history, when he becomes humanity's companion in order to accomplish his plans, which teach us that he is Love and Freedom. Beyond that there is only a blank. To choose another dimension, another point of view, or metaphysical concepts is to challenge the mode of revelation chosen by this God himself.

This mode of revelation—and, I would say, this alone—is the heart of Christian faith and the thing that differentiates it from all other beliefs; it's not its ethics or metaphysics but its revelation that includes no explanation for God's decision to

---

16. Torah is generally translated as Law, but is better understood as Teaching or even Revelation.
17. I apologize to readers who may have read these same ideas in some of my other books, but I thought it indispensable to recall here in summary fashion what I have developed at length elsewhere (e.g., in *The Ethics of Freedom,* 1976) after Karl Barth.

reveal himself in this way. All this has nothing to do, of course, with any sort of apologetics: what we are looking at here is simply a choice, and this choice is none other than one that determines whether one recognizes oneself in this revelation or not. But I don't see why the fact of such a choice should constitute a weakening of faith or a sort of counterproof. Faith (and from now on I shall use that term all by itself, without adding "faith in the God of Abraham, of Isaac, and of Jesus Christ, faith *in* Jesus Christ") is not turned into something aleatory or uncertain just because it results from a decision where persons bear witness to their freedom.

But this already serves to make the point (which we shall meet up with later on) that this faith cannot be equated with the innumerable so-called Christian beliefs, whether expressed in Protestant literalism or Catholic magical thinking, in moralism or mysticism or politics or metaphysics—honorable forms all of them, which Christianity, insofar as it is a sociological reality, a structure, an organization, a movement, has adopted on the cultural level, but which have practically nothing to do with faith or revelation. And this brings us to the stage in our argument where we have to examine certain consequences of faith and beliefs.

These consequences, not surprisingly, run contrary to each other, and I shall not be able to keep track of all of them. One that strikes me as centrally important is that belief provides answers to people's questions while faith never does. And I would say that we have here a decisive criterion to tell the two apart. People believe so as to find assurance, a solution, an answer to their questions. They encounter the "problems" of evil, suffering, and hatred proliferating everywhere, along with those of origins (origins of the world, of their own lives, of their cities, or of some peculiar group; origins of any given natural phenomenon—thunder or storms—or of some unique feature of the landscape, such as the Dead Sea). Then they

fashion for themselves a system of beliefs, fleshing them out
in myths, legends, visions, and art to explain things and answer their own questions.

But note that faith (biblical faith) is completely different.
The purpose of revelation is *not* to supply us with explanations of this or that interesting point, but to confront us with
questions about humankind in general and each one of us in
particular, to get us to listen to questions. Having failed to
notice this obvious contrast, historians and exegetes have put
biblical myths in the same category with all the other religious phenomena. This has led them to a series of remarkable
misinterpretations: reading the first three chapters of Genesis
as an explanation of the origins of the world and of humanity,
taking the Book of Job for an account of evil, or the story of
Cain for the key to the troubled existence of the Kenites.

But all throughout the Bible we find ourselves faced with a
God who refuses to answer. When you try to pin him down,
he declares, "I am who I am." When you try to constrain him
by sacrifices, he proclaims that he detests them. When you
look for a sovereign messianic king, he sends a poor man with
no political power. And when you want to consult him to
discover his will, he sends you off to a sort of game of chance
or tarot cards called the Urim and Thummim. No, God does
not give explanations, nor does he reply to people's curious or
anxious questions. And we must vigorously reject that nasty
habit of turning to the Bible for an answer to the banal problems of everyday life (of course, any text whatsoever can always be interpreted as an answer) or, still worse, the custom
of opening the Bible at random to find some providential
verse. That's as bad as praying on and on in the hope that
God will thunder out an answer to extricate us from financial
or family difficulties, to help us get a job, to resolve our personal troubles, and so forth.

To be sure, God *can* do all that too, because he is Love and knows what we need. But in all that babbling of ours we miss the core of biblical revelation when *it* speaks to our faith and asks questions of *us*. It will teach us neither the historical nor the physical facts of how the earth began, neither genetics nor cosmology. It asks a question—a series of questions—that is; it makes people responsible (obliged to respond) and throws them back upon their freedom.

Unlike beliefs, faith consists in heeding God's questions and risking ourselves in the answers that *we* have to give. Questions run all the way through the Bible, with three high points. The first question asked of us is a double one: "Adam, where are you?" and "Cain, what have you done to your brother?" In other words, Adam, the perfect communion between us has been broken; where have you gone astray? What have you become? Or, as they say nowadays, where are you coming from? And you, Cain, like Adam you were a guardian, a protector; what have you done to the one closest to you?

The second question, at the heart of our discussion, is the one Jesus poses to the disciples: "And you, who do you say that I am?" He doesn't proclaim himself, he makes no declaration; instead it's up to us to discern this. God in Jesus limits himself to asking the question—the real question, the only important one: whether we are alone on this earth; not whether "there exists a God hovering in the clouds," but whether we are met "where we're at" by God himself.

And the third, in the last days, after the resurrection of Jesus Christ: "Whom do you seek?" and then, "If it is my will, what is that to you?" These are questions about the reality of our search—whom *are* we seeking, after all? What are we searching for? Where is it all going, this human history where we cannot recognize the figure of the Crucified-but-Risen One? And at the same time we have a decision to make: Jesus says, "if I will . . . this or that, what does it matter to you?" What really *is* important to us, with our pretentious little claims to knowledge, science, judgment . . .

All through Scripture these three questions serve as a framework for the questions that God asks us and that faith is called to answer. Take, for example, the question posed by Job. As Philippe Nemo says so well in his elucidation of Job:[18] "The content of revelation is simply a Thou and an I with the world flung in my face like a question. What is revealed *is* the question. The question, 'For the sake of what?' addressed by one soul to another calls for a response through commitment. . . ." And when it's a matter of recognizing God as master, "He is Master *not* by means of the world's overwhelming silence or its idle chatter, but by that very modality of his discourse which is *to be a question* that embraces every single aspect of the future. . . ."

And on the subject of Otherness: "His essential being is like a question, one that we ask of him and he sends right back to us: 'for the sake of what?' And this question calls for nothing less than a total response, if you want to know once and for all whether God is kind or malicious. Because for the moment only the question has been revealed: God is the question of good *or* evil merging indistinctly in a single question. . . ." There's no ready made answer in the Bible. And we have to learn that *our* questions are lumped together in the "What does it matter to you?" *Our* questions are immediately minimized; they shrink into insignificance when they come up against God's, which are the decisive ones. But those can be perceived only by faith, and faith alone feels obliged to answer them. Furthermore it's quite obvious that these questions are not directed at lofty metaphysical or even theological issues, but deal instead with life on the most concrete and positive level.

18. Philippe Nemo, *Job et l'excès du mal*, 1978.

Faith is, as Barth so often reminds us, in the first instance, hearing. Belief talks and talks, it wallows in words, it interpellates the gods, it takes the initiative. Belief acts, it enters into the thick of serious action—where it can never find anything but itself. Faith takes an entirely opposite stance: it waits, remains on guard, picks up signs, knows what to make of the most delicate parables; it listens patiently to the silence until that silence is filled up with what it takes to be the indisputable word of God. Afterward, such listening can lead to all sorts of things: answers, a message, morality, action, and commitment. But all that exhausts faith, and it can restore and refresh itself only going back to listening and its silent vigil.

If the Bible asks us God's questions, it binds us at the same time to listen to the questions of others. It's a book of listening: faith turns us toward others, starting out from God's question ("What have you done to your brother?"), as it urges us to find out what others are asking. And if God, to be sure, has no answers, neither do we have to supply others with answers that are stereotyped, clear-cut, final explanations. For one thing, their questions will change. The ones they ask themselves today will cease to be so agonizing and preoccupying because those that God asks them have become more central and crucial, so that everything else fades into the background. We must listen to others, help them to hear God's questions, lead them not to any kind of certitude but to the point where it's impossible to answer (which should in no way be read as a cause for overwhelming despair, but as a joyous surrender to the incredibly liberating power of grace).

This is, properly speaking, the only way they can find deliverance from their anguish and obsessions. We must listen to others' questions and take them with the utmost seriousness, while maintaining the capacity to distinguish true questions (the existential issues where one's whole existence is at stake) from false (provoked by curiosity, sadism, amorality, political freedom, or the desire to accuse). How many questions are simply means of leveling accusations at other people. Charged with God's question, faith acts like an acid, stripping away the skin of false questions, laying bare their essential deceitfulness for all to see, so that humanity's true questions can shine forth. Naked and poor, people can throw their whole identity into these true questions, risking all they have and are by asking them. And faith invites me to take that risk with them.

But if faith makes us listen to others' questions, here is one more difference between belief and faith: faith isolates, belief (Christian or otherwise) brings together. We find ourselves joined with others in the same institutional current, all of us oriented toward the same object of belief, sharing the same ideas, following the same rituals, enrolled in the same organization, be it social or religious, collaborating in the evolution of the same culture, speaking the same language. Belief is quite useful for the smooth functioning of society, and it's quite necessary for strengthening us in our weakness. Thanks to belief we discover that we are many—and together. So, whether its object be God or the nation or our race or ethnic group or socialism or the proletariat, whatever the name, belief plunges us with a nameless feeling of satisfaction into a communion that liberates us from our own perplexed consciences (and hence from our questions). Belief is the key to the consensus we look for, the one long proclaimed as the essential of communal life.

Now all this seems so obvious that we're inclined to think that faith and belief operate on the same plane. After all, faith in Jesus Christ bids us love our neighbor, and faith ultimately produced the church and, still more, those phenomena we call Christendom, Christian society and culture. But I never said that Christianity didn't fall into the category of beliefs (a point we shall have to discuss at some length). Everything we have just mentioned, even the church (hierarchy, liturgy, ethics), is the product of beliefs at work in Christianity. So things are not that simple. Religious belief provides both a place of assembly and a framework for the people gathered there. It is thus extremely useful for various communities—but not for much else.

Faith works in exactly the opposite way. Faith individualizes; it's always an exclusively personal matter. And since I'm speaking of faith in the God of Abraham and of Jesus Christ, not in an abstract, generalized God common to all religions, let me say that faith is the personal relationship with a God who reveals himself as a person. This God singularizes people, sets them apart, and confers on each an identity comparable to none other. The person who listens to his word is the only one to hear it; he or she is separated from the others, becomes unique, simply because the tie that binds that individual to God is unique, unlike any other, incommunicable, a unique relationship with a unique, absolutely incomparable God. (How I admire those who claim they can explain, elucidate, and analyze that bond, whether they be psychologists, who in so doing show how many light-years they are from grasping this phenomenon, or believers and mystics, who indulge in lavish accounts of their "experiences.")

And this God, as the Bible reminds us, particularizes, singularizes the person to whom he says, "I call you by your name" (Isa. 45:4)—a unique name, revelation tells us, different for every individual. When God speaks to that person, he never lumps him or her together with others in a grand totality, a collectivity, a sort of spiritual magma. He separates that one from others, making that being, from that moment on, unique and different. I call you by *your* name. Need we mention yet again the fundamental role played by names in the biblical world,[19] where they are not social labels but the expression of the spiritual depths of one's being, of the most secret and authentic reality? For this God, for Jesus the state of being a collectivity, a crowd, is wretchedness. In the face of the crowd Jesus is seized with compassion, for crowds are subhuman. People in a crowd are always disoriented, never themselves, dispossessed of themselves, precisely because they are many, in which condition Jesus sees them "wandering like sheep without a shepherd." Faith isolates them and renders them unique.[20]

This is Kierkegaard's central experience, and I maintain that of all Christian authors Kierkegaard is the one who has given us the best, the most genuine, the most radical account of the existential reality of faith. We must not try to evade the issue here or content ourselves with one of Louis Aragon's lines: "The ones who believed in heaven and the ones who didn't—all united." How wonderful—total harmony, everybody hand in hand. And in the name of what was everyone united, having put aside the matter of heaven as a little difference of opinion? In the name of France. Here's to belief and myth, because naturally France is far more important than heaven. I can easily see why someone who doesn't believe in heaven should declare that such things have no importance. But Christians must be stupefyingly blind to go along with that, to make nothing of a difference established by God in order to be part of another community of belief, only too happy that people accept them and that those fine folks, the

19. Among many others see especially the fine study by André Dumas, *Nommer Dieu*. Dumas contrasts the name with metaphors, ideas, and pseudonyms; he treats it as a sign of unity, a center, a disclosure, but never a mere representation or definition.
20. See A. Maillot, *Credo* (1979), on the significance of the "I" in the Creed: "I believe," and not "we believe." The intentionality of faith, Maillot argues, demands that it be personal.

communists, agree to march hand in hand with them, dragging them along in their merry dance.

Faith separates people and makes each of them unique. In the Bible "holy" *means* "separated." To be holy is to be separated from everyone else, from the people, the world, the group, to be made unique *for the sake of a task* that can be accomplished by no one else, which one receives through faith, after being awakened to faith by the creative and distinctive word.

Immediately I can hear the worried questions: What about the church? Aren't you succumbing to that all too famous Protestant individualism? On this last point I should like to stress the fact that "Protestant individualism" is an illusion, a legend as absurd as it is persistent. In the sixteenth century there probably was a strong individualizing current in the Reformation, when both Bible reading as well as persecution gave rise to a very solid sense of Protestant identity and of everyone standing alone before God. But things haven't been that way for a long, long time, for at least two centuries if not three. Protestants now are a nice little flock of well-behaved sheep, obedient and utterly tame, though they often think of themselves as pace-setters, in France at least because they've taken up yesterday's fashionable ideas from Parisian intellectuals or some moribund leftist group. No, Protestant individualism is most certainly not the source of my claim that faith creates a unique kind of individuality, which is its only medium. On the contrary, we have to break away from the model of Protestantism and the average Protestant believer.

But what about the church? We have to keep two elements in mind here: first, if there is to be an authentic church, there have to be, as Paul says quoting Isaiah, "real men." There have to be steadfast, vigorous people; there have to be individuals. (Steadfastness and vigor are qualities transcending gender; it is possible that a sick old woman could be steadfast and vigorous, while a hyperactive businessman or intellectual might be nothing of the sort.)

Second, the church is generated out of the encounter, the union, the friendship of unique "isolates" learning to recognize one another. Once again it's never a question of a mystical magma. But there's no getting around the church; we can't do without it, and for the simplest of reasons: the faith that individualizes me is a faith in the God of Jesus Christ, the God who Jesus taught us was Love. And love makes it impossible to remain alone in one's corner. This love is not a relationship exclusively with God, because it's God who points the Other out to me to begin with.

Once again we have to come down hard on the point: it's not the presence of the Other that gives rise to love; it's because God sends me to the Other and the Other to me that love must inevitably come about. If it's not God—the God who is Love—then the encounter with others may lead us to engage in politics or play lotto but never to exist. Thus faith (which isolates) in the God of Love (who commands me to love) founds the church. Wherever individuals live that faith, they will inevitably meet and share their bread and wine. The church has no other origin; it can be nothing else. All the functional mechanisms, the institutional nuts and bolts, the whole ideological superstructure are just religious appearances, burdens that can't be avoided because we are part of a given society. But that's not the church. The church is the gathering in and through love of those who have been called individually, have been separated, set apart as *individuals* to fulfill the function assigned them by God. And if the only gathering place is love, then these men and women are united but each one still remains fundamentally alone in the dialog with God. Faith isolates; belief gathers together.

A third radical opposition between belief and faith relates to doubt. And contrary to an opinion both banal and popular I maintain that faith presupposes doubt while belief excludes it. One school of Catholic theology used to argue in the old traditional style that faith rules out the possibility of doubt, that where there was doubt, however slight, there was no faith. They used to bring up, for example, the case of Simon Peter walking on the waters of the lake: when he was seized with fear at having doubted Jesus' word, he immediately began to sink. This was evident proof that his faith was gone. They also cited Thomas's incredulity after the resurrection, as seen in Jesus' remark to him, "Because you have seen, you have believed . . ."—thus his earlier doubts were a bar to faith.

This teaching and even the examples behind it don't convince me. The thing that excludes any possibility of doubt is belief. The opposite of doubt isn't faith but belief, the attitude of the untouchable warrior, invulnerable to fear, all the more armor-plated because he is so fragile.[21] The model of belief is Calvino's nonexistent knight: a complete suit of armor operating with imperturbable efficiency and easily surpassing all the other knights, but empty inside, a perfectly abstract "behaver." That's how I view the "knights" of belief. They comply unfailingly with the law and the commandments. They are unbending in their convictions, intolerant of any deviation. In the articulation of belief they press rigor and absolutism to their limits. They precisely delimit the frontier between believers and unbelievers. They unceasingly refine the expression of their belief and seek to give it explicit intellectual formulation in a system as coherent and complete as possible. They insist on total orthodoxy. Ways of thinking and acting are rigidly codified.

All of which leads to a very high level of efficiency. The

---

21. "There is no greater temptation than to confuse truth with certainty, the intensity of belief with the quality of faith. 'He's a believer,' they say admiringly of the fanatic, but the firmness of his convictions is proportional to his refusal to think them out" (Bernard Charbonneau, *Je fus—Essai sur la liberté*, 1980).

believer is a person who gets the job done. But all this activity is hollow at the core. This may sound surprising or scandalous: doesn't every belief have at its center an act of believing that is the determining factor and that calls forth a whole sequence of acts and feelings, including the believer's rigidity? But that's just it: the act of believing is so uncertain, so fragile and evanescent that while it may have been true for a moment, it's so dangerous to put one's trust in it that you have to substitute for it all the rest of the sequence. But then that "rest" becomes increasingly monumental and exacting as the center becomes more hollow, more fragile, and more uncertain. Believers have so little internal reality of their own that they can live and express that reality only by and in a conventional established unit. This is also why, as we saw above, they are the people of gatherings. Believers find encouragement and certitude in the presence of others—the certitude that those others really believe—and so community life fills up the existential void.

This again is why we see such groups multiplying the number of liturgies, commitments, and activities that give believers complete satisfaction: in the midst of them believers have no need of questioning the truth or reality of their belief; activity keeps them busy. But in this situation you can imagine how intolerable the diversity of beliefs becomes. Anyone who speaks up for another aspect, a different point of view obliges the other believers to reconsider things, to ask themselves questions about the validity and content of their beliefs. This threatens to lead believers to the final conclusion that their inner depths are empty—something they cannot admit. There must be neither doubt nor uncertainty, for that would be radically destructive. And so diversity cannot be tolerated. Diversity is always a source of further questions, of self-criticism, and thus of possible doubt. And once doubt appears, everything snaps: patterns of behavior and traditional commandments no longer suffice; it's a debacle. This is why, when a religion undergoes rapid expansion and acquires great bodies of adherents, since the masses cannot by definition enter the world of faith, they turn to belief, which is rapidly transformed into passwords, rites, and orthodoxy.

It's inevitable: the truth of faith changes into the reality of empty belief incarnate in external forms. Hence it is belief that excludes doubt along with diversity. By contrast the whole story of faith is summarized in the words "I believe; help my unbelief" (Mark 9:24). Faith is, to be sure, compared to a rock, but the first thing it does is to take cognizance of the gap separating Jesus' faith from the faith that beats within my heart. That is, faith constrains me above all to measure how much I *don't* live by faith, how far I am from that central truth, how seldom faith fills up my life. We're not talking now about intellectual doubt, that mediocre little parlor game atheists love so much, thinking they can easily triumph over a faith that strikes them as adolescent if not infantile. Whence the questions about the historical accuracy of the Bible or the conflict between God's omnipotence (which makes him responsible for evil) and his goodness (which means he must be powerless) or the supposedly hopeless contradiction between God's foresight and human freedom. But all this is childish nonsense that has nothing to do with actual doubt.

Faith is a terribly caustic substance, a burning acid. It puts to the test every element of my life and society; it spares nothing. It leads me ineluctably to question all my certitudes, all my moralities, beliefs, and policies. It forbids me to attach ultimate significance to any expression of human activity. It detaches and delivers me from money and the family, from my job and my knowledge. It's the surest road to realizing that "the only thing I know is that I don't know anything." Faith leaves nothing intact, not because it's a joyful, trusting

(and slightly simple-minded!) abandonment of self into the
hands of Jesus, but because it's awareness of faith itself.

I've spoken of relating my faith to that of Jesus. Kierkegaard, of course, quite rightly stayed on the human level in
measuring the distance between his faith and Abraham's. If
my faith isn't the very same kind that Abraham had, it's
nothing. It's as simple as that. Faith inevitably leads me to
this measuring up, this fateful encounter—either Abraham's
sort of faith or nothing. And so the only thing that faith can
bring me to recognize is my impotence, my incapacity, my
inadequacy, my incompleteness, and consequently my incredulity (naturally faith is the most unerring and lethal
weapon against all beliefs). But that's precisely what makes it
faith; that's how it exists and how it shapes me.

Belief is reassuring. People who live in the world of belief
feel safe; God is their protector. On the contrary, faith is
forever placing us on the razor's edge. Though it knows that
God is the Father, it never minimizes his power, and so it fills
us with fear and even dread. In this context the account of
Jesus' calming the storm on the Sea of Galilee is highly significant: the disciples in the boat, full of faith in their friend
and master Jesus, go from the fear they had experienced over
the storm to dread, as Mark tells us, when the storm is
calmed by a simple word from Jesus. This is the fright one
feels upon meeting the power of God in action and up close.
"Who then is this, that even wind and the sea obey him?"
(Mark 4:41).

That is faith's question. For belief things are simple: God is
almighty, so it's normal for him to do things like calm
storms. But as soon as we normalize God, our relationship
with him is skewed. As soon as we get comfortable with
God's power, belief is sure to have led us astray. It's faith
alone that can appreciate our immeasurable distance from
him, whence the terrible and unspeakable nature of the living

God. There is no familiarity possible with *this* God. Yet at the same time it's faith that lets us cry "Abba, Father" (and Jesus is the one who in fact gives us peace and joy). These two aspects of faith are not contradictory; they make up the warp and the woof of the living fabric of faith. Thus doubt and fear constitute an integral part of faith.

Once again it must be understood that this doubt concerns myself, *not* God's revelation or his love or the presence of Jesus Christ. It is thus the clean contrary of belief. It is doubt about the effectiveness, even the legitimacy, of what I do and the forces I obey in my church and in society. Furthermore, faith puts itself to the test. If I discern the stirrings of faith within me, the first rule is not to deceive myself, not to abandon myself to belief indiscriminately. I have to subject my beliefs to rigorous criticism. I have to listen to all denials and attacks on them, so that I can know how solid the object of my faith is.

Faith will not stand for half-truths and half-certainties. That is why it constantly puts me into the position of the Other who challenges and denies faith altogether. Is this some sort of baroque intellectual gymnastics? Is it a bad conscience or scruples? By no means, it is the exclusive *modus operandi* of faith, which has no choice but to think in terms of Abraham's faith—all or nothing. But that all obliges me to face the fact that I am nothing, and in so doing I receive the gift of everything. Hence this faith, which continually incorporates doubt as part of itself, which grows out of the rich humus of doubt, is necessarily open and forgiving. Whom should it condemn? The moment the just men who were preparing to stone the adulterous woman drop their stones and walk pensively away, *then* they enter the realm of faith, then they fulfill the living law.

How could I pass judgment on the unbeliever when I myself am that unbeliever, when my faith convicts me of unbelief? How could I judge that heretic, when my faith shows me the many different roads that could have led me to Jesus Christ? How could I trace the boundary lines where faith ends and damnation begins, when faith shows me the God of Jesus Christ transcending all limits and choosing from everywhere those whom he calls to faith? But that in no way means that I will accept anything at all, or that everything is possible. This faith that sizes me up and marks off my limits leads me to perform certain acts, bears certain fruits, which, if they really derive from faith, will serve as examples, as signs of truth, for others. But the surer my faith is, the more I put my unbelief into the Lord's hands; the greater my certitude, the more open I am to others, the more I accept the diversity of individuals and things, of churches, poems, ideas, behaviors, and the more I adore both the marvels of creation and the marvels of God's patience. Since faith has brought me to acknowledge the distance between my faith and the Lord's, I can only place myself on the same level as everyone else, realizing that we are all of us the beneficiaries of one grand and unique blessing, eternal grace.

Here are four foundational texts on the relationship between doubt and faith:

> "To doubt is to wonder if a question from God comes before us and if this divine question is important for all of humanity and for each one of us. To doubt is to ask ourselves whether we are not simply crammed with beliefs, but adhering to an impossible faith, since belief is the extension of what we know already from our own experience, while faith is an answer to a question that must have really been put to us. But if I doubt the reality of the question, how can I speak of faith? . . ." Dumas then says that he chose his title, *Believing and Doubting,* precisely to stress his contention that one doesn't pass from doubt to faith because faith includes doubt. "There are first of all the words that make us believe, because they come before us . . . but with God's words having

preceded us, we find that the time comes when we wonder: is it actually possible to believe them? In this sense doubt is always there, deep in the heart of all believers. Unamuno says, 'A faith that never doubts is a dead faith.' "[22]

"Should we accept the inevitable or not: whatever reveals also reduces. Religion, culture, politics, the various mentalities all insist on identification. But this is a projection. Jesus is always somewhere else, the one you don't expect, the one who disarranges all arrangements. . . . One has to penetrate down into the kinship that links unbelief and faith. At the core of the universe is the void. At the center of belief there always remains the hollow of unbelief. At the heart of unbelief there is the possibility of faith, grafted onto primordial trust. . . . The certainties of faith have little to do with those of science. They grow deeper as doubt is incessantly overcome. For this reason they are humble, bound up as they are with grace, over which we have no direct power. But our need to inhabit a natural world, in which we are all confirmed in our beliefs by others (imagining that those others are paragons of faith), turns us into childish petty reasoners, alien to the tragic dimension. Faith arises against a background of nihilism. And the person of faith, steeped in the most virulent nihilism, recognizes the nocturnal landscape he or she has already traversed. . . ."[23]

"Everything has its cost, and the price of freedom is infinite. In the final analysis it can only be purchased with one kind of currency: anguish. Anxiety is the price of personal certitude, just as the price of free action is war with the world and other people, and the price of refusing to join the Herd is solitude."[24] While personal truth is the result of an interrogation, unlike the truths of dogma or science, nothing steadies or shores it up but the constantly renewed flow of life. It can't rely on the help of any authority, not even that of reason. Rational truth is self-sufficient; it ignores everything not in its immediate path. . . . All personal

22. André Dumas, *Croire et douter*, 1971.
23. Sulivan, *L'Exode*.
24. Charbonneau, *Je fus*.

thought goes through a nihilism that threatens to destroy it
along with the entire social order. If the thrones and
dominions couldn't stop me from calling their truth into
question, so that I can protect my truth from itself, what will
my uncertainty and weakness be able to do? It does no good
to turn Descartes upside down and say, "I don't think."
You can't find peace of heart and truth by saying, "I don't
think, therefore I don't exist." What would that "I" mean,
then, that indelible mark with which I sign my abdication
from reality? And the faith that is inseparable from doubt
can only be an act of decision: "When one gets beyond
interrogation and the drama of the will, one will choose what
he or she thought was given."[25]

"To be sure, I'm not proposing to condemn or even to deny
the name of Christians to those who find the resurrection of
Christ a stumbling block . . . if only for the simple reason
that just like the apostles, like all Christians in every age,
like the Athenians and the Sadducees, I too feel my reason
stiffen, my intelligence sneer, and my common sense mur-
mur, when I confess that the third day he rose again from
the dead. Conversely, it's probable that when the same
phrase is pronounced, an unknown longing, a mad hope,
quivers in the heart of the unbeliever. So much so that it
would take a good deal of cunning to say who believes fully
in the resurrection of Christ and who does not. There's not a
believer in the church who doesn't ask him- or herself, 'Is
this possible?' nor an unbeliever who doesn't mutter,
'Couldn't this be possible?' "[26]

But this brings us directly to yet another difference between belief and faith. Simply put, belief is always next-to-
last; faith is always final. There are two aspects to this. Belief
relates to things, to realities, to behaviors that we have little
choice save to classify as next-to-last. There is belief in
science, in the nation, the gods, money, power, and all of

25. Charbonneau, *Je fus.*
26. Maillot, *Credo.*

which is next-to-last. For each of these objects of belief the old refrain is only too appropriate, "You can't take it with you." The break must come. Exalt the object of your certitude as much as you will, one day you will die, and that object will leave you behind and become who knows what. That's what makes me lose all patience with beliefs. Those millions of men and women who put their lives on the line, who risked everything on the basis of their belief in the nation or the revolution, who cried out as they sacrificed themselves, *Vive la France!* or *Vive la Revolution!*—when all is said and done, why did they die? For the mediocre results achieved by politicians in the postwar years? And what if France hadn't struggled against the invaders in 1914? What essential changes would that have caused? In the name of the revolution, people sacrificed themselves for the gulags, the police dictatorships, the privileges of a ruling class. . . . How very next-to-last!

I'm not saying that these things have no importance or interest. I'm passionately concerned about political and social life, but I maintain that it's in no way worth the trouble of believing in or of raising to the status of an ultimate value. It's interesting, certainly, but it's all relative. As with all values, it's sometimes worthwhile even to die for such things— knowing all the while that you're dying for something relative, for the next-to-last. It's surely worth the trouble to die to save someone's life, but that someone will die someday; a person is only relative. It's worthwhile to die for honor. My grandfather committed suicide because he had gone bankrupt. Nowadays people don't do that anymore, nor do they know what they're talking about when they pronounce the word "honor." I admire my grandfather, and I have always been imbued with the value of honor. But I know that it's relative and changes with time, which is something that belief will not tolerate.

And yet belief knows spontaneously that as a matter of fact all the objects to which it would attach absolute value are next-to-last. The proof of this is that it claims to be dealing with the ultimate. What I mean is, not only does belief attribute special supremacy to these objects (France becomes Eternal, Science becomes Truth with a capital T), but it necessarily finds itself drawn to ultimateness. Belief is always inducing us to accept the idea of eternal life or a paradise or an immortal soul or extraterrestrial creatures. In other words, to the extent that it constantly refers us to an inaccessible Beyond, it implicitly recognizes its place in the domain of the next-to-last things. It sees that there is a final reality—and does no more than point to it and believe it.

I'm quite aware that this may disconcert readers. After all, isn't the act of faith a matter of believing in these final realities? Certainly, but with faith we're a long way from the order of belief described here, because faith does not consist in referring the here-and-now to some ultimate reality. Only belief (and false Christianity) could say to the poor and suffering: "Remain in the state you're in, be perfectly content because heaven will make it all up to you. In heaven you'll be . . ., and so forth." Poverty becomes a blessed condition, along with exploitation, oppression, and alienation. We have to be very careful here. It's quite true, there *are* the Beatitudes, and they're part of faith, as is the frequent affirmation in the Gospel that if you suffer on earth, your membership in the Kingdom will compensate you for all your tragedies. We have the promise of new heavens and a new earth where suffering will no longer exist; we have poor Lazarus and any number of New Testament texts that I could cite in the same vein.

As we have seen, belief transforms next-to-last human realities into ultimate, absolute, foundational realities. It turns everything that belongs to the order of the Promise, of God's Word, of the Kingdom into epiphenomena, into sweet pious words, ways of making government easier, instruments for social peace, a process of self-justification, "consolation," and finally into the means of getting rid of one's personal responsibility and the realm of the absolutely serious.

Faith and its decisions run totally counter to this. To begin with, faith acknowledges the Ultimate in all its irrefragable truth, and so it depreciates and attaches little importance to whatever offers itself as a substitute for that Ultimate. It lowers the great gods, the great taboos, the authorities and princes of this world to nothing more than next-to-last things, useful of course and not necessarily contemptible or inconsequential, but always subject to a greater reality. "You would have no power *over me*, if it had not been given to you from on high"—that is to say, if you hadn't been given permission. But the ultimate truths don't point us in the direction of a vague future, they don't call upon other truths to make them go, and they're no illusion of an artificial paradise: because they are *believed today*, these truths have to be *lived today*. There's where the question of faith lies. It's not a matter of looking to some *external* ultimate reality: the Kingdom of heaven *is* (at present) in you or among you. As of now it's you who constitute it.

Nor is it a matter of getting clear of the present in order to live in a problematical future, about which we can't know anything anyhow, since we haven't the faintest idea of what eternity would be like. On the contrary, the Kingdom of heaven must be here and now. The word must be received as a force that acts immediately. When I read "Blessed are the poor," the text is in the present tense. "I tell you," Jesus declares, "that you are blessed now." In any event, the Son of God can say this to a poor person, but I surely cannot: no believer has the right to use it to keep the poor imprisoned in their poverty. Quite the contrary, when I am told to love my neighbor, that obviously means that beside loving I am also to relieve my neighbor's misery, suffering, and poverty. In other words faith is the demand that we must *incarnate* the Kingdom of God now in this world and this age.

And here we touch on a vital aspect of faith. In Part I we saw the connections between the real world and belief. The situation with faith is altogether different. There is a "verification by reality" in the case of faith, but one that is *not* in the same category as holds for a scientific hypothesis—this verification is a constituent element of faith. It's neither a vague sentiment nor a form of escapism. From one end to the other the Bible shows us that there's no faith without the test of reality. This is no positivistic proof that God has spoken, but it's proof enough for faith. In response to faith an event takes place, sometimes different from what was expected, but indisputably linked to one's attitude of faith. What happens has to be interpreted in accordance with the singular hermeneutics of faith; what happens constitutes faith's trial. Whence the sharp contrast: "The religious person sees God as a flight from reality; the atheist sees reality as the absence of God. Faith brings reality and God face to face and verifies one by the other."[27] This is crucial.

Once again I have to insist on the validity of the contrast I've drawn between faith and belief. As I said, I've chosen to give certain meanings to terms that are often considered interchangeable, but that doesn't mean I'm being completely arbitrary. I note in the operation called "believing" patterns of conduct that are quite antagonistic. Sometimes they are mixed together; most often they're distinct and openly contradictory. I note too that each kind of behavior seems to be consistent with itself. I would say that on the one hand you have the person who rejects any kind of doubt or diversity, who affirms his or her sectarianism, attributes ultimate value

27. Dumas, *Nommer Dieu*. In this passage he is summarizing the theology of Ebeling.

to the things of this world, makes use of religion's promises to ensure his or her own righteousness, seeks to bring crowds of people together and to multiply the number of rites and ceremonies—all of which makes a coherent whole. On the other hand you have the solitary standing before God, the person who reduces the world's realities to the level of next-to-last, who adopts for his or her own purposes the biblical cry, "I hate your sacrifices and your ceremonies," who overcomes doubt and fights a way through anguish, sweat, and pain to certainty, who allows pluralistic expressions of truth and wants to live the truth here and now so as to make it real—this too adds up to a coherent whole. Given two such contrary approaches, can I really use the same word to designate them both? After all, although there is only one verb, "to believe," there *are* two nouns, "belief" and "faith," and hence it seems valid to employ these two terms to denote two different behaviors.

But, to conclude, what is the relationship between them? Belief is sometimes mingled slightly with faith (speaking for myself, I would say that the pilgrimages to Lourdes by sick people belong to the order of beliefs, but I hesitate to pass a wholly negative judgment, because there is undoubtedly some living faith at work here). Faith is often mixed in with, overlapped and enveloped by beliefs (I can't spurn the faith of Charles Péguy and Georges Bernanos merely because they believed in "eternal France" and the value of worldly nations or because they suffered whenever that truth was called into question). But in evaluating how they are related we must look not at isolated mixtures of the two but at the phenomenon as an evolutionary process. In that case I can say with assurance that one never moves from belief to faith, whereas faith often deteriorates into belief.

That first affirmation in the last sentence goes counter to a long tradition, according to which everything connected with believing was blessed. This school would contrast the vitality and energy of the irrational with desiccating rationalism, would appeal to the sources of life deep within humanity, would celebrate the *élan vital* and the expression of spiritual power. Art, the various religions, mysticism, non-Western medicine, extraterrestrial phenomena, magic, Christianity— all that was lumped together. And certain Christian thinkers professed the conviction that as soon as one entered this dimension of the spirit, he or she would inevitably be led to its summit, namely faith.

But the time came when we were cruelly disillusioned, above all by the great mystic explosions of Nazism. We could maintain a cautious reserve vis-à-vis Marxism, because it was easy for us to classify it in the rationalistic, scientific, materialistic domain, and hence (if we blinked the religious and sectarian features of communism) we might think that there was no continuity between it and old-fashioned religion, no way to confuse the two (what an illusion!). But Nazism (to take the crudest instance, and to make a somewhat oversimplified comparison because many, many people also believed in Francoism) showed itself to us as a . . . spiritual fact. Remember the Nazi propaganda for the defense of Christendom, propaganda against Bolshevik atheism, the invocations to the Most High and the Almighty, the appeal to the profound spiritual instincts of the entire people, the proclamation of the value of the irrational, of rootedness in the Soil, the Past, Blood, the call to virtue and sacrifice. All this was, unmistakably, as spiritual as one could wish.

And then what did this communion, this celebration of belief, this exaltation of the spirit lead to? To the worst contempt for humanity, to the victory of the pitiless man of iron, to scorn for the poor and weak. Such things couldn't be reconciled with Christianity, of course. But for a long time people thought they might, and the whole experience has still not sufficed to make Christians and their churches realize that you can't get to faith by way of any old religion, or belief, or some vague spiritual exaltation, or aesthetic emotions; that it's not "better" from a Christian viewpoint to "believe" than not to believe, to "have religion" than not to have it.

On the contrary, we have to firmly and rigorously assert that there is no road from belief to faith. You can't transform a conviction of the value of rites into the act of standing alone in the presence of God. You can't expect an appreciation for music to change into a welcome for the divine Word in Jesus Christ. I would even venture to say that the reverse is true: every belief is an obstacle to faith. Beliefs get in the way because they satisfy the need for religion, because they lead to spiritual choices that are substitutes for faith; they prevent us from discovering, listening to, and accepting the faith revealed in Jesus Christ. Of course, I consider Christian beliefs obstacles like all the others.

Once again we turn to Kierkegaard. It's more difficult, he argues, for people brought up on all the lore of Christmas, for those who have had all their little religious needs met by the church, to receive the shock of revelation, to discover the Unique One, and to enter into the dark night of the soul, than it is for those who have done nothing but search continuously without ever coming upon a satisfying answer. Belonging to Christendom and to one of its churches is the main obstacle to becoming a Christian. It's hard for God to make himself heard by an ear already filled with the echoes of hymns, hard for him to change a heart of stone, not into a celestial heart, but simply into a human heart, a heart of *flesh*. There is no path leading from a little bit of religion (of whatever kind) to a little more and finally to faith.[28] Faith shatters all religion and everything spiritual.

---

28. "It is in the nature of religion to put an end to religious life" (Charbonneau, *Je fus*). I would prefer to say, "an end to the life of faith."

On the other hand, we have to observe that the passage from faith to belief is always possible and always a threat. It's the downhill slide to which the church and the Christian life are always subject. It is impossible to prolong the incandescent moment of revelation. It's impossible to remain standing alone before God. Moses has to go back down the mountain, and what does he find? The people have made themselves a golden calf. Peter can't rest content with his exclusive and radical confession of faith; he returns at once to the perspective of purely human friendship and politics. In the contest with the priests of Baal Elijah can't stay on the summit of the conflict between faith and religion. After his triumphant affirmation of Yahweh, the man who had stood alone before God flees to the desert in confusion, fear, and discouragement. Faith is constantly degenerating into multiple beliefs; the revelation of the word breaks down and becomes theological discourse; the union of two or three in the name of Love sinks into ecclesiastical institutions. The ultimate reality ends by progressively recovering all the values of culture (Tillich) and politics (Barth in his second phase) and intelligence (Aquinas). The gift of freedom quickly turns into ethics.

No phrase expresses this imperceptible change better than "to have faith." I have faith, I don't have faith—the most common, obvious sort of statements. But what do they have to do with the New Birth that Jesus talks to Nicodemus about, with the tempestuous freedom of the Spirit that blows where and when it wills and that tears up by the roots or acts in the gentlest, most unobtrusive fashion? How could we claim to inveigle this Spirit with our rituals so as to take possession of it? "I have." I possess the Holy Spirit (and this "I" can be collective; didn't the church speak that way for a long time?); I am the proprietor of faith, and so naturally I will dispose of it as I wish.

"Having faith" is the worst sort of misconstruction, because the only thing we are really entitled to say is that "Faith has me." The rest is mere belief. "Having faith" is the source of a host of troubles, such as the anxiety felt by people who ask themselves, "Do I have faith?" or the facile evasiveness of those who refuse to confront the truth: "Anyway I don't have faith, so . . ." In this context the word "faith" is meaningless, because if we're referring to the God who is God, in what sense could we be the masters, positively or negatively, of our relationship with him?

All this adds up to a state of confusion and disorder because people don't understand that faith is neither belief nor credulity, neither a blow from a sledge-hammer nor a sociological accident, neither a reasonable acquisition nor an intellectual achievement; it is rather the conjunction of an ultimate decision, which I have to make and for which I'm responsible, and a revelation, which I can discern by the very fact that it sets me amidst next-to-last realities and bids me bring about the incarnation of the ultimate reality today, the Kingdom of God present among us. I am summoned to accept my responsibilities, not to acquire a new dignity or distinction. I am summoned by a Word that is eternal, here and now, universal, personal. And I accept this summons. I am willing to act responsibly; I enter upon an illogical adventure, knowing neither its origin nor its end. Such is faith, without a trace of belief, marked out by a succession of more new questions, more new impossibilities, which are resolved and fade away with each new step I determine to take.

16

Religion and Revelation

At this point we have to say a few words about the antagonism between faith and religion (or, as I prefer to put it, between revelation and religion) that we often encounter in Christian writing these days. The topic hasn't quite become a commonplace yet, but it's beginning to be at least talked about, if not generally accepted. I recall, some twenty years ago, giving a lecture on this subject before a group of ministers and priests who found it utterly astonishing, bewildering, and incomprehensible. I would never get the same response today, but I'm not sure that in the meantime the core of the problem has been widely grasped.

Let's begin by getting our attributions right. Among people who are at least familiar with the expression, the idea of religionless Christianity or the opposition between religion and Christian faith is credited to Dietrich Bonhoeffer and Bonhoeffer's interpretation of religionless Christianity has served as the focal point for debate on the issue. In fact, however, at least ten years before Bonhoeffer the conflict between religion and revelation, or religion and Christian faith, was vigorously elucidated (though not fully developed) by Karl Barth. He discussed the matter with his usual amazing intellectual balance and did so so precisely that he left no room for confusion.

Taking Bonhoeffer's religionless Christianity as a point of departure, various writers have wandered off into death-of-God theology: since God is simply a religious concept, once you clear away religion—and realize that Christianity isn't a religion, anyway—you end up with atheistic Christianity. This has enabled its adherents to revel for a decade in perfectly empty and inconsistent language, which, however, pretended to be at the cutting edge of progress and supposedly allowed its users to join together with unbelievers and atheists since they could now feel comfortable in a godless philosophical framework. At the same time it became possible to dispose of the hard scientific or metaphysical questions. Of course, to do this they had to jettison more than two-thirds of the Bible, but that was quickly arranged thanks to the notion of "culture": the Bible speaks of God insofar as it is a cultural document. Its editors adopted the language and concepts of their epoch, but anyone who can read properly will notice that this talk about God really means the absence of God. . . .

In the same way, once again using Bonhoeffer as a springboard (though I'm convinced he never would have gone along with this), certain thinkers managed to work out a dichotomy between horizontal theology (concerned with human relations), which was legitimate and healthy, the solid core of the Gospel, and vertical theology (people's relations with God), which was hollow and useless. This helped to do away with one of the difficulties experienced by Christians in dealing with non-Christians and enabled them in particular to take part in the human struggles arising from politics, the labor movement, and so forth, without any reservations or second thoughts. It was a vulgar, mediocre (if unconscious) rehash of Feuerbach, and we shall not mention it again.

These two trends have had a long career, but their vogue is over, and we bring them up merely to store them away in the museum of para-Christian fantasies. But the central problem, as posed by Barth, remains with us. To the degree that belief is obviously part of the religious arsenal and to the degree that faith is bound up with the revelation of God in Jesus Christ as it can be discerned in the Bible (which is never automatically and in itself the Word of God, but is always capable of becoming that Word—and as a Christian I would add: in a way denied to all other writings), the conflict between belief and faith necessarily reflects the revelation-religion breach.

Nevertheless, before getting to the heart of the problem, we have to consider a dictum that has gained broad currency in our day. "The twenty-first century will be religious, or it won't be at all" ranks as one of André Malraux's prophetic remarks. The spiritualist movements that have so proliferated recently vie with each other in spreading this prediction, which seems to confirm their enthusiasm. Malraux—what an authority! But, despite the immense admiration I feel for Malraux the writer and the revolutionary of 1930–1944, I have to concede that most of his prophecies have been given the lie by events. And in this case I daresay what we have is what can be called a stupid bet. Malraux says, in effect, that religious passions are going to flare up again, which sounds obvious enough, and everything is going to take on a religious coloring—politics, technology, society, culture, art, and so forth. It's quite true that we're moving full speed ahead in this direction, but there's small consolation in that. Where admirers of Malraux's phrase go wrong is in the fact that it doesn't say (far from it) that the future will become more "Christian," except in the bad sense of the term, for example, the way it was used as a label for medieval society.

Everything is taking on a religious coloring, but we have

little cause to congratulate ourselves for "baptizing" anything and everything—whether it be fox hunts or canons or ships—and making them "Christian" by a magical act. All this means is that the active, potent realities of this world are becoming religious.[29] And, unfortunately, we've seen in the dialogue between Monos and Una what we can look forward to, socially or politically, from *that*. We ought to be very worried by the contemporary upsurge in religious feeling, because this suggests that future conflicts will be of a religious nature. Even World War II was a religious war in the eyes of the Nazis, and the wars waged by the communists are religious too. That is to say, they involve the total elimination of a diabolical enemy—with modern weapons. Thus the admirable formula "The twenty-first century will be religious, or it won't be at all" ought really to be reworded: "The twenty-first century will be religious, and, for that reason, it won't be at all."

The opposition between religion and revelation can really be understood quite simply, and before working out its consequences, we can reduce it to a maxim: religion goes up, revelation comes down. Once you have truly grasped this, you have the key to the problem.

From the very beginning humankind has sought to go up. Religion was at the same time both the principal instrument of this ascent and its expression, perhaps its origin. When Adam finds himself in Eden, he tries to ascend to the level of God. When people gather to attend to their common work, they are essentially building the city, but that includes the Tower of Babel, climbing to the heavens. I admire the dewy naiveté of a certain eminent archaeologist, an expert in Middle Eastern excavations, who wrote that the biblical authors and all the Jewish and Christian commentators after them had

29. See Jacques Ellul, *The New Demons*, 1975.

grossly misread the Tower of Babel episode. The tower was quite evidently a ziggurat, one of those seven-tiered towers built in the ancient Near East to draw nearer to the gods. What a mistake to condemn it, he said, from the standpoint of those Jews. They were as religious as one could wish, so they (the biblical authors) should have understood that the ziggurat represented a marvelous effort to approach God. Instead they reacted like bedouins, ignorant nomads, terrified by such a grand accomplishment without grasping what it was about.

Alas, I fear that our savant has missed the point: this harsh biblical account is only the expression of the ban against drawing near to God. Henceforth, east of Eden there will be menacing cherubim; no one can go up there and return. God is inaccessible to humans and unknowable by natural means. As high as we may ascend (the astronauts! more naiveté . . .), we'll never come face to face with God. But humankind wishes to ascend. The cultic importance of mountains is well known—and universal. And in a flat country ziggurats are images of the mountain where one meets God. Whether symbolized by Olympus or Sinai, religion creates the need to climb up, a need Israel was not immune to: think of Gerizim, Sinai, Nebo. And the God of the Hebrews is more than once called "God of the Mountains." The Samaritans used this title, and *they* adored God on the mountain. Even in the Gospels we have the Sermon on the Mount, the Mount of Olives, and so forth. These are religious representations of the sacred place, which coincides with the idea that God is enthroned in the sky, "up above," whence the name Most High. And to reach him you have to climb.

Mystics are driven by exactly the same impulse. When the religious need to encounter God on high becomes spiritualized, it no longer induces people to scale mountain peaks but rather to climb the spiritual ladder to heaven to find God at home. All of this reflects a spontaneous natural tendency bound up with religious feeling. Religion gives simultaneous expression to needs, feelings, and sociological necessity. From earliest times humans have clearly had a kind of piety which can be called natural and whose ingenuous flavor Jean Jacques Rousseau recaptured in his *Savoyard Vicar*. One proof that it exists is the indisputable fact of our preoccupation with the dead. We don't just leave our dead anywhere, like useless objects thrown in the trash can. A dead person is not the same as a dead animal. The human body is given special treatment, buried in a prescribed posture, burned, or otherwise destroyed, so as to return the person to the group he or she has left. Humankind has never dealt with their dead as if they were nothing.

Now this expresses, on the one hand, the importance people attach to the life and death of *each individual* (in relation to the group) and, on the other, the conviction that everything cannot be reduced to the bare facts of material existence, that there is an "after-death" dimension, which inevitably means a religious dimension. There is a great deal of evidence, I think, for the religious character of so-called primitive people, which may be due to their "primitiveness"; but if that's so, that would be of small consequence. In any case there is a kind of religious need in humans, though I shall be careful not to call it natural or innate. Yet people have always behaved as if it were natural or innate. As far back as we go into our archaic past we never find people without this religious disposition. They always give evidence of experiencing a religious consciousness that attributes to a higher power—a Beyond, an Unknown, a Supreme Being—certain impulses, emotions, and profound states of soul that they cannot otherwise explain.

Let there be no confusion here: I have not the least intention of engaging in apologetics. I do not wish to argue that since humans have always been religious (apart from exceptional crises), ergo Christianity is good. Later on we shall take exactly the opposite stance. And nineteenth-century scientists were wasting their time when they declared that religion represented an obsolete stage of human history, because religious feeling has had a resurgence everywhere, adopting today even bolder forms than those of the past. On the basis, then, of this natural need or sentiment, people build up whole edifices of their various religions. *Re-ligare*, "rebind, attach": religion attaches us, whether to the past or to eternity, to our ancestors or the gods. But it also links us to the living human community and serves to bond society together, a point we shall be returning to.

It's also possible to connect "religion" to *re-legere*, "reread," which brings us to the other great edifice, myth and ritual—the rereading, repetition, and reproduction of the foundational word, the rite, the self-empowered formula. Here we have the recitation of the primordial myth, the explanation of the world's origins which at the same time holds the key to its end. And projecting outward from this rereading or "binding" is the structure composed of priests, ceremonies, temples and offerings, sacrifices and patterns of conduct: the whole religious "system."

I don't think there's anything excessive or out of order in the foregoing passage. I'm trying to show that religious systems are perfectly natural and consistent with human behavior. But we also have to recall the purely sociological side of religion, religion as an indispensable and most economical means of assuring the unity of a group. The religious bond makes it possible to establish complex group structures considered by their members as inevitable. And there is always a connection with something "higher," whether it be a higher order or a higher being. The structure of society can be either the reflection, the replica of that heavenly order or the expression of a commandment, with the divinity prescribing the various hierarchies and kinds of relationships.

We must remember that there is no dispensing with this organization. There is no society or even community anywhere that lives without rules or government, operating simply on the basis of continual spontaneous desire. Thus religion is at once the expression of individual need and the appropriate instrument of social logic. It specifies both origins and ends. Jacques Monod may tell us that biology has no final causes. Fine, but people cannot live without assigning final causes to their world. Religion is the most economical mode of social bonding, and at the same time it vouches to the members of society for the validity and legitimacy of the rules they obey. Consider how, as soon as religious feelings slacken, the law, for example, loses so much of its weight and authority. It's not necessary for law to be directly inspired by a divine source; it need only be connected to that source.

And the invention of natural law, it must be said, was a fine thing. Among other things, it confirmed the idea that religion belongs to the realm of nature, even should nature be transcended or transformed into supernature. In this light religion appears not as a superfluous mistake, but as a useful element in every human activity. And since so few people know about it, we ought to mention too that the value of religion has been gaining recognition in the scientific world, where it is seen as a tool for intellectual penetration of reality, as an interpretive key, as a framework for scientific research. Let me just point to the Taoist renaissance[30] to show how diverse scientific orientations have become.

Now that the concepts of classical physics are no longer capable of accounting for subatomic physical phenomena, Westerners must sit down and study Eastern thought. For Capra the Taoists are right to maintain that underlying all

---

30. P. Thuillier, "La physique and l'irrationnel," *La Recherche*, no. 111, 1980. F. Capra, *The Tao of Physics*, 1978.

phenomena is a perpetual cosmic flux. Matter "dances and pulsates." Rigid occidental intelligence (yang) has to be complemented by feminine sensitivity (yin) for the harmony of the world. But unlike the thought of Bernard d'Espagnat, what we have in this case is an incongruous blend of preconceived mystical notions and some laws of modern physics. It's not enough to declare that Eastern spirituality provides a philosophical framework for the most advanced kind of physics, and it's utterly gratuitous to juxtapose texts by Heisenberg or Einstein with quotations from the *Upanishads* or the *Bhagavad-Gita*. The fact that the same words can be found in both does not necessarily mean that ancient religious thought dovetails with contemporary research. No, the Tao contains no more revelations in physics than Genesis contains revelations in geology. These syncretistic efforts offer us an insupportably arbitrary melange, but it's significant that scientists should try to do such things when they encounter the void, that they should be looking to restore coherence to their own thinking. Far be it from me to exclude religion in the name of science. Its rehabilitation gives us back one of its useful features—but still leaves us hungry for a greater certitude.

There are deeper and more decisive elements in religion, one of which is the force that assures the identity and continuity of a people, their capacity to be themselves. Religion is persistence, endurance, the deepest self of a people. Consider the Jews, that prodigious adventure of a people—politically destroyed, physically torn to pieces, flung all over the world in a pitiless diaspora. It's no longer true that the Jews are a race, and it's not race that has unified them. Other peoples have know dispersion, but even when they belonged to the same race, they didn't manage to preserve any kind of connection between their scattered groups.

What has maintained the unity or, in stronger language, the identity of the Jewish world over the last two millennia?

It's the steadfastness of their religion, the holy Scriptures held in common, the reality of identical prayers, the same religious hopes that never seem to die; it's "next year in Jerusalem," it's the concept of one and the same synagogue, it's the ties to the God of the Covenant. This religious steadfastness is what has guaranteed Israel's vitality. And today, alas, we can see the opposite of this happening: Israel has never been in greater danger because political conerns are overwhelming its religious orientation, because a nonreligious, even antireligious spirit is spreading in Israel, and Israel is going to lose its identity by challenging or forgetting what has been its sole and strict frame of reference.

We can find other examples as well of religion helping to maintain the identity of a people, though they may not hold for such an impressive time span. Take the case of Poland. It has an officially atheistic Communist regime that's been spreading antireligious propaganda for almost forty years—more than a generation—and yet what has given the country its essential unity during this time? What has forced the Communists to give ground, to make concessions, to institute no reforms except economic ones, knowing they would be powerless to press beyond that? It is the Catholic religion, which has fixed and unshakable roots in Poland. Of course taking the viewpoint of a theological rigorist one could qualify this religion as nothing but ritual and superstition: the Black Madonna of Czestochowa, the attachment to religious forms and authorities, and so forth. I won't argue the matter. Quite obviously we are talking about religion. But religion is what has assured the identity and continuity of the Polish people. It has enabled them to resist the terrible pressure from the Communists. If we compare Catholicism and Communism in this instance, we find that the source of alienation is the latter. Unlike the Poles the Rumanians and the Bulgarians seem to have been broken. They seem to have had nothing to fall back upon in their fight against Communism because they were not so profoundly stamped with their religion. I say "seem" on account of the fact that twenty years ago I used to argue that the Russian people had been totally overmastered by Communist propaganda. I wouldn't say that anymore, not after witnessing the extraordinary religious awakening going on among the youth and the intellectuals of that country.

Careful molding and intense propaganda by the government have not made religion disappear in the Soviet Union. For a long time religion remained hidden, mute, apparently inert, but it was only dormant; the hour of awakening had not yet rung. Today it is clear that the Russian people are recovering their identity, restoring the links with their past, transcending the upheavals of revolution. And what should we say about the Afghans or the Kurds? They are waging war, to be sure, on behalf of their culture, their language, and their customs, but the core of their resistance is religious. And let's not say that this proves religion is naturally retrograde and addicted to the past. True, these Muslem rebels reject "progress," "science," and "the nation," but then progress, science, and the nation would have to be bought at the price of their basic identity. It's as if you were trying to feed poison to a dog, and when the animal refused it and wanted to live, you accused it of not accepting progress. Individual identity is a part of cultural identity, which in turn is the formative principle of any given social identity, with religion binding the whole complex together.

A close look at the situation shows that religion is essential for the development of human nature, that natural religion is broadly *useful* in human activities, but that religion always implies ascent, the glance directed on high. We walk on the earth but our eyes look to the star that guides us. In the long run the hope is that we will ultimately make our way to the heights where the god is enthroned.

To conclude, we recall Teilhard de Chardin, who tried to reconcile religion and science. Everything he wrote dealt with religion (without in any way calling into question his personal faith). And his celebrated formula "Everything that rises must converge" summarizes precisely the point I have been making. Humans attempt to reach God by ascending. The evolution of life all the way to the emergence of the human race is presented in Teilhard's schemas, and rightly so, as an ascent. At the bottom there is inanimate matter; at the summit there is the supreme union in Point Omega. Teilhard describes a process of ascent that leads humankind to the encounter with Christ the Last Word. At each stage there is a concentration, an intensification, a greater perfection of structural organization until we are brought by a qualitative leap to a higher level. The function of religion is at once to concentrate and organize human groups and to lead their members up toward God. There you have the sum total of religion, completely legitimate and useful, indispensable to the person at whom belief is aimed. It inspires that belief, and then belief makes the person a participant in the phenomenon of religion.

But we are filled with stupefaction when we realize that in every aspect the revelation of the God of Abraham, Isaac, and Jacob, of the God of Jesus Christ, is exactly and entirely contrary to what we have just described. The central fact, the crucial point, is that here God descends to humankind. Never in any way, under any circumstances can we ascend to God, howsoever slightly. God has chosen to descend and to put himself on our level. It's not just that God expressly declares in the story of the Tower of Babel, "Let us go down." And yet the myth is very clear: people build the tower to climb up and enter into contact with God, to equal him, to get hold of him, and whatever else one can imagine. In the face of this God proclaims his intention to go down and see.

The lofty intellectual will smile at such a childish phrase, at a God who needs to descend, to get closer in order to "see." But it's the clever intellectual who is childish. The important thing here is to stress the disjunction: the religious person wants to go up, but the God of the Bible is a God who comes down, and it's on this God that revelation (which is thus contrary to religion) finally rests. I would go so far as to say that *this* is what revelation is all about. Similarly, the crux of the story of Mount Sinai is not that God is present on the mountain and speaks there with Moses, but that Moses comes down from the mountain *with* the revelation, written in God's own hand on the stone tablets. Revelation has made its way not to some superhuman race, but to humankind, not in images, but with God's own signature on it.

It would take forever to enumerate the passages where we are told that God comes down to humankind, while there are none (except for Elijah in his chariot of fire) where humans ascend to God. Even at the baptism of Jesus the Spirit of God comes down upon Jesus like a dove. In his ascension Jesus *is* mysteriously lifted up into the presence of the Father, but this elevation is precisely what brings to an end the revelation of the Son.

But let's put aside these specific episodes and get to the heart of the matter: the fact that God speaks. We are told that he never acts except through his word (and that the Logos was with God, as in the account of the "Creation"). This is in no sense an anthropomorphism. It signifies that when God addresses human beings, he does so on their level, not in modes that might be specific to God but in the manner most specific to humans: through speech. God does not compel us to come into an ineffable, inconceivable, inexpressible world. He enters into our language, into a world both conceivable and expressible. He comes down to our level so that we can meet him. Similarly, every time the Old Testament tells us that God "repents," it is always relative to a decision he had made to act in a transcendent, omnipotent manner, with suprahuman justice. God "backs off" in order to place himself in a position where we can endure him, can comprehend and accept him. And after God has been characterized as "a god of the mountains," he goes right ahead and reveals himself as the god of the valleys and plains (1 Kings 20:23–28).

Here is where the split occurs. For us God is up there, in the sky, which is the whole message of religion. And, of course, every time we aspire to grasp God, to get control of him, to know him, to penetrate his darkness, we run up against the ironclad law: "God is in heaven and you upon earth" (Eccles. 5:2). So there is no chance of an encounter: earthlings are not about to ascend to the place of God. The moment we declare that God is up there, the moment we dream of knowing God's thoughts, of fastening him to heaven, of defining him in terms of "up there," we immediately learn that "my thoughts are not your thoughts, neither are your ways my ways" (Isa. 55:8). The text is very clear: "your human thoughts consist of efforts to ascend to me and my divine thoughts run counter to this: *I* am the one who comes down. Your way mounts, mine descends."

Naturally this entire revelation attains its full meaning and consummation in Jesus Christ. One need only cite the admirable confession of faith in the second chapter of Philippians that recounts the successive stages of God's "descent." Though he exists as God, he despoils himself of everything that makes his greatness, his power, his immortality, to enter into the human condition. He becomes a man, purely and simply a man, in everything (even in temptation, but not in succumbing to it). Although he was a man, he did not seek human power; he did not try to show that he was *also* God. He rejected the three temptations: to perform a miracle as a way of meeting his needs, to seize political power, and to give religious proof of his mission. Later, hanging on the cross, Jesus refused to do a miracle to show that he really was the Son of God. He refused to act by means of any sort of power. He entered on the way of suffering (which is God's way) as a mere man. All that the Apostles Creed says about his life is that "He suffered." His entire life is summed up in suffering.

As a man he took upon himself the miserable condition of the lowly human being, not the life of a successful artisan but that of a vagabond. "Foxes have holes, and birds of the air have nests; but the Son of man has nowhere to lay his head" (Matt. 8:20). From the state of vagabondage he descended a little lower. Arrested on false charges, he was ranked among bandits, assassins, and evildoers (to call them this is more important as well as theologically more accurate than to say that they were valiant warriors for the people's cause, revolutionaries, guerrillas—or some such contemporary twaddle). And he was condemned to the punishment meted out to rebellious slaves. This was the fourth step in the descent to the bottom of the abyss, the last being death itself—unthinkable for God. And with that we have the capstone on the radical contrast between this God's revelation and all religions.

Before getting into the many consequences of that contrast, let me briefly refute an argument one often hears raised against the incarnation. Many of the religions of antiquity have gods who become human. The inhabitants of Olympus often transform themselves into humans for a few days, but such stories, it must be noted, are no more than amusing ribaldry. Jupiter metamorphoses into a bull, a swan, a man, whatever. Venus has a mind to sleep with such and such a man, so she turns into a woman. Jupiter plays pleasant tricks on human beings, turning himself into Amphytrion, and so forth. But how is any of this comparable to the incarnation? And above all how could one see in it the element that I find essential: the continuous working out of a plan, like that of the God of Israel?

The Greek gods follow their whimsical fantasies; they bend to the flow of circumstance. The God of Abraham, Isaac, and Jesus carries out, from start to finish, a unique and strictly consistent project: he comes to humankind. At each stage he descends to human level; that is, the means he adopts are accessible and comprehensible. This has led certain writers to speak of either a divine pedagogy or progressive revelation. They have made some serious errors on this point, all of which boil down to the idea that as Israel evolves and its culture becomes more civilized, it works out an ever more refined and improved image of God. But the Bible shows us just the contrary: it's not Israel that elaborates a vision of God, it's the eternal God who reveals himself at each historical stage in Israel's cultural development, so that people can grasp then and there what God has to say to them. There is no "progressive revelation." There are cultural changes that result (because of God's constant will to encounter humankind, to find them wherever they may be, within human limits) in God's revealing himself in accordance with forms accessible to humans. But the essential factor in all this is the movement of revelation toward humanity.

Now this downward movement of revelation entails a number of radical consequences, which are precisely the opposite of those brought on by the ascending movement of religion. Revelation leads to the affirmation of powerlessness, the destabilization of human communities, the shattering of unity, the invalidating of law, and the impossibility of establishing an explicit, definitive content for faith. In that religion ascends, it always expresses itself in a show of power; and when religion has God enter the scene, it's always for the purpose of having a little more power. On the contrary, as we have to keep repeating, the revelation of God (even when it's the

"Lord of hosts," the God who leads his people to victory in countless battles) guides humankind in the direction of powerlessness, toward the choice to abandon human means of domination in order to become a people that entrusts itself to God's hands, to the free decision—and the free grace—of that God.

Because God's guiding hand is present too in that business of combats and victories in a world of war and military power; it's bringing people to give up their own paths to victory, their clans, armies, and mounted troops, to rely exclusively on God's protection, confiding in him. Hence the boy David has no need for arms or armor. This is opting for human powerlessness so that God can act as he sees fit. And it corresponds exactly, on the ethical plane, to the theological revelation of the God who comes down to humankind. Since I have often elaborated on the theme of powerlessness elsewhere, I won't go into it any further. I simply remind readers that, as always, it is Jesus who represents the complete fulfillment of this pattern of powerlessness (which goes far beyond nonviolence), in particular when he voluntarily allows himself to be arrested.

While religion founds communities and leads to unity, revelation shatters and tears asunder. Wherever it intervenes, it brings an end to society, to all "convergences." The sword of the Word severs the strongest ties of nature. But we must be careful not to jump to conclusions: this doesn't mean that human communities, that social or intellectual or cultural unity are of no significance or against the will of God. That's not it at all. We have to live, and God knows this. We are no longer in Eden and not yet in the heavenly Jerusalem. There is no period that does not have value in the eyes of God. People have to manage somehow to live and to live with as little misery as possible. There must be law and public authorities, certainly. Without them human relations would be impossible; there would be danger everywhere. There must be communities with an interest in peace, where people can unfold their gifts and find happiness on the human level.

All this is fine, but it's not God; it doesn't bring us any closer to God, nor is it in keeping with "the will of God." No, these are just precarious arrangements for living while we wait for the end and Christ's return. So it makes no sense to try to express God's will in the way we organize our cities or our legal systems. Values are a human invention, and not a bad one at that, but there are no "Christian" values. We don't have to baptize them. When we do, we're entering into the religious process, and things get very dangerous. Yet God intervenes in this human system to repair the bonds linking him to humans that he refuses to see broken. God shatters the community's consensus by the bestowal of what has never been said, never been seen before.

God makes it plain that law is not justice (the justice that God himself establishes as such), that human peace is not peace, that human virtue is not the blessing that God alone can say, that the human community is not communion with God, that human love is not Love. In other words, religion and revelation cover the same territory, though while religion sacralizes and absolutizes human realities, revelation desacralizes and relativizes them—the latter of which is extremely useful as far as humans are concerned. And yet we might well feel like saying: "But why doesn't this God let us work things out all by ourselves? Why not let us organize our little societies and blunder through in this world, a job we handle fairly well? Why does this God come to disturb us and cause confusion?"

The reason is, precisely for humanity's sake, so that people can't take themselves for God, with all the consequences we have seen deriving from that. If the nation is not a religious value, any more than law or science, if one lives in a relative world where everything is constantly being relativized, then peace is infinitely easier, as are compromise and reconciliation. But you can't relativize things except vis-à-vis an absolute, and this is a self-revealing absolute.

What an admirable decision on God's part: he does not reveal himself as a religious absolute, but as love, as powerlessness, as one who comes down to our level and thus devalues everything else. Other things have to exist, in their way, and they have their uses—a bike, for example, a pen, a spade, a plate. "Values" belong to that order of things, along with institutions, arts, and ideas. And so we can enjoy the passing moment without giving in to the temptation to cry out, as Mephistopheles suggests to Faust: "Ah, fleeting instant, you are so fair that you deserve to be eternal." No! The biblical God comes with his revelation to humanity precisely to repudiate that cry. Even the moment of encounter with this God must not be immortalized—look at the Transfiguration. When the disciples, overwhelmed with astonishment, want to set up a tent and install themselves there, with Moses, Elijah, and Jesus in his glory, the whole scene vanishes into thin air.

Contrary to religion, revelation destabilizes. It turns the game upside down; all bets are off. It makes a shambles of foresight and probabilities. It brings an imponderable, unexpected, incalculable element into our policies and contrivances. It always takes us by surprise: "For the Son of man is coming *at an hour you do not expect*" (Matt. 24:44). At *that* time and no other. As long as there are religions, organizations, rituals, sacrifices, and structures for governing our relationship with God and to receive the Son of man, then he won't come. The Event will happen when no one is looking for it or thinking about it.

Revelation calls into question everything solid and taken for granted. It shakes the foundations of the most elaborate cultural edifice; it stirs up uncertainty. Indeed, it creates un-

certainty—never the narrow-minded, rigid, unshakable certitude of the person who believes the way a cow chews its cud.
It seizes hold of everything that constitutes our humanity, our
states and societies, our hierarchy of values, our morality and
our religion, and puts it all in the crucible. It leaves us totally
uncertain as we try to decide how to rediscover and rebuild a
livable world. And this uncertainty is all the more overwhelming because we can't rely on any clear evidence from
revelation itself.

The revelation that arouses faith is never so univocal, so
rational and incontestable that we can both fully comprehend
it and maintain constant certitude. When revelation occurs,
the one who receives it experiences a constant reappropriation
of the connotations, dimensions, and depths, the "levels" of
that revelation. Once again we are full of uncertainty. The
question is not "Will I still have faith tomorrow?" but rather
"What will I make of this revelation tomorrow? How will I
come to renew my understanding of it? What will come surg-
ing up into my conscious mind from the past/present revelation planted deep within me in the unconscious or whatever
one wishes to call it?" Revelation acts in an unforeseeable
fashion and makes me act the same way, because "The wind
blows where it wills, and you hear the sound of it, but you do
not know whence it comes or whither it goes; so it is with
every one who is born of the Spirit."[31]

So then the content of faith becomes indefinable and ungraspable. Faith is born of revelation and is directed to it, but
like revelation itself, it cannot be defined or stabilized. Of
course, it's not altogether inexpressible, although its innermost core is ineffable. And the experience of meeting that
revelation is ineffable too—"Joy, tears of joy"—as is the al-

---

31. All too often the comparison of the wind that blows where it will is applied to
the Holy Spirit, but John 3:8 is quite clear: it's the *person* born of the Spirit who
is changeable and unpredictable.

teration that we undergo within ourselves. As a result we are left speechless when we try to seek out the consequences of faith in our lives. (I would say that only the negative proof is to a certain extent applicable here. We mustn't ask what has changed in us because of revelation, but what would become of our life if we stopped believing in that revelation. Then we get an answer, and in each case it's beyond dispute.)

But revelation also turns out to be ineffable when you try to spell out its content with any precision. What bitterness arises when people get into theological discussions of things like the two natures of Christ, the term *homoiousios* ("likeness," as in reference to Christ being one in substance with God), the subtleties of the virgin birth, and all the complex criteria and definitions that have provoked so much mockery from anti-Christians, and with reason. Readers cannot expect me to repudiate the effort to get some understanding of these matters, but it's essential to begin with the awareness that revelation is ungraspable and inexhaustible, that faith is indefinable because it all relates to God—who wouldn't be God if I could plumb his depths and define his being. Taking that as a starting point you try—timidly or forcefully, stressing prudence or bold intuition—to speak a truth that is never closed, never finished, never sealed off.[32]

In these attempts there are two dangers to be avoided. The first, typical of the premodern period, is the temptation to take faith too circumstantially, to break it down into propositions, to define it and nail it down and then declare that everything outside these definitions and formulas is a "mystery." Mystery ought never to be invoked in a philosophical context, because it always looks like an evasion or a counterproof. I want to stress the contradiction involved in explain-

32. See the two fine studies by Dumas, "Dieu objectif" and "La Critique de l'objectivité de Dieu dans la théologie protestante," in *Nommer Dieu.*

ing *everything,* in analyzing the hair of the Virgin and every letter in the Bible, but then getting rid of whatever is left over by sticking it into the category of mystery. This dichotomy is intellectually untenable. Those who employ it forget, on the one hand, the humility befitting the person who speaks in the presence of God and, on the other, the fact that in this case the intellectual activity arising out of revelation, which has revelation for its foundation and its object, is necessarily and uniquely included in the commandment, "You shall love the Lord your God . . . with all your mind" (Matt. 22:37). Thinking becomes an act of adoration. One thinks in order to adore him who is the only Lord and Savior. When this occurs, empty discussions of the mystery and attempts to fit things into its category are both made impossible.

The second danger arises out of the permissive attitude already spoken of that will preach "anything at all," on the grounds that the content of faith can't be defined. This approach is particularly characteristic of our time, which is in all respects the epoch of "anything goes."[33] True, faith can't be clearly demarcated or frozen in place, but it's always addressed to some individual. It's completely unique and if not knowable, it's at least perfectly "believable." The myths that foretold it and the personal testimony that made it known to us are susceptible neither to whimsical interpretation[34] nor to syncretism.

In reality, faith contains within itself a principle of interpretation. This is called the principle of the analogy of faith according to Paul (2 Tim. 3:16, Rom. 12:6) and was explained by Calvin. It consists in using only Scripture itself to interpret Scripture, viewing revelation as a consistent, continuous whole and rejecting any principle that involves out-

---

33. See the detailed analysis of this point in Jacques Ellul, *L'Empire du non-sens,* 1980.
34. On the complexity of interpretation see Paul Ricoeur, *De l'Interprétation,* 1972.

side interference, because of the very nature of revelation. This does not mean that it rules out rational methods. It rates them as perfectly legitimate but ancillary, as means and tools rather than as supreme criteria or self-contained guides to the truth. The criterion of truth is to be found in truth itself, not in a scientific proposition or some other sort of method. This is another way of saying that "Only God speaks well about God," an indisputable statement as far as faith goes, but worthless for belief. And here we have another contrast between the two: belief remains convinced at all times of its legitimacy, thanks to various means of demonstration. It's always trying to work out a rapprochement between itself and science. All the research to prove that what the Bible says is (scientifically) true belongs to the order of belief. Such attempts, like everything human, are altogether respectable but have nothing to do with faith, with the truth that faith deems itself related to.

The antitheses (rather than mere differences) we have outlined between religion and revelation make it clear that revelation never satisfies people's religious needs. We are now at the heart of the problem. We have seen that people have spontaneous religious feelings and to what extent religion is a response to those religious needs. Remember all the items we mentioned in the discussion of Feuerbach. Mystical belief has roots in all cultures, as do religion and the ensuing forms of social organization that get fashioned as a result of them both. Religion has a perfectly explicit and analyzable function. It's a human phenomenon, by no means negligible, and we don't from this particular point of view have to deny it in the name of faith.

But revelation and faith in revelation, as we have seen, run totally contrary to religion. In other words, they don't answer any of the questions belief spontaneously asks (what must be done to win favors from God, how heaven is set up, what powers the gods have, etc.). Nor do they satisfy the human need for marvels and extraordinary happenings, for explanations, guarantees, or security. Revelation speaks of a God who is simply content to be God, leaving us the responsibility of making our own decisions, a God who doesn't snare our lives in a network of constraints, obligations, rites, and prescriptions both moral and religious that we yearn for in our search for peace of mind. This God sets us free to rush out on a series of adventures where we will be our own guide, with faith in an absolute being who slips away when one looks to him for exact instructions about one's choices and decisions.

This God doesn't supply his faithful followers with power or glory or success, except when it suits him, when he has decided to do so. But in spite of the fact that decision always lacks any apparent motivation, it's not a matter of divine capriciousness—it's only afterward, long afterward, that we perceive the reasons for what he did. Then we begin to understand the origin of it all, or rather the final goal toward which God was tending for our sake. This is not a God with whom one can sign a contract and then rest easy. This God is free grace, which is utterly intolerable, doubly intolerable, because that means both that we are at the mercy of his unforeseeable decisions and that our human resources are useless and impotent—all of them. That includes the religious resources we draw on to try to win his benevolence or a decision favorable to us as well as the technical resources we employ in all our undertakings ("Unless the Lord builds the house, those who build it labor in vain"—Ps. 127:1).

This God is unpredictable, and it's no good performing rites or drawing lots or turning to horoscopes or haruspices: none of these things can forecast his decision. His intentions are inscrutable until he makes his decision, and he is bound only by that decision (which, once again, is neither irrational nor inconsistent, but follows a logic of its own that is no more our logic than eternity is merely the continuation of time). It's impossible to reach an agreement with this God on fair and reasonable terms, because his word is not ours, his love is not ours; he is not ruled by some ideal goodness. It would be so convenient if we shared common values with him, justice for example, but all the parables about the Kingdom of heaven show us that God's justice has absolutely nothing to do with ours (the workers hired at the eleventh hour, the foolish virgins, the prodigal son and his brother, the servant who hid the one talent, etc.).

If we could come to an understanding on the Good, if there was a value of goodness that, standing higher than God, might serve as a common point of reference, then we men and women might decide about it and come to terms with this God. But no, not at all, we are told all along that the Good is whatever God wants. Period. When God gives the order to Abraham to sacrifice his son, that is the Good. And even when we read in Scripture about the terrible injunction of *herem*, that too is good, no matter if it turns our stomach and sorely offends our humanitarian instincts.

So there's no way to agree with him on some consistent, commensurable basis. But that shouldn't surprise us, since the distance between us and God is, in fact, incommensurable, *if* that God is really God. There is nothing to which God owes obedience. There is nothing above him to which we could appeal. And since his understanding of the world is not the same as ours, since his eternal decisions are not subject to human reason, we have no possibility of working out a system of religious, moral, or ritual laws to bind both God and us at once—which has always been the goal of religion.

Religion binds people, but at the same time it's meant to bind God. I give you this sacrifice and from now on you are bound to do such and such. Here at least we're on ground that's solid and completely satisfying to our religious instincts, to our feelings and needs. But the biblical God is not one whit like that. The people offer feasts and sacrifices in his honor (even sacrifices that he himself had commanded), and he replies: "I hate, I despise your feasts, and I take no delight in your solemn assemblies" (Amos 5:21). They meticulously obey the Law revealed to their ancestors and he declares: "Moreover I gave them statutes that were not good and ordinances by which they could not have life; and I defiled them through their very gifts . . . ; I did it that they might know that I am the LORD" (Ezek. 20:25–26). And, furthermore, when the Law had been perfectly known, probed, expounded, applied with love and attention to every detail, God's Messiah arrives and sends it packing: "You have heard that it was said . . . But I say to you." This radical statement by Jesus is a scriptural constant; all throughout revelation God is the one who intervenes to set things right by proclaiming, "But I say to you . . ." Just when people thought they had heard the message of the Old Testament so clearly, thought they could finally relax and stride firmly along on the right road, Jesus appears and God's holy will is known at last!

The really unbearable thing for us is grace, because while it is, to be sure, the expression of infinite love, it's also totally gratuitous. You can't buy it or exchange it. You can't deal for it or get the hang of it. You'll go nowhere with influence, indulgences, collusion. Grace is what sets apart God's sovereign freedom, whose causes, we said, we can neither grasp nor still less foresee. "I will have mercy on whom I have mercy" (Rom. 9:15).

No pronouncement is more revolting than this one to the religious feelings, the clear moral conscience, the need for security that religion instills in us. Grace is the hardest thing for us to be reconciled to, because it implies the renouncing of our pretentions, our power, our pomp and circumstance. Hence it is exactly the opposite of everything our religious sentiments are looking for, of everything we expect from God, namely that he give our lives some security (he makes them even more insecure) and that he lift up our souls (he harshly reminds us, "I am in heaven, you are on earth," and that's where you'll stay). We wait for God to provide us with a meaning for everything that exists (and he sends us back to find it ourselves), to make things easier for us (he never stops complicating them), to guarantee our future. And he tells us that the Spirit blows where it wills. Free grace is the expression of love itself, but religion has never tolerated love. Religion is the radical contrary of love, both as *religare* and as *relegere*, because love never binds the beloved and love never rereads the same lines. To leave matters entirely to free grace, even if it comes from one whom we acknowledge as Love, is to proclaim, "I know that you can do all things." (Note that this is not a definition of God as Almighty, not a metaphysical affirmation, but a confession of faith.)

"Not my will, but thine be done." This is unbearable for the religious mind, which aims at getting hold of, or actually being, the place where the divine phenomenon occurs. It aims at regularizing and normalizing the acts of that unknown reality. Free grace is, inevitably, the only way God expresses himself, if he is God, but that won't satisfy any of our lofty sentiments, any of our needs for security, for models, for a fixed and calculated absolute, for ethical systems and social organizations. On the contrary, grace is the force that disturbs us and throws us off balance, puts us in front of a mirror and throws us back upon ourselves, while at the same time it liberates us—but without our having any merit or the right to deal with God as his equals. We have often said that Mikhail Bakunin was right to reject the God presented to the nineteenth century as the Almighty, but he would have rejected just as vehemently the love of free grace, because there is nothing that goes more against our grain than accepting the perfect gift of an inexhaustible grace from Love itself.

We saw in the last chapter that faith can be transformed into belief, but never the other way around. Here we discover the exact same evolutionary relationship holds for revelation and religion. Revelation, alas, can always be turned into religion, but religion never bears witness to, and still less does it end in, a revelation.

All throughout the history of both Judaism and Christianity, which are founded on the revelation of the same God of Abraham, Isaac, Jacob, and Jesus, we can trace the same falling off. People invariably succeed in gaining control of the contents of revelation. That is to say, they objectify it, transform a momentary illumination into a permanent establishment, a promise into law, hope into an institution, love into a series of works and charities, the Holy Spirit into a jurist, and the explosion of the Word into rituals and feasts. God's will *hic et nunc* is turned into a rigid commandment, dialogue into the catechism, symbolic offerings into a kind of purchase, death to oneself into good deeds, truth into dogmas, grace into a system of predestination, chosenness into privileges and superiority, and the gift of salvation into damnation for others. In effect this is separating the word from the one who pronounces it. People seize the contents of revelation, when the revelatory moment can never be reduced to such objectified contents, to things that have been analyzed, flattened, expurgated until they can all be satisfactorily adapted to meet religious needs.

Speaking of the moment of revelation, I would like to stress that I am not an illuminist or quietist. I'm aware that God's word says something, that the moment has a communicable content, and that God has chosen language so that our words too can get into the game and "return the serve." I'm

trying to underline the contrast between the living power of
revelation and the dead weight of institutional religion.

Judaism has its endless proliferation of commentaries, of
imperatives based on the Torah, with all the flaws for which
Pharisaism is so readily criticized including its harsh piety;
Christianity has its church structures, the legalism of its canons and denominational disciplines, the accumulated decisions of its councils and synods, the will to dominate the peoples of Christendom, the formulation of strict and complete
dogmatic systems, the claim to have sole possession of the
truth, and proselytism—all of which amounts to nothing but
the establishment of religion on the basis of something that
was originally the incredible revelation by the God who loves.
(In this context I see no difference between Catholicism and
Protestantism or Orthodoxy.) In each case the process of
decay has resulted from human weakness, from the pressures
of everyday necessity. Everyone needs stability and security,
and (however much we deny it) we detest the freedom into
which revelation casts us headlong.

But it's impossible to get to revelation by way of religion.
Religion has got everything organized and planned for, including sudden outbreaks of trances, visions, mystical experiences, miracles, and glossolalia. It has anticipated everything,
which is to say that it even includes the appearance of revelation, but it excludes revelation itself when it comes to upset
the established order—which it does, though not by histri-
onic shouts and gesticulations aimed at convincing bystanders
that this is a possession of the Spirit.

Dostoyevsky makes this very point in the story of the
Grand Inquisitor. There we have religion as the power that
maintains order, religion as superior to the State, because it
manages to encompass and assimilate all spiritual disorders.
This is also what Paul says when he proclaims that he could
speak in tongues, perform miracles, give all his goods to the

poor, even sacrifice himself and become a martyr, only to have that all mean *nothing* unless it were the expression of divine love. Such a love does not spring from the human heart (which is why Paul contrasts *agape* with eros) but comes solely and exclusively from the revelation by the God of love.

I know the objection can easily be raised that many religions consider themselves based on a revelation. There are the Mormons and the Jehovah's Witnesses, the Kimbangists, the Brothers of the Free Spirit, not to mention Islam. Why should I say that only the Jewish and Christian revelation seems true to me, but the others don't? I am, as a matter of fact, caught in a trap here, because if I try to *prove* what I think, that would mean that this revelation is dependent on intellectual knowledge and therefore subject to rational proofs and procedures. If I give up the attempt, I'll be told that my choice is arbitrary, and that if I had been born a Muslim, I would be singing a different tune (but I wasn't "born" Christian!). Is it faith then that gives Christian revelation its substance? That sort of fideism is quite tempting, but I think I can answer this question without playing the apologist or trying to demonstrate anything, by saying simply this: there are indeed many revelations, but they are *all* consistent with the religious mentality, can be translated only into religious forms, and in the strict sense do not exist outside of religion. There is a rigorous, exact continuity between the Koran and the various forms of Islamic religion. The Koran cannot give rise to anything but religion as we have defined it.

I am practically certain that only Jewish and Christian revelation is radically contrary to religion. That is, every time one returns to the written word of that revelation, to its always new Good News, one finds a challenge issued to all religious institutions, to all churches and religious philosophies, to all religious moralities, dogmas, and interpretations—Christian or otherwise. When we relearn how to take this revelation seriously and reacquire the habit of listening in silence, then a kind of earthquake occurs that brings on the collapse of all religion. This is the great divide between all other revelations and the revelation of the God of Abraham, Isaac, Jacob, and Jesus Christ.

17

Believing for What?

From here on in our discussion I shall use the verb "believe" to designate faith in revelation, and not religious beliefs. We have already attempted to show the inanity of the phrase "What I Believe." We are, in truth, faced with two questions, the only two that make sense and are worth asking: Why believe? and Whom to believe? Each question also divides itself in two: Why believe? and Believe for what? Whom to believe? and Whom to believe in? By combining and recombining these themes judiciously one could come up with any number of clever expositions. But having come as far as we have in our discussion and understanding of faith, I'm going to have to disappoint those who like reassuring answers by saying that there is no reason to believe, and that faith has no ultimate purpose. If we try to come up with reasons, we are right back in the line of thought leading to so many affirmations of "What I believe."

Why believe nowadays? Of course, I could draw up a list of a hundred reasons, each one as true, perhaps, but in fact just as futile as all the others. You might believe in order to console troubled souls, to give an answer to the doubt that vitiates our society, to exorcise the demon of anxiety, to understand, to recenter your personality; you might believe because you can't go on any longer this way, because people need certainty in this world, because you are falling prey to discouragement, anomie, aimlessness. We all need a landmark, a North Star, grand enthusiasms and big ideas to pull us out of the gray-on-grayness of everyday life, the nausea of consumerism. One might believe because TV no longer quite fulfills the desire for eternity that still beats darkly in the heart of every creature, however blighted or disheartened.

We could continue to pile up reasons for believing, but before long we must realize that we're talking into the void, because none of them is capable of winning anyone over to faith. For the thousandth time we're back doing apologetics, and it's impossible to avoid this trap even when we're not looking to triumph over some "adversary." Apologetics tries to prove that Christianity is true, that it's superior to other religions (which of course leaves us arguing on the religious level), and that it answers all human questions. On these three points we can show that Christianity makes a reasonable case, but we know very well that these debates among intellectuals are utterly sterile: nobody ever succeeds in persuading anyone else. No apologetics have ever brought any unbelievers to faith, even when they could see that they had been beaten by their adversary's rhetoric.

This sort of theological tourney still made sense back in the days when the champions of different religions were called before a hesitant public or, still more, before a prince to see who would win the debate on whose outcome hung the adoption of an official religion for an entire kingdom. *Cuius regio, eius religio.* One such debate was the celebrated contest at Peking that pitted the champions of the major religions against one another in the presence of Kublai Khan, to decide what religion would be imposed on the Chinese people, who had been conquered by the Mongol hordes. In the end the Buddhist was awarded the victory, after the Jew almost carried the day. But in this case and others it was still just a matter of religion, and official religion at that.

The apologetic genre has fallen on hard times lately. You can always come up with reasons, run through proofs, and pile up references and authorities to demonstrate that people have a need to believe, that religion is an inevitable and specifically human secretion, that science and belief are not only compatible but indissolubly linked. But none of this will bring anyone before the Lord to say, "I believe." Why believe? There are a hundred reasons, as certain and convincing for someone who lives in faith as they are dubious and debatable for the person outside it. There is no intellectual road to the attitude (and more than the attitude—the life) of faith. The logical, intellectualist approach winds up in a ditch. Even the person who may have been convinced by your reasons can't make the transition from intellectual demonstration or even intellectual acceptance of a proposition to the deep life of faith. These are two different worlds and the intellect does not call forth or show the way to faith.

We keep coming back to Paul's cry: "For I do not do the good I want, but the evil I do not want is what I do." Even if some have been persuaded of the excellence of the revelation in Christ, that in no way necessarily implies the surrender of their lives into his hands or the birth of hope and trust or the discovery of love, any more than it necessarily means the intoxicating sudden acquisition of freedom or the dazzling, blinding light of a truth that floods through them. We have taken our companions by the hand, led them along a line of reasoning, and then all of a sudden they are overwhelmed by misfortune, because, though they may have gotten as far as intellectual conviction, they haven't entered into faith: Elisha still on earth, on the bank of the Jordan, while the flaming chariot carries Elijah off to heaven.

But there are more approaches to the question of why to

believe than just the intellectualist one. I find, for example, that many theologians, especially from the seventeenth to twentieth century, make use of terror, which they evoke with the notion of God's wrath. You know those sermons where preachers describe the abominable tortures of hell, where they whip up fear, and the threat of judgment, condemnation, and eternal doom hangs like a sword over the heads of their audience. Then, when they have thoroughly terrified the congregation, they open the little door that lets them out of hell and into the blissful landscape of salvation. This method of educating the faithful is now, fortunately, obsolete. Perhaps, though, it may not be *that* out of date—some use the atomic bomb today to take the place of hell. In any event this approach never fails to lead to religious superstition, but not to faith. People try to protect themselves from the ire of God by wearing amulets, making vows, going on pilgrimages, fulfilling religious duties, or leading a life of puritan virtue (which fits in well with the "infernal school" of preaching). But none of this has anything to do with faith.

If the questioner insists, "But why believe today?" there are plenty of contemporary reasons for belief: wars and rumors of war, atrocities, massacres and famines, whole nations tortured and imprisoned. There are signs in the heavens, but a bloody rain need not fall from the clouds for we have taken it upon ourselves to make such a rain. We have terrifying new powers to put an end to our world and powers no less terrifying to change everything and even to create life. The whole universe, mind as well as matter, is teetering on the brink. We have plenty of reasons today. But reasons for what? For fleeing, for seeking refuge in some impregnable certainty.

And here we are face to face with another impasse: belief as a refuge and flight from reality, the degradation of faith when it's seized upon as protection, as a guarantee or insurance policy. This is altogether contrary to its real nature, because

faith is taking risks, leaving behind safety and security, scorn-
ing guarantees, stepping out of the boat onto the Sea of Galilee. It is walking across the deep water in the middle of a
storm. And the point is not to be afraid, as the disciples were.
"Why are you afraid? Have you no faith?"

In other words, not only is fear the sign of our lack of faith,
but it leads us far away from faith, to a sort of "magical"
mentality. We turn to Jesus because the times are bad, because we feel incapable of mastering the powers at work in
our lives, of standing up to the challenge of politics and technology. But this is not the way faith acts; on the contrary it
indicates the absence of faith. Jesus himself says so: when he
announces the coming onslaught of disasters and catastrophes, what he tells us is not "Turn to me," but rather
"Take courage" and "Be watchful." In other words, faith has
no why or wherefore, but it calls forth a certain attitude
toward life. It makes us vigilant, lucid, resolute, not like
those who blink the horrors of the world nor those who run
away and take refuge in the Almighty. Faith is watching and
waiting, observing all the disasters, but knowing that the
glimmer of dawn isn't far away.

If we live the faith—faith in the Lord Jesus, the Messiah of
Israel—then there is no need to plead with him to save us
from danger. It's enough to know that since he's there, even
if the danger should prove mortal, whatever God's love
wishes is being done and will be done in us, no matter what.
For our part, we have to do all we can, and even a little more.
But nothing will happen without the presence of the Father,
hence we can come to no harm *in the end*. So, however we
take the question "Why believe?" we have no answer for it,
because the total and complete answer has already been giv-
en. It speaks to faith, ignoring obsessive, hyperrational reason. Nothing above and beyond this answer can convince us
or heal our wounds. There are no footnotes or appendices to

it, only the huge index finger of John the Baptist on the Isenheim Altarpiece, pointing to the crucified Christ. Why believe? "Because Jesus ..." And that's all there is to say.

But from the depths of the Christian past the questions come pouring out: Believe for what? With an eye to what? To achieve what? To get what? And my answer here will be as disappointing as it was before, because without contradicting itself Scripture replies: believe for nothing. "Does one serve God for nothing?" the Book of Job cries out. Well, that unthinkable possibility is, as a matter of fact, the truth. One does serve God for nothing. Job was the irreproachable believer, just before God and the world. There was nothing to fault him for, contrary to what his friends say, as they repeat the traditional syllogism: "You suffer, therefore you sinned." No! He's suffering, but there was no sin at the bottom of it all. And the fact that he was flawless in the eyes of God did him no good. He loses his fortune, he loses his children, and he is filled with pain from an incomprehensible disease. His wife leaves him because of his absurd attitude, as Job cries out that despite his suffering God is still God. And his best friends rebuke him, ceaselessly telling him that since God is just, if Job suffers, it must be a punishment.

Right from the beginning of the book, we see a Job who loves God and serves him for nothing (which Satan wrongly doubts). Then when one calamity after another descends upon him, he continues to love God anyway and to acknowledge him as God, for nothing. This is loving without reason, believing without reason, without any other justification than the intrinsic worth of love and faith. Satan cannot grasp this; for him loving and serving always imply getting paid. But people find themselves called to believe for nothing, because God reveals himself as one who loves for nothing. And when Job has his endless argument with God and demands an explanation for his suffering, he never learns the "why," but he comes to see the "for what," when he discovers that God takes care of things and what matters here is *how* God does that: the Father gives himself, in his Son, to the world's suffering.

There is no objective reason for believing; you have to live it. Ultimately we are left with paradox. Job truly believes, truly loves God, after God, at the end of his "answer," has shown Job the mythical monsters, Behemoth and Leviathan, which symbolize absolute evil, after God, as Nemo says, has revealed to Job the superabundance of evil.[35] Believe *for what?* For nothing, to be sure, but we are to believe precisely at the time when the utmost evil has been revealed to us, and when we have learned that in the midst of that evil we are closest to God, and that in it we meet the very love of God.

Faith has no origin or objective. Furthermore, the moment it admits of any objective, it ceases to be faith. If you believe in God in order to be protected, shielded, healed, or saved, then it's not faith, which is gratuitous. This will prove shocking, especially to Protestants, who have talked so much about salvation through faith, about faith as the condition of salvation, that they end up saying you believe so that you'll be saved. But we have to keep coming back to grace and its gratuitousness. If God loves and saves humankind without asking any price, the counterpart to this is that God intends to be believed and loved without self-interest or purpose, simply for nothing.

It's scandalous, and yet so easy to understand when you think of love. The moment that a man and a woman love one another *for* something, whether it be for money or prestige or beauty or job, it's no longer love. Sometimes it's because of selfishness and sometimes because of weakness. You get mar-

35. Nemo, *Job et l'excès du mal.*

ried to have a wife at home to wait on you or a husband to
support you, to have children or to settle down, to get reha-
bilitated or to assure your future, but these reasons have
nothing, absolutely nothing, to do with love. Love is without
cause and selfish interests; love is without reason. No one can
say why two people "click" or why a relationship works—it
simply does. And the same holds in our relations with God.

We can't say why God loves, except that he *is* Love itself.
He doesn't have, he never had, any aim or objective in creation. He just created, for nothing. He loved, for nothing; it
was simply the expression of love. He became incarnate for
nothing. God has no plans or designs. There was no metaphysical calculation ("Let's see, the problem is to save
humankind—now how am I going to go about it?"). Jesus let
himself be crucified for nothing. He had no plans either, nor
did he know of any grand blueprints drawn up by his Father.
Jesus obeyed because he loved the Father above all. He rejected Satan's temptations with horror, because they would
have separated him from what he loved and would have
served neither to carry out some plan of God's nor to save
humankind. Jesus was Love on earth. Love doesn't calculate,
and in God there is no split between means and ends. He is
the perfect end at the same time that he is, day after day, the
constant means, always renewed, always enough. And this
love takes the first step: how, then, can one not follow the
same path, how not follow this example, that is, simply to
love in response to love, to love so as to end in love?

God shows mercy for nothing, and his grace goes before
everything. Thus we have to overturn the purposeful pattern
we inevitably find lodged in our heads expressed by such formulas as "believe so as to be saved," or faith is the "condition
of salvation," or—to echo some more lines favored by the
theologians—believe to find consolation, to see justice done,
to lead a moral life, to put a solid foundation beneath one's

life or one's philosophy, and so forth. But all these "reasons" are contradicted by the Bible. God's grace precedes us, and so faith is born. Thus Job himself was an upright and just man before God insofar as he had received from God grace upon grace, insofar as God had loved him first.

But then a certain disillusionment, perhaps a bitterness, irresistibly comes over us. If that's the way it is, we think, what good does believing do? And there is no strictly rational answer, only personal experience can tell you: live in this gratuitous faith, live this weightless existence of grace, live this liberating faith—and then you'll see. So instead of saying, "I believe in order to . . . (be saved or some such)," we have to learn to say, "I believe *because* God loved me, saved me, reconciled me. It was done apart from me, before my time, without me; it was a gratuitous gift to me, and I'm going to share it with others gratuitously."

Note the marvelous shift that God's commandment has made us go through: God is first to love us, so naturally we love him back. But this quid pro quo is not what counts, for how can we ever love God in himself? We relapse immediately into the pattern of obedience, laws, rituals, and sacrifices. But the logic of God's love is not like ours which says, "I love you so you love me. You love me so I love you." For lovers like these the rest of the world doesn't exist; how wonderful, how delightful—and yet how egoistic. Scripture tells us something quite different, however: God has loved you first, so now go out to *other men and women* and love them in turn, with no aim, no goal, no purpose (not even to convert them); love them because you are loved.

Let's not forget the parable of the wicked servant in Matthew: the master forgives him his debts. But this doesn't mean that he's supposed to bow and scrape in gratitude to the boss. No, he ought simply to pass on the grace he received and forgive his own debtors all their debts to him. You serve

God for nothing. God saves regardless of whatever decisions people come to. He does not necessarily give human support to the people who pray to him, go to worship, take communion, and believe. God treats equally (because he loves equally) those who have long been in his service and those who have done almost nothing (the workers hired at the eleventh hour). God makes the rain fall on the just and the unjust; he makes the sun rise on good ones and evil.

And, conversely, believing doesn't give us any guarantee in the presence of God, who is still and always sovereign, as he reveals at the end of Job. He doesn't have to answer to anyone, and Job humbles himself before God's majesty not simply to acknowledge his omnipotence, which would be easy enough, but to admit that *God is right to be that way.* Here is where faith comes in, as when God declares to Isaiah that the earthen vessel cannot call to account the potter who fashioned it. And, as Jesus too proclaims, many will come and say, "Lord, open to us" (Matt. 25:11), and "We ate and drank in your presence, and you taught in our streets" (Luke 13:26). And he will reply, "I do not know where you come from" (Luke 13:27b).

And if, following Kierkegaard, we have recognized the impossibility of believing, of faith—which cannot be less than Abraham's, and yet we fundamentally cannot live it as such— then faith means to accept just this impossibility of faith. Faith will always express itself in this way: "Who am I that you should turn to me and take an interest in me? Who am I that you ask me to believe? Me, Moses the stutterer, Samuel the child, David the little shepherd, the Samaritan woman, who am I that you should call me?" The God who reveals himself in the Bible implies that we should serve him and believe in him to the limit of faith's impossibility, for nothing really, because when we face this God the one reality that thrusts itself at us is precisely the impossibility of faith. The only relationship with him is one of gratitude, pure gratitude, wholehearted and unfeigned.

But the other side of the question remains, not *what* to believe but whom. Whom to believe? In whom to believe?[36] In whom should I put my faith, whom should I rely on, whom can I trust, since we have learned in the world that the first and most basic rule of the game is Don't Trust Anybody. We have heard so many meaningless words; so many people have delivered so many empty messages to us. The language of politics, like the language of idealism, the call to revolution, like the call to charity, meditations on philosophy, like meditations on art—none of this means anything anymore. When people talk to us or call upon us to believe, the only important question is, *"Whom* to believe? *Who* is worth the trouble of believing in?"

Words refer us back to one who says them; to believe them is to believe in that someone. There has to be someone behind them, otherwise speech is no more than Panurge's famous words that froze in midair or some sort of rigorously impersonal, robotlike discourse. And it must be said that such anonymity is heightened every day by TV and radio. Who is speaking? The radio station. And on TV, despite the skill of the actors and the elaborate pretense of real life, it's not true that anyone is talking to *you.* It's only an image, a bit of make-believe. They try to snare you with those pleasant, seductive faces that appear to look you in the eye, but that in reality are peering into the camera lens pointed straight back

36. Maillot properly stresses that in the Creed you can't separate the "I believe" from him *in whom* I believe. And he goes back to the fine expression, "I don't know if I believe, but I know whom I believe." He clearly shows the Creed's intentionality: "Even if I didn't believe, that wouldn't stop God from existing and existing for me. The 'in' (as, I believe *in* God) demonstrates that neither I nor my faith create God, but that on the contrary God has created not only me but also my relation to him: my faith. . . . 'I believe in,' becomes: I put myself in the hands of. . . . The primitive 'I' is no longer important, but the God in whom I believe . . ." (*Credo*).

at them, the way you yourself look at a glass plate. No one is talking to you. There's no human odor, no hands you can reach for, no facial changes responding to yours, nobody there.

Whom to believe when we meet with so much pretense? We've been lied to so often, not least by the people denouncing the lies that have done us so much harm. And yet the truth of the Bible's assertion is fundamental: the word is nothing without the one who says it. The peculiar feature of revelation is that it specifies God not as one speaking subject among others but as The Word, which in turn implies that the human is defined as faith: there is no way to get out of this relationship. "The event of the word provokes the response of faith."[37]

The word does not exist in itself. The word itself does not call forth faith; it simply challenges us to believe in the one who pronounces it and never lies. I know that on this point I'm going to offend a lot of intellectuals (who won't read me anyway) for whom language must be studied in itself, apart from its human and social context, without any reference to a speaking subject. The subject itself becomes obliterated. Discourse must be analyzed, its structure delineated as we find it; our assignment is to look not at a face but a text, not to enter into a personal relation, but to discern what has not been said in the interplay of linguistic structures.

Well, no, faith will have nothing to do with dissociation of speech and speaker, whose unity is part of faith's basic design. But on another point I have more unpleasantness in store for those who refuse to consider anything but the message in itself, the independent transmission of a truth. Listen to the Beatitudes; notice how beautiful and true they are *in themselves*. Read the Gospels, with their admirable lessons in

37. Dumas, *Nommer Dieu.*

wisdom, which after all are valid for anyone. There is only one obstacle, one source of annoyance—the enigmatic, blurry, ambiguous character of Jesus. If it weren't for that Jesus, how easy it would be for people of every conviction to come to a solid consensus on the basis of the Gospels' splendid language. When you come down to it, the message of the Gospels repeats the prophets' word to the letter, and that would reconcile us with the Jews. In the same way Islam takes up so many of those wise sayings that very little separates us from their symbol system, their ethics, and ascesis. Then there is Buddhism, some of whose ideas are so closely related to the Christian message. How can we reject these converging opportunities for union? There's only one problem—Jesus. To the Jews he's not the Messiah, to the Muslims he's only a prophet, to the Buddhists he's nothing. So wouldn't it be more sensible to put this burdensome Jesus aside and revere him instead merely as a sage, a source of renowned words of wisdom like Confucius, Lao Tzu, the Buddha, Epictetus, or Socrates? Wouldn't it be better to stay away from that madness of a supposed Son of God, not to fasten upon the drama of the crucifixion—a touching story, to be sure, but slightly repugnant too—not to delude oneself with the empty tomb? Best clear away that personage and retain solely what the disciples heard from his lips and passed on to us—the message itself. What does it matter who said it?

We can see why Paul should become public enemy number one for certain readers of the New Testament. Paul "pushed" the figure of Jesus, insisting on what he *did*, what he *was*, and what he *is* for the person who believes in him (and not in this or that word of wisdom). Paul is the one who bound the word to the man, the man to the word. And, unfortunately for the savants and other well-meaning souls, Paul is right, and that argument was right long before he used it. For, beginning with the story of Creation, and even before then, the Word is creative, not in itself but because God has said it. It's God who gives force and weight to that Word. And if Jesus was not crucified and raised from the dead, then I have no reason to believe that Word.

It is *not* true that the Beatitudes are just and fair in themselves. Taken at face value, they are absurd and full of pious idealism. They can be true only insofar as the one who says them has the power to *create* this new situation by living a reality that corresponds to those same Beatitudes. From the Bible's point of view the word cannot be separated from the speaker, whether it's the word of God or the word of Jesus or my own words. "By your words you will be condemned" (Matt. 12:37b). Not, "Your words will be condemned," but "you." And I rejoice when I hear young people, Marxists or those sympathetic to Marx, questioning a statement because of the person who made it. "Where do you get your terminology?" they pedantically inquire, "where are you coming from?" And they're right. Our speech has no autonomous existence; it's bound up with our social and cultural life, with the "where" that we're "coming from."

I am a professor, an intellectual, converted to faith in Christ; I occupy a certain place in society; I have a certain past history. For all these reasons my words carry a "message" that has to be read in that context, has to be understood as part and parcel of my self. The same words would have a different tonality, a different coloring, a different background, if I were an African, a laborer, or a magnate. The same words wouldn't mean the same thing. The same sentences carry more or less weight, depending upon whether the speaker has authority or lacks it. There *are* some evident facts, but these too must be accepted on the Bible's terms.

Only the person of Jesus gives meaning and authority to his words. His word is creative because he rose again. I can test the truth of this for myself. But there is no dissociating the question of truth from the question of the person. There is no truth-in-itself, about which some well-intentioned words might speak to us with more or less eloquence; there is a person who is more or less credible. If the person is credible, then we can believe his or her words. We know what a drastic devaluation has hit statements by so many intellectuals and politicians, because we have learned in a hundred different ways that such people are *not* credible, that nothing in their lives matches what they say. And so their words are merely so much hot air.

Look at the one speaking, study that person's face, learn that person's life, and then take his or her words seriously— or don't. Neither oratorical art nor rhetoric will be able to bring us to faith, only the one who speaks. This high level of faith has only one equivalent: trust. But we can put our trust only in a person. If we know that a certain intellectual who talks politics is a time-server, that he has changed his opinions again and again, that he goes in whatever direction the winds of today's events are blowing, then the man can be as brilliant a rhetorician as one could wish, but his words are nothing more than the sound of a tin can tied to a cat's tail. Language is true when we can trust the one who speaks it. And to trust that person is to put our faith in his or her word.

It's not the content of the message that calls forth faith. We can take a set of texts and compare them, arrange them in a synoptic table, in semiotic squares, or any diagrammatic pattern whatsoever, none of which will give rise to faith; at most all we'll get is a hierarchy of intellectual values. Thus the Christian faith is in no way comparable to others: either it is "Christian," that is, it relates to the person of Jesus as Messiah and Christ, or it is just one more entrant in the field of beliefs, which, as we have repeatedly said, are by no means to be despised—but they're not faith.

And why, then, would we trust Jesus? We have no way of knowing him anymore except through his words. Once again it's a matter of trust in people, in the men and women who lived with Jesus, knew him, acknowledged him, and spoke about him. Did they simply make up a pretty story? Were they false witnesses? (This question was asked fairly early on: in First Corinthians Paul raises the issue of "false witnesses.") Were they narrating (at the risk of their lives?) a "golden legend"? If that is the case, we had better be careful, because it makes *history of any sort* impossible. There could be no history at all, because the whole science of history as we know it rests on the trust we have in the witnesses who tell us something, directly or indirectly. If we refuse to trust those men and women, let's burn all our history books at once (to the unending joy of dictators present and to come!).

The classic, monotonous, peremptory "trial" of witnesses from the past that ends by disallowing their message does away with vast stretches of our knowledge of humankind. But how can we judge whether the witnesses are credible or not when we're well aware that a person's credibility can never be scientifically demonstrated? You can pile up proofs for and against, but you won't get anyone to believe. You either feel it or you don't. You believe someone or you don't, which is the definitive wisdom on the subject of human relations, as experience has shown a thousand times and shows here too.

I trust those witnesses who tell me about the person of Jesus (and who had no "interest" in doing so). I trust the person of Jesus and I enter the world of faith in the words that he spoke. The mission of the "good news" has been accomplished, and yet it still remains to be accomplished, because Jesus is who he is, and nobody else. I don't offer any proofs or rational justifications. But the one who suffered, who was crucified and raised in his glorified body, *he* still speaks to me today with words that burn, that start me off and push me into being something other than what I am, even while fulfilling every particle of myself as I am.

And if I go back over my life, carefully reading it in the light of the Bible, I see that the trust I put in Jesus has never been betrayed (though his answers to my prayers were sometimes different from what I anticipated!). This is exactly what the Bible says so forcefully: that God's promises were not empty, that he always kept them (and note that we're talking about *promises*, not *threats*). His word, once it has been uttered, flung out into human history, has never come back to him without having achieved its full potential. The ultimate Speaker is nowhere to be found except in his Word, which is never inert but always charged with his presence.

So everything fits together perfectly. What the word of Jesus shows us above all is that *he* has total, fundamental trust in the Person of the absolute Speaker. And because he has that trust—not without passing through doubts and temptations, obstacles and crises, but nonetheless having an unshakable trust–he has limitless faith (literally, without any finitude) in the prophetic Word, which he fulfills in its entirety, not as if it were a law, a Torah, or a decree, but as the expression of the one in whom he has total trust. And he can, in fact, say that everything has been finished, consummated, because, identified as he is with the Father by that trust, he accomplished the totality of the Father's Word through faith. Thus, and in the same manner, our trust in the person of Jesus opens a path for us into his own trust, his own faith. We become participants in the faith of Jesus, and that way we have faith in the Word of God. But everything goes awry when we leave this personal relationship behind, when our faith becomes objectified, when the words of the Bible are torn from the Speaker's mouth and made over into either cultural documents from a specific period or else timeless dogmas.

And everything goes perversely awry when faith, instead of

being confidence (childlike but not childish) in a person and that person's word, turns toward, and against, others, to convert them, to judge and condemn them, to convince them or triumph over them. Here we see those who wish to impress others as profound believers, shining examples, not to mention those who abjectly exploit the word of faith as a means of self-justification or a stepping stone to leadership of a sect or religion. We need only hear individuals declare themselves prophets or gurus for us to know that they are false prophets and liars, because their faith is oriented toward themselves and they hold themselves up for adoration by others. When guru followers say flatteringly to Jesus, "Good Master," he sends them away empty-handed. Only God is good, and don't call anyone master or lord. Jesus was not a guru, and we know that he gave himself no other title than Son of man.

Faith operates counter to beliefs (as does revelation to religion). Of course, faith in Jesus the Messiah, in the ultimate Speaker, can be corrupted, as it has been throughout church history (though not always or unremittingly!), by being directed toward others as a way of achieving domination. The faith we have in the Son and the Father ought to be extended beyond them, but only in the sense of trusting others, all others including those who we know don't deserve it. We trust the iniquitous judge and the flagrantly crooked manager, the extortionist in the front office and even the executioner. "Do your job, hangman, but do it right."

We must restore relationships based on trust, but not in the style of simpletons or imbeciles who blindly and naively trust swindlers. We must trust like those who spot the crooks or the torturers from the very first instant and are never taken in by their snares, but who see beyond all that, beyond the first blow to common decency, beyond the immediate evil. Hard as it may be, we must learn that beyond the glaring fact of evil (which they always try to mask and which we must always lay bare), above and beyond all that, in truth and for all eternity the ultimate Word has been said concerning the imperialist, the Chekist, the S.S. man, the plantation owner. This Word is not spoken in condemnation but in pardon, in a love that embraces all the horror and takes in all the shame and ignominy on earth. If we put our faith in the Word of Love, we will see this.

And, seeing it, we will in spite of everything trust those who don't deserve any trust, who are, from a human point of view, absolutely guilty as charged. But from the very moment that trust is given and vouched for, things change. The hangman doesn't stop being a hangman, but the human situation changes nonetheless because the truth that is love has been lived here and now. In the final analysis the choice of power-lessness, the word of truth, wins out, historically speaking, over all the apocalyptic trumpets sounded by humanity. Faith is not conquest and superiority, but liberation, breaking the fetters that bind together the master and the slave.

Some people of complete integrity have failed to recognize that connection between a person and his or her words, have not understood that faith is trust in somebody and must be an outpouring of reciprocal trust. Because of this they continue to miss the point, suspecting that faith is a cloak for fanaticism or magic. Of course, they have their reasons for thinking so, and Christians can only blame themselves for having played the conquerors, the apologists, the convert-makers, superiors in the knowledge of truth, the models, the exemplars—which they were not. But faith is not fanaticism or magic; it doesn't fit into the category of what Grosser calls magical thought.[38] "For me ideas like the Creation, the Incarnation, the Resurrection constitute myths . . . and with

---

38. A. Grosser, *La Passion de comprendre*, 1977; "Non à la pensée magique," *Le Monde*, Feb. 1980.

my penchant for logic I have always been puzzled by the strange Christian argument that accepts the Scriptures as true because the Truth is expressed there, and believes the Truth is expressed there because they are true."

This is a fallacy like those of Bakunin, which are based on a reductionism incompatible with personal belief (but quite consonant with the "What I Believe" genre). Grosser forgets that truth is not a thing, but, as faith sees it, a person. Faced with a friend expressing friendship toward him, Grosser would apply the same kind of thinking he attacks: that is, he would say, "I believe his words of friendship because he is my friend, but he is my friend because he expresses his friendship." Are friendship, love, and trust either unthinkable or forms of magical thought? I don't deny the fact that Grosser's objections show us the dark side of Christianity, of the Christian religion, of Christendom, and of the beliefs and practices of a Christianized people. He reminds us of the God of the gaps, of guaranteed answers, of Christians who claim ownership of those "incarnate capital letters," Love, Truth, and Justice, who are convinced that outside Christianity there is no way for people to love one another.

But all that is irrelevant, nor does it mount any real challenge to revelation, which, as we have shown, is something different and whose faith is not of this order. If you want a more cutting question, ask me, "But where are they, these people of faith?" I admit that from the beginning of Israel, from the beginning of the church Scripture has always been quite clear on this point: they're very few in number, a little flock, *never* the dominant force, never grouped in a body that could be weighed and measured sociologically.

Faith isolates. Individuals carry the cross of faith, and they alone repeat the question that God asks of us; they alone are the prophets and saints. "I shall always maintain," Grosser writes, "that the Christian method of giving the idea of mystery as the answer to a logical question is inadmissible." But those who have received the living Word in their hearts can only agree, first of all because they're not trying to give an answer, but to ask another and more fundamental question, and second, because for them "logical questions" can only get logical answers, regardless of who is capable or incapable of supplying them—but none of this concerns the Christian.

Mystery, which most certainly exists, has nothing to do with the little game of questions and answers. You don't put it in the catechism. To declare "It's a mystery" is to talk nonsense; mystery should be met with silence and adoration. On the other hand there is a real kinship between Grosser and the authentic believer, when the former announces the difficulty he has in justifying his values and his concept of human relations, his permanant uncertainties and self-questioning, his desire to show tolerance and respect for others. All this is one of the main features of a life lived in faith.

Grosser's diagnosis, however, looks rather feeble when he says that the meeting point for Christians and nonbelievers is to be found in ethics, because here the difference between them concerns something altogether essential: for Christians morality derives from God, while for people like Grosser the Christian image of God is a function of their morality and changes with it. Once again we're dealing with unalloyed religion at the level where one is analyzing haphazard expressions of opinion (and on this score my judgment is even harsher than his).[39]

The real point of convergence between Grosser and the person of faith lies just where he locates their widest divergence. The real point of divergence lies where he thinks he has found a similarity, because the morality he speaks of as a potential common bond, though it's a product of Christen-

---

39. For example in my *L'Idéologie marxiste chrétienne*, 1979.

dom, differs radically from faith. Christian ethics as an expression of faith is simply impossible. All this amounts to saying that views such as Grosser's are correct only insofar as they separate words from the one who speaks them. For Grosser the solitary individual discourses about and constantly refers to him- or herself. But for anyone who understands speech this way, words remain an impenetrable secret, and hence contemporary semioticians have been gradually obliged to have recourse to something beyond speech. The unity of the word and the speaking subject reaches a unique depth in the Logos made flesh, who places before us the question of life itself and of love.

18

Critical Faith

Faith never fails to provide me with critical distance, because it makes me see the world, my society, and the people around me in a different light, from a different perspective. It obliges me to take off the mask—mine and others'. At the same time it effects in human relations a sociological dis-identification and a displacement of being. As Scripture puts it, The Lord is a God who does not consider appearances but the heart. So we find ourselves involved in both a critical faith and a critique *of* faith. But when I talk about a critique, which deals not just with faith but with ideas, ethical systems, and patterns of behavior, I am by no stretch of the imagination according any intrinsic superiority to persons who "have" faith, as opposed to the poor wretches (however brilliant they might be) who "don't have faith." Faith does not confer any superiority on people, still less any power to judge others. Some of the first words in the Gospel that faith hearkens to are "Judge not."

"Critical" refers to something altogether different, namely that faith is the critical point, that is, the point of separation and breaking off, which is to say the situation and expression of holiness, the severance that occurs when one is set aside by God to undertake some service. Faith is the point where one breaks with oneself (the death of the old Adam), with the world, with people. But we mustn't forget that this rupture is intended to locate all human relationships in a different sphere, in a rediscovered world based not on nature, or society, or politics, or philosophy, or human rights, or humanity —but exclusively on love. Faith as the critical point is the power of breaking away. But it comes from the God who is Love and hence it must be the creative initiative of love's new connection with humankind.

Faith is constant interplay; it never stagnates or settles down. One can never be "all love" or "holy" in and of oneself, nor can one incarnate faith in some static, definitive fashion. In its attempts to live out this love faith is the perennially new critical point. Thus faith necessarily moves right ahead to criticize itself. It constantly measures the distance separating the faith of Jesus and of Abraham from the faith I myself am living. It disconnects me more and more from myself, from the encroachments of my self-critical ego. It keeps a watchful eye out for whatever might imprison it in arrogant solitude (proud of its own righteousness and unrelenting conviction), as well as for whatever might transform it into belief. Faith therefore implies the continual presence of temptation and an ever clearer vision of reality; it implies criticism of Christian religion, of civilizing missions, of Christian moral codes imposed from the outside, of a Christian truth that excludes claims to it from any other area of human culture. The first task of faith in Christ is inevitably to criticize all of faith's "constructive" extensions in politics and morality, which are inevitable but nothing more than so many forms of betrayal.

The model we should always keep in mind is Kierkegaard, a man whose faith really did reach a critical mass. And let's not have any silly talk about masochism. What I'm referring to is what traditional biblical language calls repentance, but the idea has been cheapened, coarsened, hackneyed, softened into a kind of *moral* regret. But there's nothing of that in revelation. The Word of God holds out a mirror to me in which I see myself as I am, where I discover simultaneously how impossible it is for me to believe that word and how impossible it is to break away from it. Again, this has nothing to do with masochism: from one end to the other the Bible keeps telling us that God's judgment *begins* with the judgment of his faithful. The Old Testament announces that judgment begins with Israel (as we have seen, alas, over and over again). In the New Testament judgment begins with the church, which is the first to be weighed in the scales. This, and nothing more or less, is what faith as the critic of faith means in the concrete reality of our day-to-day lives.

But this can't be separated from its other aspect, faith as the point of rupture (not with our fellow human beings) but with religions. Starting from there faith *must* proceed to criticize, to judge (in this case, yes), and radically to reject all human religious claims. We have to be careful here: it's not people who are being judged or criticized here; it's their will to power and the expression of that in religion. Faith does not reject human speech, quite the contrary. Faith is always listening, always on the alert, always attentive to people's words, to their fears, their hopes, their passions, and their hymns. It never judges anything against the norm of an abstract, frozen morality. It has its ears open to questions, knowing that it can't answer them intellectually. Instead it puts us at the heart of the same questions, the same dramas, the same impossibilities. The only answer we have to give is ourselves, such as we are, while pointing to the one who transposes our questions into others that we can, in fact, answer, because we have been made answer-able by love.

Thus faith leads me into the midst of humanity, without any break, but it provokes a crisis when people make their religious claims, when they shout "Me, me" and nothing but "Me," or when they fashion a god for themselves from a piece of wood, thereby earning Isaiah's denunciation. Or when they proudly announce *L'Italia farà da se* (Italy acts on its own), or that *gesta francorum* (the acts of the Franks) are *gesta Dei* (the acts of God). Nowadays we would translate the latter motto as "revolutionary acts are the acts of God," adding that "the state is the sum of all things; it represents God on earth." The religion of science or of reason or of Marxism, of revolution, of society, of the American Way of Life, or of messianic socialism—all these secular religions must be radically (down to their roots!) criticized, ruined, struck down, ridiculed without pity or respite by faith in Jesus Christ, because, as we said before, religion is what alienates people.

It is religion that people fashion for themselves in order to hoist themselves up to the level of God, who every time this happens becomes their implacable negation. Marx's view was accurate but incomplete: the religion that was invented by the ruling classes does not just alienate the oppressed classes. The ruling classes are themselves caught in their own trap and alienated along with the others. Alienation as the result of economics is not, in the first instance, what really counts, since that only comes in the wake of spiritual alienation. The objectification we're speaking of now is the peak of the religious explosion. We adore things while treating people as objects, and we ourselves turn into objects. This is the fulfillment of a three-thousand-year-old prophecy: "Those who make them are like them; so are all who trust in them" (Ps. 115:8). *We become what we choose for gods.*

Such is the critical discernment faith gives us. This is why we have to launch out from faith, for the sake of humankind and in their name, to engage in a fight to the death with those gods, those religions. We have now arrived at the one undeniable point of rupture—provided, of course, that our goal is not to subject our fellow human beings, now unburdened of their "false gods," to some allegedly higher religion, which is unfortunately what the Christian world has all too often done. It has substituted one form of alienation for another, a deeper kind of alienation (because it has as its source the true Word, and since it always contains some parcel of truth, it's harder to criticize) than the earlier one. This is why faith's critique of religion can be rooted only in its critique of itself.

This critique implies a process of distancing. Faith in Jesus Christ produces a double effect that appears contradictory. Faith permits, indeed it demands, all sorts of approaches, because its very nature is to give rise to love. So nothing can be foreign to us; nothing can leave us indifferent or unaffected. But at the same time, because faith refers to the Absolutely Other, because it places us in a qualitatively different universe, it will never let us be assimilated into any group or cause or person, into any idea or reality whatsoever. Faith situates us at a literally infinite distance from all of that. But if everything around us is put at such a critical distance, nothing can be objectified (here, as far as I am competent to judge, Hegel's thoughts on objectification are ultimately non-Christian), transformed into a thing and examined like one.

Faith leads me to take part in everything, while at the same time it shows me everything in a light that is not that of reason, experience, or common sense. This is not an intellectual operation, but an existential attitude. Hence it can neither be learned by appropriate methods, nor is it reserved for intellectuals. Faith brings about this form of the "new person" (to use the traditional term), manifested in love and lucidity. Love believes all things; the discernment of spirits judges all things. In faith we find both of these together.

This is simply because faith makes us share in all human

reality and shows us how *in*human it is, with a clarity neither related to the scientific method nor derived from some epistemology. The God of Abraham and Jesus knows human reality infinitely better than any of the human sciences do, and even so he gives himself in his Son to save a creature that is in no way lovable. Faith follows the same path, or it ought to, but this love is not incoherent, sentimental, thin-skinned, feeble. Nietzsche was undoubtedly right to blast the sniveling piety and sanctimonious railing at the world typical of his age, but he hadn't the slightest idea of what the revelation by the God of Jesus Christ was all about.

Faith prescribes ways of acting that are harsh and unyielding. They spring from love but they imply the labor needed to change our inhumanity. We spoke before about alienation. There must be ongoing criticism of all civilizations. Or rather, in each generation we must develop a critique of the society, the culture, the civilization in which we find ourselves. Once again this must not be a superficial critique, or a rationalistic or vitriolic one, but a summons to judgment aimed at driving out the inhuman elements of that culture. And we have to keep at it, starting over again and again.

Now I maintain that faith alone makes possible a critique that is both radical and generous, because faith implies the double movement discussed above. In each generation we confront the assumptions behind civilization, and in each case they are just in their origins but baneful as they work themselves out. Faith is always primeval, always there "in the beginning." Every time the churches have come to grief, it's because they have forgotten this. Faith puts us at the starting point, and from there we have to wander off on our adventures. The same rule holds for the society we belong to, namely that we must criticize it in order to lay the foundation for new beginnings. This is one of the reasons why it is so stupid for Christians these days to sharpen their knives and call for the scalps of capitalism or imperialism, echoing hundreds of millions of socialists, communists, anticolonialists, and so forth. Back in 1848 such cries represented a real genesis. It was then that the churches had to transform the world, to struggle against inhumanity.

But nowadays all that is antiquated rubbish, dangerous to both the Right and the Left because, like a decrepit building, it threatens to come tumbling down on everybody. But faith compels us to look elsewhere, to search for a new beginning, which is by no means impossible insofar as faith gives us both the closeness of love and prophetic distance. We can no longer conceive of basic changes in our society without this double approach. *Nobody* can conceive of them. These transformations are such that they call for commitment to almost absolute risk, something only love could endure. But they are also so difficult even to think about that they can be imagined only by placing them at a qualitative distance from our socioeconomic reality, that is to say at an infinite distance. The task calls for rediscovering the immutable, when we know that everything passes, that everything is history, that our grasp of truth depends upon our culture, that reality slips between our fingers, and that ultimately everything ends up being subjective, save for the determinations that make us all take our cue from the identical source and prevent us from noticing the illusions of which we are victims. We must rediscover the immutable, or what the Bible calls the Eternal, the Living One, him whose word and promises never change. And on the strength of what he lets us come to know as immutable, we must learn to see our situation.

This is the first condition that must be met before we can understand, imagine, and accomplish radical changes in our society. Are we, in effect, viewing the earth from Sirius? Exactly the opposite, because the whole idea is not to be detached from the world, but, placing ourselves at a critical distance, to love it at the point of our involvement with it. To borrow another comparison from astronomy, there was no way to navigate, in bygone days, without the North Star. We now know that Polaris is not as fixed as the Vikings and Phoenician mariners thought, but it was stationary enough to let them plot their earthly courses with precision. The compass will not work without the magnetic pole, which of course doesn't point us to the true geographic pole. And magnetic storms throw our calculations off, but still, were it not for that magnetic pole whose steady position we know, there could be no sea voyages.

So it is with the unchangeable reality of the God of Abraham and of Jesus Christ. Our cultures, our theologies, our doubts, our systems of interpretation may give rise to errors of "declination," but faith can only orient itself by the immutable being who alone says "I am." And from the point of reckoning it enables us to trace a feasible route. This is why the responsibility of Christians strikes me as bound up in such a terribly immediate way with the adventure (the last adventure?) of our world. Christians have constantly gotten bogged down in supposed short cuts, turning off from the high road where the two inseparable elements of faith go together. At times they have gone off on a purely heavenly route, marked by inflexible piety and dogmatic thinking centered around a transcendent God, paying no heed to the reality of the world we live in. At other times they have plunged into the heart of the crowd, into the midst of humanity with all its struggles and grief, without maintaining the least critical distance, swept along by whatever historical choices, temporary scientific findings, and political commitments happened to be around, lacking any North Star or transcendent frame of reference. If the world collapses the way it is collapsing now, in filth, blood, and hatred, the first who must answer for it are Christians and the churches, who have not adopted faith's attitude of critical distance, so as to build a new beginning.[40]

It might seem that we have just taken a quite different approach to our old question, "Believe for what?" "You see," someone might object, "there *is* a reason for your faith; it does have a purpose. Your answer that one believes for nothing is false." Not so, we have merely changed the focus of our discussion. We first looked into the matter of our salvation and of our relations with God. We asked whether we could count on our faith to get something from God and in that context we answered no. We now turn to the question of active intervention in the world, of how we are to behave, and our answer here is simply that faith has some basic consequences. But again we need to dispel the twin errors of falling prey either to the Christian temptation: "I'm going to believe in order to change the world"—which explains, at long last, why one believes, but if faith does have such an objective, it's not exactly faith in the Unconditioned—or else to non-Christian skepticism: "This is the worst sort of apologetics, exploiting the present crisis to badger us into believing."

But, just as the existence or nonexistence of God can't be proved, I don't claim to be able to convince anyone that faith in the God of revelation makes possible what I have said it does. This is something you either live out or you don't; that's all there is to it. And I can't make someone who doesn't live faith actually experience what the person who does live it experiences. Nor can I bring the nonbeliever to adhere to a doctrine or profession of faith, which wouldn't mean anything even if I could. I'm merely saying that to prompt the

---

40. "It is clear that the atomic bomb is a parody of the Creator, a challenge thrown in the face of the Reconciler, a negation of the Consoler. It is a No to faith, to love, and to hope. Pollution launches a direct attack on the Creator.... The ravaging of the Third World attacks the one who will come to judge the living and the dead" (Maillot, *Credo*).

transformation called for by the terrible conditions of our time, by the frightful complexity of the problems and trage- dies overwhelming us, we need nothing less than an *absolute* frame of reference, a qualitative critical distance, a differen- tial index, an outside "viewpoint," an epistemology that is not connected to our sociocultural mechanisms.

Otherwise there is no way we can grasp the situation we're in. Only this orientation to unchanging reality can give us the courage to intervene in the world (knowing as we do that the changeless One has become incarnate, has therefore already intervened, so that in fact everything has been accomplished) along with a motivation to act: we know that this unchanging God is Love, who expressly calls upon us to love in his foot- steps and as an expression of who he is, to love the world and humankind and hence to work so that the world lives and that men and women have a chance of surviving, before we try to convert them to their Lord.

"Maybe that's how it is, maybe faith moves mountains. But we have yet to see it happen, and it would take more than a little intellectual demonstration to convince us." This objec- tion sounds justified to me. That is why I insist on throwing it in the face of Christians, who are entirely responsible for the political, economic, and social situation that is now upon us. Their faith has gone astray. Their obsession with the con- tents of faith (theologians quarreling over technical terms) in- stead of with the movement and life of faith is what has trig- gered our worldwide crisis. But the unchangeable remains unchangeable. The Ultimate One, the Unconditioned, the Wholly Other has not changed. We have to pull ourselves together and find our place. We shouldn't expect any tailor- made solutions, or hope for some magic wand to wave over us. We shouldn't turn to God as the Great Repairman. Once again, God doesn't answer people with designs on him.

God is not a machine that dispenses solutions. But we need

only know that if we don't take his road, there can be no way out. There is no humanly acceptable answer. And, let me repeat, God is not the one who will give the answer; he is not the refuge of those who have given themselves up for lost; he is not the burst of illumination in the night; he is not a magician. Yet it remains true that it is in the light of God that we see light. God makes it possible for *us* to come up with an answer and discover the way out, however concealed and obscure. When we are radically alienated, he restores us to freedom, that is, to a situation where we can start afresh, undertake new risks and responsibilities. But we have to seize the moment and take the risk. As Denis de Rougemont says, the future is our business.[41]

And now to conclude this section with an exasperating term: the Transcendent. The one we have designated in various ways is, when all is said and done, the Transcendent, the one on whom everything depends and who depends on nobody and nothing, the one who is never an object. This is where all religions err so spectacularly: the god is always an object.[42] The god of religion is the object of veneration or prayers, the object we fabricate to make up for our weakness and ignorance, an object located in some place or nonplace. Even when we invest this god with every conceivable metaphysical quality, he remains an object. *We* have made him what he is.

This is exactly what the prophets describe when they speak of "false gods" and "idols." Such gods are the kind we set up as guardians over our lives, our temples, our thresholds, our homes. And they have to carry out the functions we assign to them; they have to work miracles and cures to make us succeed and win. As far as the object-gods are concerned, all the

---

41. Denis de Rougemont, *L'Avenir est notre affaire*, 1977.
42. Of course, God can be "objective." See Dumas, *Nommer Dieu, Croire et douter.*

critical barrages at religion by skeptics are perfectly on target. Once again, if God is God, he is never an object. He is the one who takes the initiative and keeps it. "I will have mercy on whom I have mercy. . . . Has the potter no right over the clay, to make out of the same lump one vessel for beauty and one for menial use?" (Rom. 9:15, 21). His acts are the sovereign decision of a subject whom we cannot bend to our will, as the prayer of Abraham reminds us. Yet we can place our trust in him because this unalterable, indefeasible Subject is at the same time the one who declares to us that he wishes our freedom, our salvation, our cooperation. He is the one who establishes our dignity by treating us not as objects but as subjects in our own right, because the sovereign Subject cannot be himself except by creating other subjects capable of responding to and loving him.

God frustrates all our efforts to pin him down; he baffles all our definitions, but he "gives himself away" in certain words, certain decisions for (not against) us. He is not a subject except in relation to other subjects. And all the other gods are nothing of the sort. Consequently we can at best point him out and name him on the basis of revelation. We can designate him, give a sign of him, about him, toward him, a sign derived from what he has let us know about himself. No more than that.

I admire the subtlety of theologians who analyze God's works or his reality *ad extra* and *ad intra*. As far as the first category goes, it is surely possible for us to see, hear, and perceive the signs of his activity precisely because these are part of his connection with us. But as for the second, which deals with the internal relations of the godhead, with the substance or specific quality of the Father, the Son, and the Holy Spirit, I believe that any attempt to grasp them is not only doomed to failure, but an affront to the majesty and sovereignty of God, the sovereign Subject. We cannot grasp him in any way whatsoever, and we must not use the revelation that he graciously gives us as if it were a means of comprehending or defining him.

It is evident that the very terms we apply to God are contradictory: com-prehend means to take hold of him in his totality, to catch him in the net of relations we create. To de-fine is to mark off limits for him, to grasp him as finite. It can't be done. Whatever we can comprehend or define is precisely for that reason not-God. He is, inevitably, beyond our comprehension, our definitions, our limits. We can only point to him from the things we have seen him do. We can know that he was there after he has left; we can discover his traces and recall his words after their sound has died away. Thus we can bring forth signs of an ineffable and incontestable reality.

But we must not confer on these signs a value they don't have. We are not to make the Torah into God himself, nor the Bible into a "paper pope." The Bible is only the result of the Word of God. We can experience the return of the Word of God in the here and now, the perpetual return of the actual, living, indisputable Word of God that makes possible the act of witnessing, but we should never think of the Bible as any sort of talisman or oracle constantly at our disposal that we need only open and read to be in relation to the Word of God and God himself. And so we de-signate God, which is to be witnesses, concrete signs of what we point to. This is as far as we can go: testimony about God. There can be neither proofs nor demonstrations nor conclusions nor objective knowledge nor repeatable experiments nor a process of falsifiability. And when we talk about signs and designation we have to be careful not to get caught up in the linguistic mechanism of the Signifier-Sign-Signified, because the signified is strictly relative to the signifier. But God surpasses all the signs and signifiers in every way possible. Any statement I can make may be the signifier of an act or word of God, which are thereby signified, but not God himself, who is always above and beyond and outside, dwelling as he does in the innermost core and the most personal depths. In the same way God as subject is bound by nothing but his own unfathomable, unfounded decisions (which to the human eye seem arbitrary and irrational), and so we have no way to come to grips with him except in the relations that he establishes with what is traditionally called creation. In other words, we know God is an irrational being but we also know that he has integrated himself into this world. This arbitrary being has bound himself up with justice and can be "taken in" by human minds only as justice and not as arbitrariness. This "unfounded" God has no ties with us save through his foundational word. And the Eternal or Transcendent does not exist except here and now.

Why this abstract digression on God? Because it's crucially important for us now that God should be transcendent. With the way things are going that's our only hope. Everybody agrees that everything making up our world has a total or totalitarian character. It's no longer the state or government subject to totalitarian doctrines that is totalitarian. The state has become totalitarian in itself, whatever its political doctrine. Whether it be liberal, democratic, socialist, or communist, nowadays the state is inevitably the universal refuge, charged with handling all missions, coordinating all activities with an all-embracing administration, extending its vast grid, or tentacles, everywhere, out of internal necessity, not malice.

The state, the government takes upon itself the whole life of the nation. It is the total state, the nation-state. There's no use talking about peripheral powers, about the catastrophic breakdown of politics, about the impotence of the state. The state is total. And the same thing goes for society, of which it is only one aspect. Here too there is no ill will—there is no will at all. This has happened, as Charbonneau said half a century ago, "by the sheer force of circumstance." Our societies, without exception, become all-engulfing; nothing can escape their control. We are confronting the increasingly familiar process of "integration-exclusion." This involves an effort to make everyone identical with everyone else. Anyone out of the ordinary or unwilling to conform is locked up. Or else such people are marginalized, excluded, rejected, which makes their lives as intolerable as would a formal curse or banishment in primitive society. You have to speak exactly as everybody else does, or you're insane. We've come a long way from the bourgeois morality and benign conformism of the nineteenth century!

And the computerization of society will raise this tendency to the nth degree. It will provide the means for carrying out the blind process of categorization and rigid, airtight centralization, though with the best of intentions and the conviction that the welfare of humanity is at stake. Never has there been so much discussion of humanism and human rights, but the talk is all coming from society and its language is more monolithic than that spoken by dictatorships. Then there are the convulsive resistance movements: prison unrest, strikes, assaults on the power structure, terrorist attacks, extremist feminism, the hippy movement, anarchic communitarianism, and so forth. But all they do is strengthen the oppressive centralization of the system, by being "retrieved" and absorbed into it.

We note the same pattern (however unconscious, involuntary, and with the best of good intentions) in the development of the sciences. The more they progress, the more attention they pay to humans and human values, the more this leads inescapably to the absorption of humankind into the scientific world. Science carries no built-in guarantee of respect for people, for human freedom, autonomy, or individuality. As science expands, it continues to look upon people as objects. All sorts of investigators train their instruments on these objects to get to know them better and, of course, to bring out their specific features, but that's no safeguard against exploitation.

The more is known about human nature, the more people insist on the importance of creative disorder and at the same time the more humanity becomes assimilated to a highly regulated order. Similarly the more humane bureaucracies become, the more they become, in reality, rigorous and absolute. And all this culminates in pantechnocracy, which leaves no earthly domain unplundered. There is no foreseeable limit to the spread of technology that has entered on the path of complete ingestion of natural resources, of nature itself, of human beings, and everything in existence. The process of technological growth is intrinsically totalitarian. Nothing can stop it except the actual disappearance of the fuel it feeds on: raw materials, space, objects of every kind, and ultimately human beings. All the nuances and fine distinctions are useless here. Technology can't come to a halt until it has reached the barrier of absolute finitude, when *everything* has been technologized.

That means that these manifold powers combine to form an ensemble that is doubtless incoherent but even so constitutes a totality that has never existed before, other than as our galaxy. This is, in effect, the disappearance of the human being as an individual and a person, and the emergence of the human as fragment, as cell, cog, switch, coded number, of the human as an opportunity, a bacterium, a pretext, a microprocessor of the unified ensemble that absorbs all things into its unanimous disorder. The only hope, given this situation, lies in a reality utterly beyond the reach of that limitless expansion, that is, located beyond finitude, outside the realities accessible to technology, in an essentially inaccessible reality. That is to say, God.

Vahanian was right, from faith's point of view, when he said that humanity is the condition of God. But nowadays we must reaffirm the fact that God is the only condition guaranteeing that we will endure. This is not, let it be noted, the old argument according to which we can't exist unless God exists, since God is our necessary condition. We are no longer talking about the genesis or first appearance of the human race; the question is whether we can continue to be human, that is, free subjects. The only possibility of achieving this in the face of the totalitarian absorption of our world would be if some reality totally impervious to that process were to become our own reality.

But at this point it's crucial for us to speak precisely. In affirming such a reality am I not once again giving an answer to the question "Believe for what"? My imaginary opponents speak up. "Look, if your description is accurate, then we should believe so that people can escape this devouring force, this reductive mechanism, this overpowering assimilation. We should believe so that people, in the real world where we live, can continue to be human. There's your answer. And so you yourself destroy your case for believing for nothing."

There is a regrettable confusion here between believing and God. I am in no ways saying that if people "have faith in God" they can escape the oncoming wave of conformism. Faith has already been exploited so often by being transformed into belief in order to make people conform that we can safely assert that in itself faith guarantees nothing. On the other hand, I might suspect that at any moment it could be taken over as a technical means of assuring people that they were not mistaken in committing themselves to technology and in building themselves a hermetically sealed cocoon to imprison them forever.

But our topic here is neither faith nor, still less, belief. It's the reality of a transcendent objective, regardless of whether people believe in it or not, a reality beyond any possible absorption, assimilation, or utilization. And I mean reality, neither some objectified human belief, nor simply truth. Truth and reality have to be united, wedded together— "truth-reality." Truth is not hidden away in some inaccessible transcendence.

What good would it do us to know that truth exists but is absolutely unknowable and unrelated to us? We know scientifically that when the galaxies and the whole expanding universe began there was at one "point," billions of years ago, an incalculable condensation of energy leading to an unimaginable explosion, the "Big Bang." But what do we gain from such knowledge? What does it matter to us that this energy exists, that it continues to act, to penetrate everything? Neither the knowledge nor the energy will be of the slightest help in preventing our disappearance as human beings. What we need is a truth of similarly cosmic dimensions, but much more complex, much more qualitative, but also possessed of will, choice, and the power of decision, possessed, still more, of attentive care for everything in creation, and finally of love, since everything holds together by mysterious ties, a love effectively directed at the forlorn hope all of us are.

Nothing less than that will do if we, amid the dangers now surrounding us, are to survive and maintain our humanity. If the truth that has chosen to be our reality does not exist, then our end is really in sight. But then aren't we resorting, as so often before, to the "God of the gaps," to God as the escape hatch from our difficulties, as the solution to a problem that we ought to solve on our own, in a word to God as a convenience? I would hope that readers have grasped my meaning: in all that I have said there is no room for solutions or "usefulness." And as for solving on our own the problems we're tangled in—we don't have a chance in the world.

My thesis is that either there exists a "truth-reality" that cannot be assimilated by the forces unleashed in our time—and if so we have a possible future—or else it does not exist, and then we might as well resign ourselves because human history is finished. As of now. In this context faith is our responsibility to see to it that the Transcendent, the Unconditioned, the Totally Other Being, becomes an active reality here and now, because it's not simply God's existence all by itself that gives us the answer. And we must not count on his waving the magic wand to change our situation. Faith moves mountains only when it speaks to the omnipotent Creator, and when it also accepts its role of hearing the word of faith. But this faith must bring us to decide on our own course of action, which will find its source, its origin, its *raison d'être* in the unassimilable and unknowable Truth, which becomes by way of faith the reality that sets us free.

PART THREE

"YET FORTY DAYS . . . "
SAID JONAH

After analyzing belief and faith, the only thing left to do is to cry out. After an analysis that, I know, could not have convinced anyone but that I had to do out of intellectual honesty, after a speech that couldn't get anyone to change or make a move, the only thing left is the prophet's cry. How many of us cry out? All the singers these days cry out so as to hypnotize their audiences and lull them to sleep. "But the power of cries is so great that it will break down the harsh measures decreed against humanity," writes Kafka prophetically. May his prayer be heard, and may this prophecy be as true as the others he composed on his descent into hell.

Jonah cries out, "Yet forty days and Nineveh shall be overthrown" (Jonah 3:4b). I cry out because I see the end. I cry out because I have been ordered to. "Watchman, what of the night? Watchman, what of the night?" The watchman replies, "Morning comes, and also the night. If you will inquire, inquire; [be converted and] come back again" (Isa. 21:11–12). Jonah echoes Isaiah's words, be converted. Such was Jonah's cry, which still rings in our ears. And all my books, cold as they are, must be heard as cries. I cry out like Jonah, "Yet forty days . . . " We are approaching the end.

There is nothing I desire more than that Nineveh should not be overthrown, and perhaps it won't be, just as Jonah's prophecy was not fulfilled. But he had to cry out, as we have to cry out today. Yet forty days, soon enough, and it will all be over, because God has turned away—when *we* turned away.

In my innermost being I feel the rising tide of disaster. How can I express it? How can I tell you? Who will listen? I'm back in Berlin in 1930, when the communists were afraid of anything and everything (especially of social democracy) but paid no attention to those frenzied, crackpot Nazis. I'm back in 1947, when the French elite scornfully rejected basic anticommunism, not wanting to blame the Soviet Union for anything, lest it drive Billancourt to despair. And now here I am in 1980, and I see the same delirium. You're all afraid. You feel in your bones that it's impossible not to be afraid. The communists proclaim their class struggle, the technocrats chew over their statistics, and the masses in the Third World swear death to the colonialists. Imbeciles. "History is played for the first time as drama and for the second time as farce." We are putting on the farce of the next to last disaster. And there is no one there to stop the avalanche of cement that will shut our mouths, no one to turn off the unconquerable universal motor of technology, so lovingly perfected by us, which will take us in a flash to our last, truly last, objective.

19

We Never Wanted That ...

There is just too much evil. I am going to talk about banal things that everybody knows about, but I'm not going to spare you, not in the least. Look at Brazil, Argentina, Chile—pitiless dictatorships ruled by the most brutal torture, by the most cynical oppression, by death prowling everywhere. There are secret or not-so-secret groups that settle their private scores with police protection; there are overflowing prisons amidst a population crushed by terror and injustice; great landowners have immense power, all opposition is crushed, while absolute misery reigns among the peasants and workers who can no longer say anything; even guerrillas don't seem to be able to do anything any longer. And all of this is covered with the veil of Christian idealism, so that hypocrisy, lies, and imposture triumph in the name of Jesus Christ.

Then there is the incomprehensible furor of reciprocal massacres that has gripped El Salvador (1980), a typical example of manic, unchained violence comparable to what struck Lebanon in 1975. There is Cuba, where leftists are the dictators, with exactly the same results, including torture and internment camps *and* economic misery. Cuba is as deeply dependent on the USSR as the others used to be on the United States. Cuba has become the Soviet Union's handy little mercenary. The great Soviet chief whistles and Cuba comes running to do the dirty work that its big socialist brother doesn't want to touch. Instead of trying to make its people happy, Cuba mobilizes them to invade Angola, Ethiopia, and Cambodia (to bolster the Vietnamese). And all this goes on under cover of socialist idealism, so hypocrisy, lies, and imposture triumph in the name of the brotherhood of nations, the proletariat, and the revolution.

Then there is the whole Sahel, from Niger to Somalia, struck down by absolute starvation, with millions dying of hunger. This is not undernourishment; it's living skeletons and children with enormous skulls and swollen bellies who have no more than a few days to live because there is nothing left to eat. The desert marches implacably southward, gnawing away at lands barely fertile to begin with. Hundreds of thousands of people die of famine each month. In the meantime we continue to produce useless gadgets and to overproduce food that gets thrown away, because the laws of economics and international price levels are inexorable. We throw away fruit, milk, fish—and with every item we throw away, we cause the death of a human being. And we claim we can come into God's presence with clean hands and justice in our hearts.

As if there were not enough misfortune from nature gone amok (though *we* are responsible for that), people have to add on even more calamities. Countries decimated by famine are racked by war. Ethiopia fights Somalia, the Ogaden will once more be plowed up by mortal hatred, and bombs and flame-throwers will be added to the desert's meager harvest. The Soviets were on hand, stirring up trouble from the first.

Look at anywhere in Africa. Military dictatorships grow more and more numerous. We were all jolted by the atrocities of Bokassa and Idi Amin, mad, blood-thirsty tyrants, maybe even cannibals. Theirs was not the cold hatred of the Latin

American generals. In them we saw the wild excesses of megalomaniacs showing their power in murder and blood, seeking to degrade a population already thoroughly terrorized, men whose cruelty was simply unrestrained and bestial. We saw children slaughtered and countless assassinations.

But if Amin and Bokassa were particularly monstrous examples, what can we say about all the other African dictatorships, every one of them founded on the same principles of despotism and terror? In each case we find a camarilla, a small but powerful group governing by violence, who together with their protégés carry off all the country's wealth, leaving behind only desperate and spreading poverty. True enough, we colonialists have a share in the guilt. We have reduced nations to slavery, we have toppled their social structures, and we have wiped out their food crops for the sake of industrial monocultures. And the misery of those peoples comes indeed in part from that. But, despite these facile denunciations, we are no longer the key to their wretched condition. It's pointless to only accuse American imperialism, because Chinese and Russian imperialism are at least as active in black Africa; and when a tyrant backed by the West falls from power, he's replaced by a Red tyrant whose regime will be marked by the same violence and cruelty.

Look at the massacres in Angola, a whole population forced to take flight; look at the massacres in Zaire and the Republic of Congo. Where can the Africans flee? Everywhere they run to, they find the same hatred, the same starvation, the same police, the same search and seizure. And in the meantime the new African bourgeoisie ruthlessly exploits their own proletariat, as ruthlessly as the worst French or English industrial bourgeoisie ever did. They are just as hungry for wealth and comfort as their Western counterparts, but with this difference—they build nothing, make no permanent contribution; they merely grab what isn't nailed down and reduce the people to utter misery.

We see them by the dozens, military, bourgeois dictatorships of both the Right and the Left. Black Africa has become a continent of wretchedness and extermination. We used to take slaves from there (as did the Islamic Arabs before us) and transport them to our plantations and mines. But it's no longer necessary to lead military expeditions and capture the vanquished warriors. The whole black population has now become on their own home ground the slaves of native tyrants. And where you don't have demonic madmen in charge, there is the contagion of tribal and ethnic hatred— southern Sudan pitilessly starved and enslaved by the north, the Islamic North against the animist South, as evidenced also by the terrible war in Chad.

There are only a few places where the situation is not so grim, Senegal perhaps or Dahomey, Tanzania perhaps or Zimbabwe, but only perhaps. Everywhere else it's evil unchained.

The land of Africa lies riddled with assassins' bullets. I maintain that "neocolonialism" is demonstrably harmless, compared with the native strains of bloodshed, waste, and starvation. But we have to say a little bit more about the opposite ends of the continent. First there is the slavery that Muslim traders continue to practice among the blacks—*real* slavery, that is, the capture and sale of humans who have it no better than animals, who do every sort of task for the lords of the petrodollars. Admittedly, this outrage was denounced at the United Nations, but they quickly proceeded to the order of the day. At the other end, the Republic of South Africa, with its apartheid, torture, omnipresent police and repression, has been condemned so often that nothing further need be said. One of the rare points of world unanimity is our abhorrence of that country, but wherever there is unanimity, we have to be suspicious. I have explained elsewhere why South Africa has been chosen as everyone's scapegoat. What is going on there is unforgivable, especially since it's draped with the mantle of the Bible and Christian civilization, but it's just as bad everywhere else in Africa. Such terrible suffering is unfathomable, and the evil done to people by their fellow human beings seems inexpiable—literally inexpiable: on the human level nothing can redeem it.

Readers may not like this discussion, but we have to continue with it, because it is the true way of the cross for us as it was for Christ, who shares the whole immensity of this pain. Look at the Middle East, the hatred of the Palestinians, the assassination attempts, the slow strangulation of Israel, which within a short time will vanish beneath the bombs of its enemies a thousand times more numerous. Israel is not without reproach, but that tiny nation wants to survive, and step by step inexorable destiny, like a concrete wall, advances to crush it. This to the endlessly repeated cry of "Justice for the Palestinians," and so in the name of justice millions of Jews will be massacred. I say that all those who are now defending the Palestinian cause with an eye to set up a Palestinian state in the heart of Israel are the potential assassins of the chosen people.

Lebanon is torn in pieces. It is more than ever the victim of civil war at the same time it is occupied by foreigners, Syrians on one side, Israelis on the other. The tenuous equilibrium of tolerance, mutual respect, and dialog between the different communities has been shattered at one blow, and there's no going back, no possible restoration. And Lebanon slips into almost total destitution, while alongside her in the oil-producing countries the most fabulous wealth the world has ever seen piles up. But these riches produce nothing; in no way do they benefit either society at large in those countries or the poor and disinherited, whose condition grows steadily worse.

Within the lands where "egalitarian" Islam reigns justice violated cries out louder and louder.

And the tragedy goes on. In Turkey (1980) fear provokes daily massacres on both sides. Extreme leftist groups open fire because they're afraid of being murdered by the extreme rightists, who claim they're only defending themselves from the leftists. Then there's Iran—what's the use of talking about it, except to say that it's not as dreadful as the propagandists charge. There aren't that many victims or persecutions or crimes against justice in all those revolutionary outcries and decrees, which Westerners find so insane, but the dangers are accumulating. Conflicts are growing between religious Islam and communism. And how could the Islamic movement not be swept away by the immense ground swell of communism, with the Soviet Union so close? The time will come for massacres and deportations, but until then we can save our tears for Iran.

Yet Iran is not innocent either; it has its share in causing the plight of the Kurds. The Kurds are a people torn apart, persecuted in Iraq, persecuted in Turkey, persecuted in Iran. When they flee from one country to the next, they fall into the clutches of an enemy worse than the previous one. No one cares about the Kurds, unlike the pseudo-Palestinians, those darlings of the righteous and of the strategic Left. Injustice and misery are their lot.

And what is there to say about Afghanistan? A people almost entirely unarmed puts up heroic resistance against napalm, tanks, and MIGs. It's reminiscent of the horrible Italian butchery of the Ethiopians, but here the disproportion is worse, and there the dictator didn't talk about anything but power. But the Soviet disease is permanent hypocrisy, the lie of socialism, the lie of freedom brought to a nation that supposedly begged for it (in 1940 the Nazis too came to "liberate" the French from the odious Republic), the lie of help given to that country to "protect" it against its frightful, menacing neighbor.

The USSR is the land of every kind of lie, oppression, ignominy, and torture. There is nothing positive there, only evil. And when I say that I'm not talking about communism —the Soviet Union is not communist. It is the most imperialistic country in the world, a cold, savage conqueror, the new Tamburlaine, but no longer limited to a single human lifespan. It has enslaved and manipulated huge populations, part of which have miraculously (and I mean miraculously in the full Christian sense) escaped being lobotomized. They have survived as human beings and managed to stay on their feet as they confront the monster. The Soviet Union is not only the gulag of gulags, but the universal steamroller—Berlin in 1953, Poland and Hungary in 1956, Czechoslovakia in 1968— and all that, we must recall, during the benign rule of Stalin's successors.

Later came the takeovers in Cuba, Angola, Ethiopia, and now Afghanistan. And all the while the Soviet Union is incapable of guaranteeing its people peace and economic progress on the domestic scene, not to mention basic human rights, freedom of speech, and so forth. It is a land of terror, for which the only biblical parallel is Babylonia. But like the Babylonians the Soviets might well be the flail that threshes the wheat, that bursts open the heads making the grains shoot forth. The flail—the scourge—of God, that's how I see the USSR, with its pure distilled cruelty, its imperturbable conscience, its quenchless thirst for conquest, its seductive attraction for wretches who have nothing to lose and for imbeciles wearing blindfolds.

The Soviet Union is the land of death and the purveyor of death, though by different means from those of Babylonia— just as the punishment it inflicts will be different from the one that struck Israel. In those days Israel was *the* chosen

people, and the Eternal whistled for the Babylonians to attack. Now the people of God, thanks to Christianity, are
spread all over the world, and we find ourselves confronting
the final scourge, which will strike the entire world through
the injustice of those whose lives ought to be full of love and
freedom. We shall not escape it, and this time the judgment
will probably be terminal.

Finally we move to Asia to complete this worldwide cham-
ber of horrors. Is it necessary to talk about the deportation
camps, little known but just as heinous as the gulags, that are
scattered throughout China? In any case we cannot keep silent about the way the Chinese crushed Tibet or the heroic
resistance of the Kham, who for twenty years have fought
assimilation. More unknowns. And then we come to the great
tragedy of recent years, the massacre of the Khmer people
and the collapse of their society. I hear the word genocide
thrown around a great deal, but since the Jews endured it
under Hitler only the Khmer have known genocide. From
1975 to 1979, three million victims died in four years out of a
nation of seven million, from massacres, famine, and over-
work. And one's revulsion approaches the absolute limit
when one thinks that the disaster was purely gratuitous: no
one among the Khmers asked for a dictatorship to bring order to the country. They were a peaceful and contented
people who had no need of anything or anybody. There was
no proletariat, no class struggle. All that was imported from
outside, along with the Vietnamese, the Chinese, the Ameri-
cans, the Russians. And the result was ignominy, the most
unspeakable act of our generation. How could it not come to
judgment—God's judgment (because we must never count on
history to judge fairly)?

After Cambodia we can make a rapid survey of the rest: the
correctional camps of Vietnam, the executions of South Vietnamese by the Vietminh, the continual victories of the Ton-

kinese, the prisons of Saigon, the tiger cages of the American
era . . . the tortures in Korea and the Philippines, the massacre of the Communists in Indonesia—wherever we look on
the map of these places we see only suffering, oppression,
exploitation, and death. And because we are no Abel face to
face with Cain, but a vast living body of humanity that has
been marching for the past half century over mountains of
cadavers, all of us have to hear the voice that asks, "What
have you done? The voice of your brother's blood is crying to
me from the ground. And now you are cursed from the
ground, which has opened its mouth to receive your brother's
blood *from your hand*" (Gen. 4:10–11). These words are
meant for every single one of us. Here in the West we go
about our quiet little lives, but we have nonetheless set the
machinery in motion; we have raised the curtain on a tragedy
that will unfold until its end—our end.

Look at the Western world, Europe and the United States,
islands of tranquillity and happiness. Despite the police and
the authoritarianism, despite poverty and racism, prosperity
is everywhere. Never has there been a world so rich, so
blessed by fortune, so full of avid consumers. And never have
people reached a comparable degree of moral, spiritual, and
psychic decadence: stricken by anomie, *taedium vitae*, the
longing for death, a collective suicidal hypnosis, wherein the
West has already begun to feel its chastisement. Prometheus
has been bound anew, but this time he has done it to himself,
with great care and effort. As an historian I can say—and this
is not to glorify the past—that never has humanity reached
such heights of power or such universal depths of suffering
and despair.

I am sick over the world I shall leave behind, sick at heart,
physically and intellectually sick. I had been so hopeful when
at the age of twenty I first committed myself to action, when
we hoped to change the course of the world. In 1930 we could

already see the oppression and disorder of that world taking
shape. And we had the absurd hope of turning it away, however slightly, in a different direction, toward humanity and
freedom, toward justice, toward a true democracy. I tried
everything. I seized all the opportunities that seemed favorable. I thought and thought, but managed only to understand
what was going on. Marx has some nerve proclaiming that it
no longer suffices to understand the world, that one has to
transform it. To begin with, the results of his career have
worsened the situation literally everywhere. Second, the
world in 1930 was ten thousand times more complicated than
in his day, and merely understanding it was a *tour de force*. I
saw correctly, I spoke, I gave warning—it all went for nothing.

When the time was ripe no one listened, and when my
message gradually found an audience, it was too late. We had
started down a slope that we couldn't climb back up; we had
accumulated powers that were indestructible; we couldn't get
back to our origins anymore from which to strike out on a
new path. It all went for nothing. Inexorably it has become
the worst of all possible worlds. We never wanted *that*.

It's too simple to accuse the capitalists, the imperialists, the
colonialists: they didn't expect things to turn out this way.
It's too simple to accuse the communists: they never wanted
bloody dictatorships, nor Pol Pot's massacres, nor the gulag,
nor the imperialism of communist power. I can vouch for the
fact that the communists I have known never imagined that
their marvelous ideal would produce only the most powerful
armaments and police in the world. Einstein never wanted
the atomic bomb; people of good will have never wanted the
evil they so abundantly reaped in all their activities—science,
technology, economics, politics. The whole harvest has been
evil. It's as if in some terrible hallucination all the wonderful
flowers of progress in every area had wilted at once, leaving

behind only horrible poisoned fruit, and nothing, not a thing, to eat.

Having been left with only two alternatives, belief or hemlock, young people are right to react violently to the world we shall bequeath them and to call everything into question. Everything *is* rotten and poisonous. But they accuse the adults, my generation, and somebody has to tell them that we never wanted all that. We were the rising generation after World War I; we solemnly swore, "Never again." We struggled for peace, for social justice, for deeper analysis, and more disciplined tactics. As early as 1935 we rejected both Hitler and Stalin and what they stood for. We saw things clearly. We had long since damned capitalism and liberalism across the board.[43]

We were looking for something different, and we refused to believe in either historical fatalism or the victory of the devil. We had an ideal; we wanted a free and brotherly world; we tried to learn as best we could and take the most constructive action possible. We sought universal happiness and equity—and look what we turned out. In things as they are today we recognize none of the hopes and ideals of our youth. We weren't greedy for money or power or eager to dominate and consume, but everything we tried to achieve was relentlessly perverted, deformed, transformed into its opposite as we looked on with horrified incomprehension. Most of us couldn't foresee what was coming, and those who did were unable to act. We never wanted *that*.

I know it's a shabby excuse, the favorite line of impotent idealists, but with the precipice yawning beneath us it's the only thing we can say to attest to our good faith. And there was no one villain to blame it on, no one dictator or class responsible for our plight. We have to get away from false,

43. See A. Dandieu and R. Aron, *Le Cancer américain,* 1927.

simplistic explanations based on the "class struggle" and the responsibility of the ruling class. Even that group is led by forces more powerful than itself—and not by its "interests." We all played the game according to our lights; we all had our reasons, which were good ones.

Now we are overwhelmed by the world we have made. All of us made it, together, but made it through some inconceivable power of perversion. And then when some people did finally understand, it was no use or it was already too late. I am ashamed of the world we're leaving to the young. And my fears are all the greater because I see these young men and women with exactly the same hopes, the same words, the same goals, the same judgments we had fifty years ago. What will they do differently from us? Maybe the perverse power of fate will be cancelled in their case; perhaps the tragedy was only for us, and the resolution of the crisis is at hand. Perhaps.

We never wanted things to resolve themselves *that* way; nobody wanted the world as we have it. But who cares what we wanted? Who still remembers how powerfully and energetically we longed for the revolution, how we believed in it, as deeply as the rebels of 1968, and that on two occasions we thought we could get it? What a wretched feeling to hear young people scorn us for what we were, thinking themselves the first to want such a revolution. But we were more demanding than they are; we were more rigorous both in our analyses and our choice of means. And it all crumbled into ashes. We did everything we could, and I sometimes feel a bitter wave of mockery sweep over me when I hear ideas praised as new that we were talking about in the 1930s— exactly the same ideas. I have been accused of treating society and technology as if they were machines that functioned without human help, but this is something I learned from the

failure of all resistance movements, all revolutions, all de-
sires, all analyses, all proclamations, and all programs.

Worst of all, as I see it, is the perversity of history in bringing about the opposite of what we were fighting for, after
victory appeared to initially give us what we longed for. Each
time we got exactly the reverse of our expectations. Socialism
led to Stalin. Hitler's fall led to the widespread use of his
police tactics and methods of government; it led to the triumph of the totalitarian state, of torture, of one-party politics, of concentration camps. The democracies learned at Hitler's school.

And every time one of our discoveries was taken seriously
by those in power, every time it was accepted by public opinion, it came back to haunt us in a shape that was false, deceit-
ful, and noxious. In 1930 we fought against the grotesque
hypocrisy of bourgeois morality, hoping to foster a morality
of freedom and life, only to end up with eroticism, drugs,
anomie, the dismal repetition of slogans attacking the family
and cheering abortion, a kind of alienation much worse than
before.

We were among the first to analyze and try to grasp the
phenomenon of technology. We had hoped that this would
enable individuals to regain the power that was slipping away
from them, to return to authentic subjectivity, to control
what was controlling them. But for ten years now our message has been taken up by a thousand spokespeople; it has
been turned into a cliché, into hatred of technology, an approach that looks down on our research from the 1940s as
ridiculous but that in fact furthers the spread of technology
and grants it greater autonomy. Hundreds of fuzzy-minded,
self-indulgent books on technology are now rolling off the
presses. Their very abundance serves as an ideological smokescreen obscuring reality, while their banality contrasts so

sharply with the seriousness of technological growth that they seem to justify it.

The same thing goes for the French "ecology" movement, which began as a prophetic message and became a sociological trend, a springboard for political success, and a way back into the industrial system. We never wanted *that*—or did we? Where did we go wrong? Was our analysis false? Were our objectives vague or futile? Did our rigorous critique of means and methods contain the seed of our failure? No, absolutely not.

We were right, our vision was clear, and we stood at the center of the drama of our time. We had the key, but we have been beaten. The very success of our ideas, by remaining mere ideas, by undergoing metamorphosis into slogans and aberrant behavior, spelled our defeat. The whole thing turned false when it was embraced by the public and the politicians, the media, and even those whom it had directly challenged, worse yet when it was made a plaything by insane works of art, graphic evidence of how insignificant our achievements were. A doctor examines a child, diagnoses a serious illness, and prescribes a drug to cure the disease. But while the parents are out of the room, the child makes the prescription into a paper airplane and it sails out the window: something like that is what happened to us.

20

An Ever More
Perilous World

Our troubles keep piling up, thanks to the way people keep hurting their fellow human beings. But beyond these failures and evils, a much grimmer species of catastrophe is spreading through the innards of our society. People take it for granted that atomic power plants are reliable, that there's no danger in the stockpiles of missiles, submarines, and rockets, no danger in the neutron and hydrogen bombs, the nonmilitary toxic substances, the barrels of radioactive wastes and dioxin, the accumulations of mercury and lead, the ever increasing amount of carbon dioxide in the atmosphere. These things are no more threatening, they tell us, than gas lamps were in the 1850s or the first railroads.

What pathetic imbeciles we are, we critics of progress—we never understand anything! No one will ever wage the terminal war, 500,000-ton oil tankers will never run aground, offshore oil rigs that drill 3,000 meters down will never spring an unstoppable leak. Genetic engineering will never go astray and produc monsters or regimented clones; the vast quantities of tranquillizers, uppers, and downers used will never become a collective chemical straitjacket. The artificial food-

stuffs manufactured by agile activated bacteria won't ever be
filthy swill. Data processing will never be the tool of a universal police state; television cameras will never be mounted to
scan city avenues, replacing the eye of God and judgment
after death. The state will never become truly totalitarian; the
gulag will never spread.

We have to trust. Trust the experts, the laboratories, the
statesmen, the technicians, the organizers. All of them have
only one wish—the good of humanity. They have a firm grip
on the mechanism and they know which way to go. Trust the
forecasters, the data processors, the hygienists, the economists, the guardians of the City (ah, Plato, we have guardians
now!). Trust them all, because our trust is an indispensable
ingredient in this witches' brew. If a catastrophe were ever to
happen, it would be our fault. We would be as much to blame
as someone who throws a monkey wrench into the works or
slams on the brakes at the wrong time or needlessly causes
panic (everybody knows that in a burning building it's not
the fire and smoke that kill but the panic created by people
shouting "fire!"). We would be as guilty as those who prevent plans and programs from materializing, but who have no
plans or programs of their own, people who just wish other
people would damn well leave them in peace (and that's
where peace begins) and not try to draft them to fight for
every cause under the sun. But they have been drafted;
they're already in uniform.

The world is becoming an increasingly dangerous place because of three crimes. First, there is the material accumula-
tion of a thousand means of power, which is now reaching the
absolute limit—since I can conceive of nothing beyond the
ability to annihilate the entire human race and to transform
the surface of the earth into vitrified rock; and we now possess—and continue to stockpile—a hundred times more
equipment than we need to obtain that result. What blind

beasts, those Nobel prize winners and brilliant politicians of ours, indefatigably pressing on in the race for power, afraid of being overtaken by their competitors. And what despicable idiocy we find in the recurrent slogan, "Let the whole world go under, rather than see France in second place" (France or Niger or the proletariat or a viable return on investments . . .).

The second danger is the incompetence, impotence, and ineffectiveness of the forecasters.

And the third danger is the fashioning of a human being driven to submission by violence and fear. I won't cite any statistics on our various means of destruction and the dwindling chances of survival, since everyone is familiar with them. It's sheer mockery, the way we are gravely informed that our average life expectancy has soared, thanks to medicine, hygiene, and the rise in the standard of living, when all the while we know perfectly well that the most trifling incident might blow up the crate of nitroglycerin that our planet has become, and then our life expectancy would be zero. What we have to say, actually, is that if there's no war, if there's no famine, if there's no cataclysmic release of radiation or toxic gas, if some little-known carcinogens don't accumulate in our bodies, if, if, if, *then* our life expectancy is on the order of seventy-two years, assuming we belong to the better-off classes of Western society. In other words, if everything works out perfectly—if death doesn't get us first—we will live a long, long time. But I want to dwell on the two other dangers.

There is no end to the forecasts, future projections, and future scenarios we hear about today. Methods have been refined (no more simplistic extrapolations), and statisticians now delight in simulation models, levels of probability, and so forth. But I should like to bring the forecasters up short by reminding them that their forecasts have never come true and that, conversely, history has always turned on events that no one, or almost no one, had foreseen. Recall that all the demographic projections made since 1945 have been belied by events. Similarly, as everyone repeatedly points out, not one economist (except Schumacher in his report on energy in 1961) predicted that there would be an energy crisis. Around 1970 all calculations were based on the assumption of a continuous supply of cheap oil. Nothing, in fact, or at any rate no scientific reasoning process, could have led to the prediction that the oil-producing Arab nations would rebel and seize control of this main source of energy, treating it like a weapon. And yet from an economic point of view everything turned out to depend upon this rebellion.

But these are only two examples among many. Who really saw in advance the worldwide movement toward decolonization? As late as 1950, despite the goings-on in Indochina, almost nobody did. People were still making complacent noises about new types of relationships with the Third World. Going back even further, who saw that Hitler was telling the truth when he announced what he planned to do, or that Stalin was lying when he said he was doing one thing and was actually doing quite another? Go back and look at the analyses written by the specialists, the sociologists, economists, and political scientists of the period: to the extent that they stayed within the bounds of their scientific expertise, they were all mistaken. The ones who saw, who predicted, who announced what was coming were the nonspecialists, the intellectuals, religious thinkers, artists, and politicians from the "other camp." There was a vast hurly-burly of opinions and counteropinions, and of course somewhere in the middle of all this you could find people who did as a matter of fact foresee what happened. But their vision was founded on their convictions, not on science, and there was no reason to believe them rather than other people who were saying just the opposite.

Again, more recently, who predicted the collapse of the dollar in 1976? Who forecast the breakdown of economic growth and the plunge into unemployment and inflation? Nobody, literally nobody. Or, to take one small personal example, at the time when Castro first launched his revolution, I had great confidence in the man. I was convinced that he was going to use that revolution to liberate Cuba and that he might set up a genuinely new regime. Unfortunately, not long after his accession to power he proclaimed a "day of justice," when the mob was unleashed and went on a murderous rampage. It was unimaginable—and in the worst rabble-rousing manner of dictatorships. I wrote an article around that time to explain that Cuba had entered on the road to dictatorship and that since it rejected the United States[44] it would have to align itself with the Soviets. I was roundly insulted by Claude Jullien, who responded by writing an article to explain that I didn't know what I was talking about, that I wasn't, like him, a specialist in Latin American affairs, that I was completely ignorant on the subject of Cuba, and that the new government would take its cue from neither the United States nor the Soviet Union.

That was the peremptory judgment of the *specialist* in this area. One could write an entire book tracing step by step the enormous errors made by all the specialists, all the scientists, all the economists, who are barely capable of putting the facts together after they have occurred and of explaining why it turned out the way it did. And then it all becomes extremely clear, so clear that you can't understand why nobody saw it coming. How is it that today's enlightened communists didn't understand yesterday what happened the day before, although they explain it so well to you now?

The danger lies in this total incapacity to forecast anything

44. Current official history would have it that repeated mistakes by the United States drove Castro into the arms of the Soviets. But if one carefully examines the facts, it becomes readily apparent that the contrary is true.

whatsoever. I know readers will say, "But it was always that way. People have never known the future, which is why they invented the gods. In the old days there were seers, wizards, oracles, the Urim and Thummim, haruspices, prophets, and so forth." Well, our problem has nothing to do with that. Back then people wanted to plumb the dark depths of fate, the uncertainty of natural events, or the mystery of the gods' will. Nowadays it doesn't concern any entities outside ourselves; we are the only ones who matter. We are the savants, technicians, politicians, and economists who control forces that once were hidden and beyond the natural sphere; we are the ones who use them to make things happen.

And that is just what we have become totally incapable of predicting. Events are simply the result, the consequence, the effect, the conclusion of our own undertakings. That's the joker in the deck. That we can't predict an avalanche, a flood, or an earthquake does not put humanity in general in any irreparable danger. But that we can't predict the outcome of the spread of nuclear reactors, of experiments in genetic engineering, of our interference in the water cycle is a different story. We foresaw none of the consequences of the Aswan dam or of modern city planning.

When we set events in motion, we are in effect betting. We bet, for example, on electrification. We run a senseless advertising campaign to get people to consume and overconsume electricity for any reason whatever. (And indeed the consumption of electricity in France has increased fivefold over the last twenty-five years, 1955 to 1980.) Then suddenly we have trouble on our hands. Naturally, we have to go on producing electrical power. We can't just stop or change the whole system, so atomic energy is now a necessity. But this supposedly ineluctable necessity is something we have brought on ourselves with our total lack of foresight—based on wonderfully precise scientific calculations that have determined that this is the required solution. The upshot is that the twenty percent of France's energy production that we now get from nuclear power plants equals one hundred percent of what we consumed in 1955. And all those plants would have been completely unnecessary if we had moderated our demand for more electricity. The world has become so dangerous because while our sources of power have proliferated we are utterly incapable of controlling their future.

All this relates directly and significantly to faith. Faith implies an altogether different attitude. Knowing how unpredictable things are, that it's impossible to proclaim "the future is mine," faith inclines us to go slow, to be prudent, to consider dangers, risks, and the most improbable of probabilities. It fits in very well with certain perspectives of contemporary science—unless it's science that is now seeing the wisdom of faith. Lagadec has done a study, which I think highly significant,[45] showing that any estimate of probabilities has no validity at all when the risk being calculated would have infinite consequences. In other words, figures proving the extreme unlikelihood of a serious nuclear power plant accident are worthless. The risk, we are told, is negligible, but that's false: since the effects might be close to the absolute limit, the risk is actually enormous (in the true sense of the word going back to its etymological roots).

This latest scientific judgment approaches the attitude of faith, which assigns no value to future projections. Faith demands that we give free play to uncertainty. In the face of the innumerable proofs that the forecasters can't forecast, of the accidents that were unforeseen and unforeseeable but happened anyway and upset all our expectations, we have to go back to the wisdom of faith. The worst is always possible,

---

45. *La Recherche*, no. 105, 1979. With catastrophes the exception is the rule, hence statistical reasoning has neither probative nor predictive value.

and no one can prevent it from materializing. We will never master the forces we unleash. The distinction between good and bad uses of technology, as I never weary of repeating, is idiotic.

Accordingly, we must stay within limits, be prudent and judicious, do things on a small scale, respect mysteries, starting with the mystery of the future, which is the condition for respecting the mysteries of the present. We have to admit that unpredictable chance is a factor in all our enterprises and that it can be a negative factor. We must admit that even though we believe that fate, destiny, and necessity truly come to us in and through Jesus Christ and through him alone, there are nonetheless in human affairs inexorable, ineluctable connections that manifest themselves with all the force of destiny. We have caught our fingers in the powerful machinery we started up, and there's no way left to get them out except by a miracle, which will have its costs. We may have to sacrifice the hand, cutting it off so that our whole body doesn't get pulled in. These dangers are of our own making; yet we can't tell in advance what will come of them.

In this context, then, I would strongly maintain that faith offers us a greater capability of foreseeing the future than does mathematics. Faith frees the mind and allows it to have a clear-eyed view of what could happen. Faith calls for the prophetic attitude, not the absurd illuminism that proclaims any fleeting "inspiration." Faith is clairvoyant; it never lets itself be taken in. Having nothing to fear, it has no pessimistic conception of humankind's future, but an optimistic one, since Christ is alive and victorious. For that very reason faith can see clearly among the likely catastrophes as it stands facing the proliferation of powers, forces, means, enterprises, and information. It can see clearly and speak out—not to terrify people and start a panic, but to bring them around to a sober evaluation of what can be accomplished without creating some terminal danger.

Since we can't predict anything, we ought to be prudent and move ahead slowly. Let's move at a human pace, since humans, whether we like it or not, remain, as long as they inhabit this earth, the measure of all things. There we have faith's statement on the story of creation in Genesis where Adam and Eve *are* fact that measure and where their temptation is to go beyond all measure, into the excess of evil. We have succumbed to it in science, after having succumbed to excess in religion. We must stop doing this. Is faith still for nothing? Yes, but living in faith also lets us see what is coming and warn others about it.

The third danger is the "forgetfulness-fear-violence" syndrome. We have just spoken of the inability to foresee the future (which is a danger only because we are unleashing unsuspected forces). But at the same time we are witnessing the disappearance of the past, the widespread loss of both collective and individual memory. A few years ago an important book was published with the title *Hitler? Never Heard of Him*. People in our society are creatures without memory; step by step they forget everything. This means that they have no past and no roots. And so these people—us—have no foreseeable future and no past to build on, neither familial, nor local, nor communal, nor national, nothing at all.

How, then, could you expect them not to be afraid, these people from no-place, who don't know where they're coming from or going to? And when they become afraid, how could they not get violent? Only the fearful are violent, as we know in the case of dogs. It's the same with people.

Forgetfulness or amnesia is one of the striking features of today's psychological landscape, spontaneous forgetfulness, erasing a past without glory, adventure, or satisfaction.

Sometimes this oblivion is an unconscious blotting out of remorse, of our own perverse acts—and we have been well
schooled in the necessity of getting rid of guilt feelings. But
there is also a free and deliberate forgetfulness in the face of
powers aiming to obliterate our history at any cost. No, this is
not 1984. But it *is* a reign of amnesia in all quarters, all
classes, all governments. The past is rejected, and everything
is staked on the future. People rush headlong to prepare
themselves for the twenty-first century. It all makes one think
of a rudderless boat cut adrift and swept along with the current.

The mad passion for progress stays with us, though we can
already taste the bitterness of its fruits. Onward, ever onward, tomorrow will surely realize the dream of . . . And so
each one of us carefully buries in oblivion the self we were
yesterday. I shall not go into what I consider the outrageously
facile denials and contradictory affirmations of which Sartre
was the master, the model, the guru, but which one now
hears from almost all intellectuals, scientists, politicians, and
the militant followers of various movements.[46] They have long
since left behind the stage where they clearly realized, and
had qualms of conscience over the fact, that they were in the
process of worshiping what they had condemned the day
before and of condemning what they once worshiped.

You meet fervent communists, once Stalinists, who brazen-
ly tell you, "But of course, everybody knows Stalin was a
bloodthirsty tyrant, and anyhow he never represented real
communism." Or you meet anti-Christians who have had a
sudden illumination (of what?) and converted. But unlike
Paul or Augustine (no road to Damascus here), they never
recall either their life of debauchery or their violent resistance
to Christianity. Oh no, that never existed. Conversion is the

46. Ellul, "De l'Inconséquence."

great miracle. God exists; they have laid hands on him. Before this? There was no "before"; it didn't exist. Simple as that.

It reminds one of M. Mansholt, the eminent and revered economist whose plan hastened the liquidation of the French peasantry, but who was suddenly touched by ecological grace and now sees the essential importance of the life and work of the peasants, who has become a bard of natural beauty. But don't think that he criticizes his celebrated plan, which did so much harm. Not at all, it's been quite forgotten. As far as M. Mansholt is concerned, there never was such a plan—tell that to those peasants whose lives and flesh were trampled by "progress" as a result of it.

We have become totally irresponsible in the political and economic positions we take; we have forgotten ourselves and our fellow citizens. As I said twenty years ago, one piece of information dislodges another. There is no continuity, no coherence. We live in a culture of forgetfulness, a culture that suits us very well, enabling us to be blown about by every gust of wind, while we gravely affirm the stability of our opinions (like the politician accused of being a turncoat who replies, "But my coat was on inside out"). This is a culture that also suits our governments, because a people without memory is infinitely easier to manipulate. History is being eliminated from the schools for the same reason. All education is being reduced to the indispensable prerequisites for "taking part in the society of tomorrow"—a grotesque proposition since nobody in the world knows what that society will be.

There is, as Montaigne says, a "science of forgetting." The first one to describe it was Orion,[47] who properly calls it *lethotechny.* But it's so dangerous to bring up this technique

47. In his admirable introduction to Girouettes's *Nouveau Dictionnaire,* 1948.

and to denounce it that not one of our eminent intellectuals, not one psychologist, philosopher, or analyst has gone back to that essay, now more than thirty years old. Orion notes that the pattern of forgetfulness appears to be anything but random, so that we can make out a few simple rules.

The most important kind of forgetfulness is political. Our recent experience of this runs deep, as we have seen how literally everything can be forgotten, by writers, by the public, even by the opposition party. How prophetic were Nietzsche's words in *Beyond Good and Evil*, "Blessed are the forgetful, for they shall recover even from their own stupid mistakes." That is most certainly true, but people who live submerged in forgetfulness cannot help being beset by fears about the present, which seem incomparable, unheard of, insurmountable, because they have lost all their memories of war, famine, errors, obstacles, lies, wandering in the desert, persecution, all the things that past generations in their obstinate will to live managed to overcome.

But we don't overcome anymore, the art has been lost, and people are afraid of everything. They are like a body no longer capable of immunizing itself because it has lost the "memory" of previous diseases. Our society as a whole has become incapable of producing the antibodies needed to triumph over adversity, because their source could only be, not programs, plans, or doctrines, but vital social and political experience. They could arise only from memory, from the flesh and spirit of everything we have lived through, from all the lessons painfully learned, all the meanings laboriously built on those human experiences.

But when everything is obliterated, people become afraid. Here we see what I have often denounced as the singular frailty of moderns, their inability to take on the *real* risks of life. (By contrast they're ready to take all sorts of false risks—solo ocean voyages, mountain climbing in the Himalayas, automobile races, and so forth—provided they have nothing to do with the harsh reality of everyday life where our survival is at stake.) Modern individuals are afraid of their shadow, and of everything else. They seize on a vision, a hallucinatory apprehension of the world where they find themselves, and then they attribute the fear and anxiety they genuinely feel to fictive causes.

They become frightened of sickness, of other people, of the young (or of the old), of imaginary dangers, of world war, of bosses or unions, of revolution or reaction, and so forth. I don't deny, of course, that there is a certain reality in all this and in part a fearful one. But the more important fact is that everything takes on gigantic dimensions in our imagination and sensibility while at the same time we assign our uncontrolled fears to insubstantial realities. The fact that people are basically fear-ridden leads them to frighten themselves even more with images of those social objects, thereby justifying their experience of ontological fear.

But in the meantime the true origins, the causes if you will, of our anxiety have been totally obscured, misread, or treated as far-fetched notions invented by intellectuals. And in such matters psychiatry is completely powerless. With no more future or past or frame of reference or meaningful connections, contemporary people confront the solitude in time and space that gives rise to their unconditional fear. But over this deep structure of fear a complex superstructure is erected, whose elements are the (real) facts previously alluded to, which are recognized but blown out of proportion in the universe of fear. Every item in the news feeds our anxiety (oil shortages, muggings in the subway, etc.). People often accuse the media of creating such anxiety, but radio and TV reports are simply responding to what the public wants to hear. The whole business of the news has become part and parcel of the climate of fear we live in.

But there is one reproach the media deserve, and it has two aspects: first, they are in effect selecting and broadcasting only bad news. Only accidents and catastrophes seem to qualify as information, which makes the world itself look catastrophic.[48] All this is aggravated by the tendency to dramatize things for the sake of a livelier story. And then there is the effect of *mass* communication, which is felt even if unconsciously. Millions of people share the same emotion, and so the fear is compounded.

But even so this syndrome would never occur without the underlying fear in the depths of our soul, hidden but coloring our every attitude. Now fear dictates two modes of behavior: violence and rigidity. The violence it arouses affects not only the life of the state—with the police on one side and demonstrators, rebels, and young people on the other—but all human relations. Let me mention some forms of violence we don't usually think of; to begin with, violence against morality. This is altogether fundamental, since it's one of the constitutive elements of fear. In their universal violence aimed at morality (as seen in the movements promoting homosexuality, radical feminism, and sexual freedom, or attacking the family and decency, etc.) people are voluntarily destroying what could calm their fear and in so doing they heighten and encourage it. They act like the sailor who smashes his compass and radio.

Another kind of violence is the endless cycle of people accusing and informing on each other. It degrades everyone involved and reflects the universal suspicion, the impossibility of trusting others that is once again both the source and the effect of fear. Then there is the violence that flares up as soon as different ways of thinking or being appear, the vio-

48. See my study of this situation entitled *Propaganda: The Formation of Men's Attitudes*, 1965.

lence against everything foreign to us. In the church every deviation leads to incredible outbursts of verbal violence (and I don't necessarily mean on the part of church authorities, but also by the enemies of that authority, on both the Left and the Right). And the same thing exists in the unions and political parties.

Violence pervades literature: a book can't find readers unless it contains some kind of violence, either in the scenes described or the thought or the language, whether the work be a thriller or a pseudo-scientific essay. In each case the idea is to destroy the things we hold most precious—friendship, a mother's love, the things that keep us going. Literature is made to glorify assassins; criminals become the most exciting characters, the ones most worthy of respect (Sartre started this off properly with his *Saint Genêt*).

Violence inevitably spreads everywhere when a culture destroys the opportunities for people to recognize good and evil, when "goodness" (rectitude, honesty, fidelity, chaste love, etc.) is denounced as absolute evil (as a manifestation of hypocrisy and constraint), while evil is loudly extolled and transformed into good. This transformation is the burden of all present-day literature, theater, cinema, and TV. And so it makes sense to speak of the most archaic sort of collective fear, the fear of contagion, which has been stirred up by the spread of this inversion.[49]

Widespread mediatization lies at the roots of oral violence, of the veritable epidemic of news overwhelming us. The authorities that ought to provide some sort of security against it now become the headquarters of this terror, which both provokes and is produced by violence. Violence plays at one and the same time with both official power and its negation. The police, who ought to protect and reassure the population

49. H. P. Jeudy, *La Peur et les média: Essai sur la virulence*, 1979.

become a machine that wreaks violence upon it and arouses it to violence. City planning as practiced over the past fifty years is both a result of violence (by the capitalists) and a cause of violence (by the city dwellers, through the way of life imposed upon them).

Public administration is a constant source of violence. It behaves violently because it fears that none of its decisions will be implemented, and it provokes violence (by ceaselessly attacking those it controls), especially through arbitrary and authoritarian decisions. These are applied without consulting those affected and without heeding any legal norms that the citizen could look to or rely on. Fundamental fear and unleashed violence are an inseparable pair. We are returning to "primitive" times, an age in which we all think we have to be our own bodyguards. But people have simply mistaken their enemy. They will never succeed in mastering their fear, which springs—and will keep on springing—from a basic flaw in their very being.

Meanwhile the second effect of violence, its equally certain corollary, is rigidity. The more one is afraid, the harder one's (supposedly protective) armor becomes, the more it turns into a part of one's own body like a kind of carapace. Like fear rigidity too manifests itself in every area of life. We find it in religious movements as a return to dogmatic narrowness, formalism, scriptural fundamentalism. We see rigidity in administrators and planners—a sure sign that dictatorial tendencies are reappearing. When fear sweeps over society, a security grid will have to be imposed upon it. And this will necessarily be some kind of fascism, whether of the Right or the Left, which, before bringing on the terror, will have people heaving a great sigh of relief, glad to think that at last they know where they're going, that someone is protecting them.

Rigidity in religion will be matched by rigidity in politics.

Communism has already given us an instance of perfectly stereotyped discourse, of wooden, leaden language. Communism is becoming a tranquillizing beacon of authority precisely to the extent that it shows itself incapable of evolving and continues to interpret the world in a fashion that is both utterly obsolete and inadequate (e.g., explaining everything by the class struggle) but that restores people's trust by remaining immutable in a time of incoherence. In this way it raises the level of incoherence by instilling false visions and false ways of acting in today's world. It creates a defensive rigidity that gives people a false kind of roots, a false morality, a false confidence, a false past (artificially reconstituted), a false future (of unremitting oppression), but that also gives them a strong and comforting sense of security.

21

Politics: The Realm of the Demonic

Everything we have described up to this point is more or less directly the result of politics. Jonah cries, "Yet forty days . . ." to Nineveh which was the political city par excellence, the imperial city, ruled by the most powerful of kings. If evil has piled up upon evil, if the tide of danger is rising, the reason lies in politics and nowhere else. Politics is the contemporary image of absolute evil. It is satanic, diabolical, the home base of the demonic. And when I say politics, I am not pointing at the state—that's another problem again. The point I want to make concerns those who would conquer and use the state for their own purposes. Nor am I accusing a specific kind of politics, rightist or leftist.

No, the issue is politics itself, whatever form it may take, whatever its objectives, doctrines, methods, social roots, intentions, or rationales. I am talking about politics in the concrete, as put into practice by the political world. I won't bother with those sententious allusions to the Greek *polis*, which has nothing to do with the United Nations we're all familiar with; I won't bother with those pious definitions of politics as the quest for the common good or the public interest, as the art of living together, as the blissful key to harmonious construction of the ideal city.

All such nonsense is worse than the worst religious trickery designed to cast a veil of modesty over naked reality. Politics is the acquisition of power: the means necessary for getting it, and once you have it the means for defending yourself against the enemy and so holding on to it. But what does one use it for—for goodness and virtue? No, one uses it for power; it's an end in itself. And that's all there is to politics. All the fine talk about politics as a means of establishing justice, so forth and so forth, is nothing but a smokescreen that on the one hand conceals harsh, vulgar reality and on the other justifies the universal passion for politics, the universal conviction that everything is political, that politics is the most noble human activity, whereas it is really the most ignoble. It is, strictly speaking, the source of all the evils that plague our time. And when I say that it is diabolical and satanic, I mean these adjectives literally.

Politics is diabolical. The devil can be the one who *divides*, separates, disjoins, disrupts communions, brings about divorce, breaks up dialog. In the Bible the devil is the one who instigates the break between God and humankind, who uses various means to shatter the communion that once linked the creator with creation. He takes advantage of perfectly natural and healthy human instincts: God creates humans free, bidding them govern creation and subdue it. The devil induces them to declare themselves independent of God's will, to seek autonomy. And in the same way he transforms the power given by God into a will to dominate.

This kind of distortion is typical of the way the devil acts, pretending to accomplish God's work, while transforming it into its opposite. And this is also where idealistic politics—the highly moral, community-oriented sort—turns into the real politics I mentioned before. To achieve this reversal, the

Bible says that the devil operates through seduction (Eve looks at the "tree" and plainly sees that it is beautiful, good, pleasing, intelligent, etc.) and through what is often called lies (the devil is the father of lies), but what is rather the exploitation of truth to produce effects contrary to those of the truth. Thus in the dialog between Eve and the devil, the latter doesn't lie. He does inform her that people will be as gods, determining good and evil, and that they will not die. But basically he seduces by shifting meanings and values. Finite reality becomes ultimate truth. And finite reality puts people in a situation different from the one they had imagined or hoped for as they peered through the glimmerings and refractions of the devil's seductive speech.

Now speaking concretely of society today, what is the father of lies? It is politics, and I would go so far as to say politics alone. France is divided into two blocs, which fact is absurd enough, because we know very well that both are largely interchangeable, that it's six of one, half a dozen of the other. But France is divided nonetheless. There are the victors and the vanquished, labeled as such by politics—and the terms are nothing but labels. There is White imperialism and Red imperialism, ready to go to war against each other. And what is it that drives nations straight to war, even though in general and on their own they have no such thought in mind? Politics.

What makes boys from Texas go off and kill Vietnamese, and boys from Estonia go off and kill Afghans? Only politics, which claims to represent the common good, collective interests, the homeland, and all that. Obviously, there are groups and clans who don't agree with each other, tribes, families, and corporations that are hostile to one another. But this doesn't have any terrible consequences—it leads at most to vendettas. But when these local interests are taken in hand by politics, then they come to stand for the general good. And then we find ourselves in collective tragedies where the innocent pay for the guilty.

When this happens, it's useless to talk about economic interests being more fundamental: without political structures, strategies, installations, and ideologies, economic interests are nothing and can do little to change conditions. It's politics that conquers colonies and markets (with a good deal, admittedly, of economic profit), politics that mobilizes people for wars that economic interests have made inevitable. And even if it isn't always true that politics is motivated by economics, still politics is the divisive force par excellence. It is politics and not economics that causes class divisions and shapes class struggle.

Look how incredibly hard it is for partisans to get away from politics. The unions are continually being drawn back into it. And when a workers' movement tries to be both revolutionary and antipolitical, as anarcho-syndicalism* was, it fails and its lifespan is short. The "progress" made by socialism has come by way of politics, not by the struggle of economic classes. And the anarcho-syndicalists who condemned politics had a clear notion of its divisiveness when they insisted that trade unionism ought not to get involved in politics, because it only creates division and it would inevitably make the working class split up into conflicting ideologies.

If you want to maintain working class unity, said Merrheim, Griffuelhes, and Pelloutier, you have to stay out of politics. They had a fine sense of what politics is all about, but nobody paid them any heed. Politicians who advertise themselves as "bringing people together" are preposterous:

---

*An anarchist movement which sought to use trade unions to attain the rights of workers through economic, rather than political, action. The movement flourished between 1895 and 1912; its leading theoreticians were Georges Sorel and Fernand Pelloutier.—TRANS.

they bring a group together at the cost of widening the gap between it and the rest of the nation. Similarly, politics doesn't bring a country together except insofar as it takes it into a war to the death with another country. This is in fact the simplest and best known way of uniting a country.

Politics creates nothing, least of all an authentic encounter and permanent ties between human beings; nor does it unify society, make it humanly responsible, or lead it forward. Politics produces nothing but division and inner conflict, which are useless, baseless, absurd. When fifty years have passed and we look at the divisions that led political adversaries to set upon each other with savage hatred, we are always stunned by the hollowness and stupidity of the motives of such hatred (and of wars in general). Was *that* the reason why those people butchered and massacred each other? We would never be so foolish.

But what we don't see is that, given other grounds, other objectives, we would do exactly the same thing. And the political motives behind our struggles will seem just as idiotic to our grandchildren. That's how politics is; it induces, lures, and provokes people into frenzied conflicts. It makes us deadly serious about the cause or the doctrine or the opinions that must be defended against those of others. It gets us to rise up against our brothers and sisters for superficial ideological reasons. And in the name of such stupidities it brings on mass slaughter. In the name of opening up Siberia to agriculture, the gulag is built. In the name of intensive cultivation (which was not needed) of rice, Pol Pot massacres a third of his people. In the name of political prestige France invades one fourth of the world.

We hear solemn, grandiloquent political proclamations, but their only real, long-term effect is discord and massacres. But for the moment people believe them, with their eyes closed. Politics makes us totally blind. It invents all the

ideologies that get us ready for war and turn us into killers. It
stirs up irreversible conflicts. To take a single example: ever
since the Middle Ages Druzes and Maronite Christians had
lived peacefully together in the Middle East. They disagreed
about everything, but through daily contact and habitual ac-
quaintance they had come to a satisfying *modus vivendi*. And
then politics thrust itself onto the scene in the 1800s. English
foreign policy competed with and tried to stymie French foreign policy. The Russians and the Austrians stuck their noses
in. Each country intervened, it said, to protect some local
community—which was doing very well without their help.
Once politics took charge of relations between the two
groups, their rapport was shattered. For the first time Druzes
massacred Maronites, and the latter replied in kind. And this
has been going on continually now since 1840. All this horrible violence was the immediate result of mixing politics and
human relations.

I could cite other examples. When people have dealings
with individuals of a different color or race, when they meet
with strange customs, with curious ways of dressing and acting, it doesn't necessarily prevent mutual understanding.
People are quite capable of respecting one another. But as
soon as politics seizes on physical or cultural differences, then
these become grounds for exclusion, and racism is born. Racism is always stirred up by politics, making use of natural
feelings of antagonism—which were never an absolute bar to
coexistence, despite occasional clashes. Thus politics makes
differences murderous, conflicts irreversible, disagreements
irreparable. This is true diabolical discord.

But a distinction has to be made here. I have never favored
any sort of conformism or rigid unification or endless cloning
of a single human or social type. I have always fought for
pluralism and against mass production. I have always said
that dialog is inevitably rooted in differences. So when I ac-

cuse politics of being diabolical, it's *not* in the name of unity. The division fostered by the devil is the sort that has no basis in reality, that leads people to reject pluralism and coexistence, to refuse to acknowledge others, not to respect varying opinions, the crazy-quilt of human relations, of multiple and divergent interests. And if you tell me that concern for all these things is precisely what defines liberal politics, I shall send you back to consult the record of liberalism, and you will see that it's been just as divisive as other forms of politics.

Second, my objections to politics don't concern either philosophy or theology; that is, I don't claim to be describing politics per se, politics as an unchanging, eternal, metaphysical essence. I'm talking, as always, about here and now, the present situation, about politics over the last three hundred years, about Western politics—which has, however, invaded and conquered the world so that Asian and African politics now fit into the Western mold. The diabolical has taken on different forms down through history, and currently the devil, the sower of discord, is politics, and politics alone. We see it diabolically corrupting the law, lying about justice, arousing false hopes (ever brighter tomorrows), driving people into a labyrinth of hostility.

That is just how the diabolical element operates: it dramatizes everything; it leads to breaches that can't be healed, to one hopeless impasse after another. And it does this by seduction, by promises, by illusions. We shouldn't forget that the principal weapon of every political system is propaganda and that propaganda is essentially a lie. In our time the father of lies speaks through propaganda, which engenders passion and false clarity, burning commitment and inner alienation. The great lie of this age is found in the celebrated phrase, "Everything is politics," or, "A people can express itself in only one way—through politics," or "If you don't take political action, you don't do anything at all." These absurd maxims show us the radical mendacity of the father of lies, who is literally and totally incarnate today in politics. Politics nowadays *is* the devil.

But it's also and at the same time Satan. In the Bible Satan and the devil are not identical (nor is either the same as Lucifer, who doesn't appear until long after the closing of the biblical canon). The devil is the one who sows discord through seduction. Satan is the accuser, the one who stands before God in continual accusation, accusing people, but God as well. And wherever accusation occurs, even when it's well founded, legitimate, and judicious, Satan is at work; Satan himself is there.

The point of contact between Satan and the devil is obviously that both of them, though they follow different paths, are the negation of love and communion, the negation, destruction, and corruption of love. Where in our time do we hear the great accusations that condemn certain persons or groups as absolutely evil? What plays the role of world prosecutor, bringing charges against a whole class or nation or race? The answer can only be politics. We have seen that in the realm of the diabolical there is some sort of correlation between politics and economics, but not here. The satanic is the pure distilled essence of the political. Gone is any reason or balance, any human consideration at all which might serve as a mitigating force. The Other is accused of all the evil that occurs; he or she is reduced to the level of absolute evil, with the certitude that if only we can eliminate that person, we shall finally see true purification and liberation.

Accusations are leveled at the communist or the bourgeois or the black or the colonialist or the capitalist or the Nazi or the Jew. How many times have I read the words (which seem to have been written in a trance), "Capitalism is absolute evil"? The writer is a Christian, as it happens. But the phrase might just as well have been, "Communism is absolute evil." This accusation leaves no room for pardon, for leniency, for conversion. Once you have been a communist, you can't change; you remain crushed beneath the weight of the satanic accusation. The enemy, by definition, has nothing good or admirable about them; the only remedy is to wipe them out completely. This is the only solution, and it was invented by politics.

No doubt some readers are already objecting, "But aren't you really talking about religion?" One thinks of the Inquisition, the interdicts and excommunications, the forced conversions. My answer on this point is direct: yes indeed, religion has become satanic, every time it has fallen into the grip of politics. The dreadful part of the Inquisition was not the church's doing, but the crimes perpetrated on behalf of and often by the state. The extermination of the Cathars was much more the work of the king who used the church than the work of the church itself. The Inquisition did not resort to extreme measures until it came under the control of the king of Portugal, the king of Spain, and the republic of Venice. Excommunication was nothing more than a *remedium animi* (healing of the soul) until it became a political tool. And who was responsible for the forced conversions? Who used violence to convert the Saxons? Charlemagne. Who used violence to convert the New World Indians? The conquistadors. (Some of the Christian missionaries who came later refused to be the servants of the political order and defended the lives and customs of the Indians.) The spirit of accusation, of blanketing good by calling something an evil that must be extirpated is always the result of politics.

The worst accusations of our time have always come from politicians, they have been based on political motives, and they have always ended in death in the political arena. Arthur Koestler makes this brilliantly clear in *Le Zéro et l'Infini*

(*Darkness at Noon*). And just as politics tries to pass itself off as the whole of reality, dethroning God in the process, conversely politics raises accusation to the status of an absolute, thereby counterfeiting—that is, utterly falsifying—divine justice. So it is no facile literary image but a far-reaching insight into the nature of politics to call it satanic, to view it as Satan's handiwork, implanted by Satan in human hearts.

Once again, this evil growth is grafted onto spontaneous human feelings, namely the desire to justify oneself and to expel one's enemy so as to achieve self-purification or catharsis. People always need to feel just, and up till now it has been the task of religion to provide people with the means of self-purification, sacrifice among others. The great classical religions have disappeared, however, or have lost their power through lack of faith. But people's religious needs are as intense as ever, especially their need to lead a pure and righteous existence in their own eyes and those of others. And the only way now available to them to achieve this goal is through accusation, through the political discovery and designation of a scapegoat.

Here all evil is concentrated into the others, the ones who are unlike us, and all that evil will be driven out when the others are driven out or, still better, destroyed. The adversary becomes the enemy, and the enemy becomes the absolute incarnation of evil. Only by annihilating them can we be assured not of a simple political victory but of paradise, justice, and freedom. When we ourselves have been incorporated into the assembly of the just, we cannot help sharing in their justice.

So everything is based on accusation, that is, on the work of Satan. It's not simply a matter of political structures or organizations, and we shall have to press beyond them. First, though, we ought to specify that the devil or Satan is not, of course, a historical character, a figure situated in a given

place, a personified will with a certain objective. I'm saying
that from the biblical point of view every time an accusation
or a break in human ties occurs, something more than a simple sociological or psychological phenomenon is taking place,
something inexplicable by and irreducible to sociopsychologi-
cal factors. There is a spiritual dimension of God's domain, a
dimension that goes beyond the human, an unanalyzable
power that makes the whole thing so terrifying. This is what
we mean by the terms Satan or the devil. In the world that we
currently find ourselves on, politics is the incarnation of the
biblical Satan.

Politics today is indeed the realm of the demonic.[50] It is the
realm of total illusion in our society.[51] Politics is the art of
multiplying false problems, of setting up false goals, and of
starting false debates, false with reference to the concrete life
of concrete people, false with reference to the actual
socioeconomic trends that politics never touches.

Having created this false orientation, politics mobilizes
everyone's energies, it involves all of society in spreading
falsehood. Everything is constantly being risked on false
problems that politics has suggested and elaborated as the
only true ones—and then finally imposed them as such. This
illusory element has to be combined with the mechanism of
political mediation.

Politics becomes the necessary universal mediator between
the individual and society. Politics offers the only possible
way to act upon society as a whole. It is invested with an a
priori legitimacy marking it as supreme in the public sphere.
It establishes a corps of officially approved mediators.
Through this political mediation everything that happens is

50. Jacques Ellul, "La Politique, lieu du démoniaque," *Archivio di Filosofia*, 1978.
51. Jacques Ellul, *The Political Illusion*, 1967.

translated into the language of politics, thereby supposedly becoming rationally comprehensible.

The final stage of political mediation is reached when the particular will is interchanged with the general will, the common good, and so on. This process of mediation pervades every aspect of our lives, ultimately prevailing upon everyone to accept it as the sum total of human life. Here once again is the demonic feature of politics: it substitutes the means for the truth; mediation replaces everything else. In the end, as everybody knows, the modern state claims to be our savior. We have already made the transition to the state-as-Providence, but now we've gone beyond that to the state as dispenser of salvation. What is actually a lie proclaims its salvific mission—such is the power of evil to disintegrate reality.

If we combine the total illusoriness of politics with its enforced mediation, we get on the one hand organized unreality and on the other the antimediation of the whole social order. Thus strictly speaking it is not the mediating function of politics that attests to its demonic nature but, first, its seizure and monopolization of the mediation process, which is then made a party to illusoriness, which leaves us with a mediation between nothing and nothing, between a lie and an illusion, absorbing all the human energies of all the people in that society. There we have one specifically demonic quality of politics, but the others are demonic too.

Besides this the demon is the one who takes possession of the interior person, who makes good on promises to accomplish what is supposedly God's will, and who, owing to his promises and their "obvious" fulfillment, takes the place of God. The demon is in all things the reverse imitation of the divine. Here we must turn to Castelli's *The Demonic in Art:* "Communion that pays no heed to Christ means believing in a kind of self-importance that only the demonic could inspire." "Unlimited, undefined horror: the feeling caused by something whose nature has been definitively perverted." "The façade of a face—this is an allegorical anticipation of the dehumanized masses, a prelude to the concept of everyone in general, that is to say, nobody." "The power of disintegration."[52] These excerpts from Castelli spell out the character of the demonic. They point out features of the demonic, all of which we have clearly seen in our experience of politics: lies and illusion, the creation of a wholly falsified universe, conspicuous evidence of a promise to accomplish people's will, the feeling of perversion, the façade of a face. . . . We could go on in this vein.

Finally, politics has an irresistible force of absorption and assimilation. The French anarcho-syndicalists active around the beginning of this century were completely right when they argued that politics inevitably corrupts—in itself and by itself—all our intentions and all our projects. They were right when they affirmed that the socialists, once they began to engage in politics, may have continued to speak from a social-ist point of view, but their praxis was antisocialist, and that likewise the revolutionaries inescapably stopped being revolu-tionary when they got into politics. These assertions were later borne out by subsequent history: Millerand, Aristide Briand, Paul-Boncour, Clemenceau, all serious, committed socialists and revolutionaries, turned out to be, once they got to power, exactly the opposite of what they had promised. In the same way Christian leaders are caught in the tragic dilem-ma: either they try to remain Christians and their politics will be stupid (Jimmy Carter), or they'll be effective politicians but no longer Christians. Rocard is correct to insist on the essential incompatibility of these two options.

Our choice of the term demonic was not, therefore, artifi-

---

52. E. Castelli, *Le Démoniaque dans l'art*, 1975.

cial or gratuitous or an attempt to dramatize the issue. Our point was not to show the difference between the theory or the ideal and practice, nor simply to acknowledge the necessities of political reality. Beyond that, there is a certain structure of the demonic that accounts for certain real phenomena whose existence and importance can never be explained in any naturalistic-positivistic fashion. (Marx had a presentiment of this when he mythicized the proletariat and the class struggle.) The surface of politics has another dimension stretching into the depths beneath it. This is a fact. The question is, how can we go along with it?

I have observed that the structure of contemporary politics corresponds point for point with the structure of the demonic. But couldn't we in turn extend and banalize this correspondence—couldn't we also say with equal justification: the economy is demonic, money is demonic, science and technology are demonic, and so on? I have done quite a few studies on technology, but I've always been careful not to say that it was demonic or diabolical. The reason is that I want, as far as possible, to keep my use of words relatively precise. If the demonic answers to the Bible's description of it (and I think it does), as explained by Castelli and others, and if we don't take the word too loosely as signifying everything unpleasant, unjust, or evil, then we can't apply it nowadays to any areas of life apart from politics, since none of them actually fills the bill. Science *as science* does not produce lies and falsification. The economy is not "the undefined horror: the feeling caused by something whose nature has been definitively perverted." By contrast, I would say that money certainly *was* the demonic force par excellence in the nineteenth century, as Marx has shown to perfection. But nowadays money has been denounced, exposed, and labelled as demonic so often and so eloquently that it no longer qualifies. When the father of lies is exposed, he disappears. He ceases to exercise his power in the place he had chosen. He moves into different realms and makes use of new mirrors. We have passed from the demonic reign of money to the demonic reign of politics. We have made a great deal of progress—in self-torture.

22

More Questions

At this stage of my reflections I am inevitably led to ask myself, what am I doing? Am I reacting this way to modern politics simply because I'm getting old and can't keep up? Because I can no longer understand what's going on? Because in any of my undertakings, however slight, that were potentially political, I always came to grief? I have struggled, but for what? The world has sped along in all its power and glory, without swerving an inch from the route one might have predicted it would take. Am I driven to speak out by my failure and disappointment, by nostalgia for the past?

I find it tedious and discouraging (the only thing, in fact, that *does* discourage me!) to have to keep saying that I am in no sense a *laudator temporis acti*. I am as familiar as anyone with the nightmare of the Middle Ages. I have no desire to return either to France's "great" seventeenth century or to the "stupid" nineteenth century. But these days it's not people of my age who are killing themselves, taking drugs, and rejecting the world. I feel impelled to speak out not because of the past that now lies in ruins but on account of today's young people. They talk of their disgust for life; they say they absolutely can't bear the world as it is; they turn away from politics; they sense more far immediately than others the power of nothingness, the fascination of destruction, because it seems that this is their only future.

What constrains me to speak out is simply my anxiety over leaving an unlivable world behind me. That and remorse for not having known how to do whatever was necessary to give our children a time worthy to be lived in. I repent of having been one of those adults who have, in the final analysis, driven today's youth into becoming what they are. But have I accused others in these pages? I should not like my remarks to be construed as an accusation, otherwise I would be playing Satan's game. I don't accuse anyone in any of my books. When I speak of modern people, I'm speaking, in the first instance, about myself. I do not condemn politicians, deplorable as they are. The most I can say of them is that they don't know what they're doing. The only one I'm calling into question is myself; the only one I've put on trial is myself.

I acknowledge my responsibility for failing to alter in the least the unfolding of that quasi-destiny we saw coming but could do nothing to combat. This book, then, is both a cry of lamentation and an appeal. The things we didn't want have happened after all; the things we hoped and longed for did not. Looking toward the future now I can only issue a warning, try to draw a lesson that might perhaps help others, might give them fresh courage, might make them realize the truth. It's a very fragile hope, but a tenacious and tireless one. It's not just the old message in a bottle—we have seen so many bottles washing up to shore, most of them empty. This is a declaration of the will to break with the status quo and go off in a different direction, but such a change of course can no longer be fueled simply by a burst of our own energy.

For our present confusion is not primarily the result of running headlong into the evil of certain facts, structures, institutions, or even the system itself. The problem arises from a lack of reaction, from the terrible submission of the new generation to a kind of fate that strikes them as completely ineluctable. But I argue that precisely because *we* have failed, *we* know the enemy better. We are trying to surround him, to point him out to you, the new generation, to teach you his forces and his limitations, his appearance and reality. We want to show you his tricks, the first of which is to make you believe in progress and politics. As long as you continue down that road, you are guaranteed to get bogged down in it. You must invent new forms of action, a whole antipolitics. Nothing is ineluctable—until the moment when you stretch out your neck so that they can either place the yoke of slavery on it or cut your jugular. Refuse to submit, but be sure you know whom you're rebelling against.

I'm dismayed by the weakness of the calls to revolt and the uncertainty of the paths they point out to us. The rebels are all correct, when they talk about conviviality (invoking Illich) or wisdom (Friedmann) or graciousness (Jouvenal) or prospective morality (Fourastié) or hope and the individual (in some of my own writings) or the value of smallness (Schumacher) or moderation and respect (de Rougemont). They're all quite right, and Garaudy too, all of us are, when we talk about freedom.

But you can find almost exactly the same ideas when you look back old issues of *Esprit* or *Ordre nouveau,* to the kinds of things Dandieu and Bernanos were saying in the 1930s. It's all true, but there's a lack of incentive, of motivation, of reasons for going in that direction and paying the price that it will cost. And there can be no doubt that the price will be high, that we shall have to labor mightily to reverse the current. We shall have to abandon our privileges, our special advantages, our carelessness, and engage in untrammeled self-criticism. That way we can rediscover the taste for risk taking for something besides money and comfort, rediscover the fierce demands of truth—at the price of ascesis.

What we really need is a sort of cosmic lever to change everything, and in our time the only lever is faith—faith in the God of Abraham, Isaac, and Jesus Christ. The God who is at once the Transcendent and the one who agrees to come to us and to join the game of earthly life in response to our prayers. But this does not contradict what we said before about faith for nothing. That still holds. As soon as we *make use* of faith in this God or set ourselves to believing in order to "solve our problems," to save humanity, to get the strength to carry on, to ensure the world's survival, as soon as faith is not simply itself, "for God's sake," but an instrument to reach some other goal, then it's just one more illusion, and the God it speaks to is no longer there. He becomes a shadow, and heaven is empty again.

23

Faith and the Exodus

"Yet forty days . . . " said Jonah. And when they heard him, the Ninevites repented. But I am no Jonah.

Jesus too refers to Jonah: "And then some of the scribes and Pharisees said to him, 'Teacher, we wish to see a sign from you.' But he answered them, 'An evil and adulterous generation seeks for a sign; but no sign shall be given to it except the sign of the prophet Jonah. . . . The men of Nineveh will arise at the judgment with this generation and condemn it; for they repented at the preaching of Jonah, and behold, something greater than Jonah is here.'" That's the only answer we receive when we ask to be shown a miracle. And yet, given the enormity of the disasters that have been unleashed upon the men and women of our time, in the face of mounting dangers that burst open to reveal even greater disasters, our common reaction is that we have to have a miracle. It doesn't matter whether we are atheists or believers. "I believe in miracles," said Paul Reynaud, "because I believe in France," a remark that ought to be preserved if only because of its stupidity. But he was desperate and that apparently makes up for everything. We have to have a miracle, but the miracle doesn't come, and it won't ever come.

Then as we confront this incommensurable solitude we go through a double reaction, one that every person in our world, without exception, can attest to: we deny God or we turn to belief. Since God lets the horrors we see come raining down upon us, since he causes or permits or doesn't prevent them, since he doesn't rule over them or, should I say, rules so badly, since he doesn't intervene and produce the miracle that we're waiting for, the sort of miracle we have in mind, then he doesn't exist. He deserves not to exist; he ought to be annihilated. Or rather, since the danger is so great, we must plunge into the unconscious depths of belief, turn away from this world and look to the next, pay no more attention to what's going on here and contemplate the heavens, even if they be empty, and bury ourselves in religious practices. We must believe, believe, believe; we must seek refuge in the Noah's ark of belief, sealed tight in the heart of the raging Flood. We don't want to understand or foresee or know anything; we only want the miracle that God can do. He has to perform a miracle, as long as we are pious enough, virtuous enough, religious enough. He owes it to us. This is the impetus behind the religious revival of the past few years. But both these attitudes are unacceptable to God.

All the overlapping elements of our world have created a tightly unified ensemble, such that any impulse striking any portion of it increases the danger of ultimate destruction, because the whole thing is leading us toward death, individual and collective. Can we resign ourselves to this death? Could anyone actually face it with the wisdom of Job, "The Lord gave, the Lord has taken away" (Job 1:21)? But that wisdom was false, as the rest of the book shows. And the true lesson of Job is not stoicism. Nowadays we would translate his words this way: "Chance and necessity have produced the solar system, life, and humankind, and all that will be destroyed by necessity and chance." But this too is false. No conscious human being can say the universe has no importance. And it's a lie when intellectuals come along with their false arrogance, their Parisian-Phariseean detachment, to announce: "The human race? It simply has to disappear; let's not make such a fuss about it."

But people *do* make a fuss about it, and with reason. That is how they made history from the raw materials of chance and necessity. Everything leads us on to death, and the collective presence of death leads us to reject God, to deny him, or to take refuge in beliefs that are nothing but a consolation for our final hour, summoning God to do a miracle for our convenience. But that God we reject is not God, and YHWH has never given in to blackmail. "An evil and adulterous generation asks for a sign; but no sign shall be given to it except the sign of the prophet Jonah. . . ."

Faith stands up against both the denial of God and self-serving belief. We must relearn what faith is all about, that is to say, steady confidence with no ulterior motives, trust in the one who speaks the word, who alone can say, "I am," who awaits an authentic relationship. And once again we must not foolishly nod our heads and repeat, "Oh yes, faith can move mountains." Faith in itself is nothing and can do nothing. If it can move mountains, that's because—and only because—Jesus Christ, the Messiah, Son of God, Son of man, said so and thereby made it so.

Faith has power only because in one sense it urges us on to the task at hand, in another it stands still and witnesses to the transcendent reality of the One who alone is. These two aspects are fused together in faith. Faith in that God implies action, and action implies the presence of God. Faith is not a place of refuge for passive souls; it implies the will to change the world. But it knows that all the action, all the politics, all the human devices of whatever kind are nothing without God. It does not demand miracles from God. It commits itself

completely to the work life bids it do, but only insofar as the
Lord of the Living *is*.

Faith lives at the cost of doubt, because it brings us to act,
to fight, to want victory for humankind, to go beyond doubt
for the sake of the Unique, the Living one, who has revealed
himself in Jesus Christ. Faith is obliged to pass through
doubt, to keep on passing through it to measure the truth of
its undertakings. It exists at the cost of belief, because it
brings us to a state of trust that lies outside of rituals, tradi-
tions, sacrifices, or spiritual transports. It has to measure itself incessantly against spontaneous human belief, in order to
gauge its own authenticity. Faith is dead if it claims to seek
asylum in the lap of a God who is not God.

It is not enough to believe in God. It is not enough to know
him, for "even the demons believe—and shudder" (James
2:19). We must not look for an explosive outpouring of the
Holy Spirit. We have to act with a lucidity that is, humanly
speaking, desperate, but filled with hope, as if God did not
exist, as if everything depended on us. We have to be inven-
tive; faith must express itself in works, in building paths to
salvation, in the structures of a new society, in responses to
the insane perils of our time.

We shall see what faith can accomplish. Seeing a miracle
the crowd "glorified God, who had given such authority to
men" (Matt. 9:8). We really do have such power. So why not
use it for salvation since we have so far proved only our ability to pile up unimaginable powers of destruction? But we
must not separate two things that should always remain strictly *unified*. That is, the selfsame works of salvation, if performed without God, don't exist at all. They produce exactly
the opposite of what we expected, as the cumulative experience of humanity's last two hundred years has shown us.

We can find the most ideal form of politics and the purest
science. We can be full of loving kindness; we can pardon our

enemies, organize justice, formulate a common body of truth, refrain from oppressing the weak, and spread happiness over the earth. But if all that is done without God (I don't mean without belief, but without the constant presence and hidden working of God), then it has no value whatsoever. At the heart of such works, even the best of them, lies coiled the serpent of human perversion and degradation. Thus, do everything as if there were no God; but realize that if there is no God, nothing has been done.

Such is the ambiguity of faith, based as it is on repentance and trust. We have to start by repenting. If some people find this religious term offensive, so much the worse—or so much the better. Repentance serves to dispel the jokers, the legalists, the complacent rationalists. I am no Jonah, but I cry out here and now, amidst a danger that threatens not just a city but the entire world. "Yet forty days, repent."

To repent is to change one's course, even more to completely reverse the course one was following up to that moment. And it is to do so not out of fear or morality or doubt (if something doesn't do any good, it doesn't do any harm) or devotion, but because with the catastrophe imminent God has drawn near. It's not "Take the right road, make the right choice so you can continue in the same snug old round," but change your life completely, change your society, your vision of the future because the Kingdom of God is near. The days of wrath are coming (but it's enough for God to let human wrath do the job); the axe is laid to the root of the world (we have the power to disintegrate everything). There is no security of any kind anymore—either religious, intellectual, or political. The Kingdom of God is coming. Now we see the point: because It is coming, because the Ultimate Reality is near, bring forth fruits worthy of repentance.

We must bow our heads and acknowledge that we have basically been deluded—all of us, rich Europeans and poor

Africans, nationalists and antinationalists, virtuous colonizers and virtuous anticolonizers, the gluttons and the starving, exploiters and exploited, liberals and conservatives, technologists and ecologists, believers and skeptics, all of us have been equally deluded because we played our game without the presence of the Ultimate; in building our world we excluded the possibility of an initiative from God—from the God who began it all and who can always lay the foundations for a new beginning, because he alone is new.

We have to pass through the extremely narrow gate of repentance, the eye of the needle. And this brings with it a whole series of consequences: to enter by this door we have to leave behind everything that encumbers and accompanies us, both our works and our wealth, our convictions and our certainties, as well as our uncertainties and our doubts (a sort of enormous hoop skirt wrapped around us!), our science and our law, our friendships and our hatreds.

Entering by that gate I find there is just enough room for my body, with no space to spare. Everything else remains on this side of the threshold and once I have crossed it, I stand there unbelievably naked, with no protection, without even the obolus to hand to Charon the ferryman. But if that's how it is, the point is not to wait for Judgment to shatter the heavens. If that's the way it is, cries John the Baptist, "Bear fruit that befits repentance" (Matt. 3:8). Get to work right away. Pay no attention to your nakedness, your weakness, your destitution. When you have become weak and naked and powerless on account of your repentance, then you can begin to bring forth works that make sense and give life.

Don't mourn for what you have left behind; don't cast longing eyes at the wherewithal that once let you have a TV, car, refrigerator, satellites and neutron bombs (to ensure your safety) and microprocessors (to make you feel intelligent); don't look back at all that. Lay the groundwork for a new beginning, for your life; for life itself choose the moment that marks a split in the fabric of time. The moment for breaking away, the *kairos* (meaningful time) has come, and it's first and foremost the moment of repentance. Of course, it has no significance in itself, but it's a recognition that the Totally Other is, is here and now. Armed with this faith, go beyond repentance; open up your new path, trace it out; begin the tasks that must be done.

We shall see that faith, in bringing forth the works of repentance, gives a point-by-point answer to our excesses and our misery. Let's have no misunderstandings here: I don't mean to try to convert you after the manner of the familiar worldly sermon, "You are all sinners and evil, you're going to hell. Convert and you'll be saved, and everything will be fine." I'm saying nothing of the sort. I don't practice that mediocre form of blackmail; I don't promise you heaven. There's no need to, since grace gives it to us above and beyond anything we could do on our own. I don't promise you the earth, since the prince of this world has it at his disposal until the Kingdom of God appears.

But amidst all the afflictions of humanity, I point out a path for you that doesn't enable you to escape your own wretchedness but lets you help others escape—and at that moment your personal misery will vanish in love. You will see for yourself and at that instant you will believe, with authentic faith, which can arise only from the encounter between the Word and experience. Once again, let there be no misunderstanding: if you repent for the sake of some result, you fall into the trap of all religions. I repeat, faith is *for nothing*. If you convert in order to flee the catastrophe that is upon us, the only thing you are going to hear is, "You brood of vipers! Who warned you to flee from the wrath to come?" (Matt. 3:7). But conversion and repentance now open up before you. We must begin.

Here we are locked in the combat of faith. We must travel
backward on the road we've taken so far. We have wound up
with those manifold answers wished for by everyone·nowa-
days who sees with any lucidity the categorical imperative
facing humanity. As in all other things faith takes us along
the same trajectory, but by going from the greatest profundi-
ty to the greatest clarity. Faith listens to the cry of "Repent,"
which indeed serves to characterize it. But we have to view
the subject in the round. I'm not saying that there is an entity
called faith, that there is a person of faith, and that at a given
moment this person listens to the word—just one of the many
varied sounds and words—calling for repentance. The truth
is that faith comes into being when someone heeds that word,
on condition that some passerby hears that "Repent!" and
takes it to heart.

This mode of listening immediately leads to the double attitude, the double orientation, the double lived truth that constitutes faith: that is, trust in the one who proclaims "Repent!" (but he at once redirects that trust to one who is
greater, to the one who comes after him, who alone is worthy
of absolute trust—and it's not for nothing that there should
be a John the Baptist before Jesus: he helps to bring faith to
birth among his listeners, who will turn toward Jesus) and at
the same time the beginning of a decisive change in one's life,
in one's activity, in one's very being. This is the reverse side
of repentance, which makes a person full of defiance and indifference into a person of trust and commitment.

Faith is this double movement. It is born through the acceptance of the call to repent. And, once again, it welcomes
that call without any calculations, tactics, or pretentions,
without ideology, self-satisfaction, self-absorption, psychological or sociological angles. Faith is simply the welcome of
the one who says "Here I am." And taking that as our starting point, we can be on our way. We moderns have an imper-

ative obligation to discover every aspect of the goal toward which the ethical visions of the future, with their wisdom, temperance, conviviality, and so on, are converging.

We asked: "How could this be done? For such a revolutionary overturn of everything inculcated in people today by propaganda and advertising, by the productions and demands of 'modern life,' by ideologies and statistics, technical miracles and opportunities for happiness, how can we get to that value that radically reverses future expectations and that, when it does, will bring on political and economic catastrophes, as well as tremendous social upheavals?" What's needed is a more profound level of motivation. And I maintain that such a motivation can be found in faith in the God of Abraham and of Jesus Christ—and nowhere else.

Faith makes the turnaround possible, because it stops turning and makes people stop turning in the same identical circle, the circle of human contemplation, human success and power. It smashes that circle by the irruption of something that is resolutely foreign to it, the Transcendent. We have tried to show that if there is no transcendent reality, there is nothing but destiny, which in our case has taken on the form of techno-politics. We are completely imprisoned by it, and completely conditioned as well.

But it is not enough that there should be a transcendent reality, if it's also inaccessible, outside, blind, and indifferent. If the circle is to be shattered, we must have a relationship to this transcendent. And the only possible relationship is faith, because it listens to that word coming from elsewhere and addresses a word to that Totally Other, because it leans on that Being whom it is slowly coming to know, because it takes its origin from him and orients us to him. It makes possible a turnaround in the conditions of existence obtaining in this world; it impregnates society with new values and a new understanding of life, which arise neither from nature

nor human intelligence nor people's inner spirituality, but
from a relationship with him who makes all things (every one
of them) new, that is, establishes a new commandment.

On the basis of that faith (and not just any faith whatsoever) we can set out from the center (conviction, spiritual
vision, ethics, thought) and move toward the periphery (action, politics, economic life). I know that all this will be treated as outdated, reactionary, and simplistic. I too have read all
the big names. And I reply to these authors, yes, Christendom has been a failure, and so have idealism and scientific
technology. Socialism or communism has been the most re-
sounding failure of our time, and the failure of psychoanalysis
is becoming more apparent every day. The deepest thoughts
of our leading intellectuals in structuralism, linguistics, semi-
otics, and the various epistemologies are scarcely worth men-
tioning, so derisory do they appear in the face of the real
monstrosities now assailing humanity.

Very well then, given the fact that we are hemmed in by
repeated failures, why not begin with the beginning? People
need a motivation strong enough so that they can build
healthy relations between themselves and others, so that together we can confront the world and the unleashed forces
that have to be mastered. There is a way to do this, but I
think we're running short of time. Each one of us must be
converted: that will determine whether there is any chance
for the emergence of kindness, renunciation, a new respect
for the world and other people. Nothing less than that will
do.

And this points the way to our next step: the struggle
against the demons, the devil. By its very nature the revelation of Jesus Christ involves us in that struggle. We can
throw ourselves into it; we can begin to track down the rifts
and accusations, the denunciations and visions (between persons, groups, institutions). We can take off the masks and lay

bare the unadorned reality in its rather considerable horror without trying to justify it. We can explode the rationalizations, and by destroying the anonymous "everybody" bring each individual to light. We can restore meaning, give some free play to the pieces of the puzzle now welded together. We can turn such open spaces to good account and melt the ice floe, renewing the nature of denatured humanity. We can get behind the façade of the face and shatter its illusoriness.

If we fail to accomplish the whole thing in our society as a whole, then there will be no more real possibilities, either social, political, or economic, only the whims of fate. What we must do is eradicate the consequences of the presence of the diabolos, the daimones, the demons of our time. Faith can undertake this enormous task because we set out "as conquerors and to conquer." We set out with the victorious certainty that Jesus Christ has already won the victory. God in Christ has overcome the powers ranged against us. That is to say, we have to exploit this victory won in eternity and make it present in history.

Once again God will not do for us what we can do by ourselves. Notice how inconsistent we Christians are: we pray every day, "Thy will be done on earth as it is in heaven." But this means, Thy will is done in heaven (which is God's "space"), and hence *we* can do that same will on earth. In the same way, precisely because the demons are stripped of their power in eternity, we too can win the victory in time. But we've got to get going; we've got to do it. I realize that you'll say, "Why haven't Christians ever done it before?" This is not quite true—there have been periods that came very close to accomplishing it. But even if we never really quite made it before what prevents us from making a start? In our urgent situation with disaster looming over us, let's stop ruminating over what may or may not have been. Walk right out on the water; try it once again.

But are all those powers the same ones that we claimed occupy the political realm, that are the sum of contemporary politics? In that case we seem to be headed toward a rejection of politics pure and simple, toward a rupture between the spiritual and political spheres. Our message then would be rather short—and perfectly useless. We do indeed have to take an antipolitical stance these days, but that in no way means to "stay out of politics" and still less that "religion and politics don't mix." The tremendous errors of Christian Marxists, Christian Hitlerians, Christian radicals, Christian royalists, and so on, and the traditional Protestant leftists— the errors of all these types must be condemned because they fundamentally distort the possibilities of faith. But this means that we have to relocate politics on another plane; we have to uncover (something no one else wants to see or think about) the truly basic problems of our society, so that we can cut into them with the surgeon's knife. In other words, we must join the political battle elsewhere, at a deeper level, and with means other than parties, unions, collectives, elections, terrorism, pseudo-revolutions, solidarity with the "poor" (provided their ideas are correct), and pseudo-conscientization. All that is a deviation from Christianity and stays firmly within the framework and methodology of politics.

Faith demands that we create new ends while constantly criticizing the means. But the point here is not to address for the nth time the question of "Christianity and politics." The question is rather the driving of the demons out of politics and restoring it to its human dimensions. And we should not set our minds at rest by arguing that this is a matter of secularization or laicization: the people *least* capable of making politics human again are those humanists now drowned in the flood tide of forces that they are powerless to control, because they don't even see them and think they are still high and dry on the terra firma of rationality.

Faith alone has the power to exorcise the demons. But Christians must also make a firm, specific commitment to this task, rather than search for ways to mingle with the great mass of society or to plunge into some disembodied spiritualism or to fashion some lifeless ecumenism or to be reliable political partners within the system. But what are we to do then? You know perfectly well, it's nothing unexpected—it's known but neither lived nor applied where it ought to be: reconciliation, forgiveness as the prevailing standard in all things, a persevering love of the enemy, the rediscovery of a superreality that transcends reality and gives it meaning, the deliberate choice of powerlessness under all circumstances, the passion for freedom (not to be translated as individualism or nihilism or liberalism), the individual treated as the center and core of all social life, an individual no longer demanding his or her rights, but voluntarily stepping out of the "more and more" syndrome, the decentralization of power and decision making, the search for a qualitative norm that excludes the quantitative (for the claim that the two can be harmonized is false).

There's nothing original in this stage of the program—yet it's here that the battle will be fought. This conflict will be harsh and terrible, and only faith in Jesus Christ will enable us to wage it, because it will be against the powers and dominions—if we are willing to take the responsibility upon ourselves, we, along with the others, and the church. Nothing gets done all by itself or by the solitary worker; even the nucleus of all action is the unique individual not bound by destiny but included in the Kingdom.

Let's go back still further. When we do we meet with fear, violence, forgetfulness, and the absence of a future. We have to rebuild the whole structure, but we have to start with the foundations, not the roof. And the foundations have to be laid stone by stone. When you try to make modifications in the institutional order, in political parties, constitutions, economic arrangements, or health services, you are working on the roof. A roof supported by nothing, because there are no more people beneath it. When you campaign for public welfare or a sane birth rate, what does that mean without human beings? When you insist on human rights and women's rights and the workers' rights, what does it mean without human beings?

Everything is reduced to the level of suffering animals, of passionate machines, of the interplay of stimuli and reflexes, but what's the sense of such animated thingamajigs wanting to have a revolution? We must radically refuse now to affirm our "rights." In this context "rights" run clean contrary to the gospel of grace. We need a politics of gratuitousness, which alone can overcome violence and fear. So stop proclaiming the value of your personal welfare and the common good. That abominable fraud is never anything more than greed, cupidity, and individual egoism, made seemingly legitimate by the qualifier, "common," which simply means "stronger" or "dominant." We have to tear off the masks, but only someone with purity of heart can do this, and such purity comes only through the gift of grace. The violence and fear that go hand in hand will not be overcome except by the knowledge that God is with each one of us, that God is the one who protects and accompanies us, not like an insurance company but like a traveler's friend who looks after one and calls in others for help when necessary. But those others have to have their ears open and hear the call and be ready to help the one in trouble.

At each stage of the rebuilding process there are extremely concrete social, political, and economic changes that correspond to the spiritual facts of the matter. I am not dreaming; I am beginning in the only way possible in these distressful times. And if I am asked *what* must be done, I answer unequivocally: invent, imagine, discover something. Faith lays a new foundation of a new beginning, and as long as we haven't, each one of us, made that start, this can mean only one thing, that we are not living in faith. *That* is the criterion.

In the third stage, face to face with oblivion and the absence of a future, we have the specific movement of faith, which is a nonstop shuttling back and forth from remembrance to prophecy (and from prophecy to "Remember, Israel"), from anamnesis to apocalypse (and from apocalypse to the total illumination of the past). In the Bible faith is constantly shown to be this sort of movement. It tells us to *remember* the great deeds of your God, remember your deliverance from the land of Egypt, and *from that* learn what the future will be, for your God is the same, he is faithful, he is the one who will make that future. The future is not a matter of chance. Amidst all the random strokes of fate you can see the traces, like a crimson line, of the will of the same God who has shown both his creative power and his fidelity in your past. Don't forget anything, neither his words nor his revelation nor your history; keep going back to the past to find the meaning of the present. But, conversely, learn the meaning of the past by looking at what came afterward (as the classic phrase has it, the meaning of Good Friday becomes apparent on Easter). Everything always has to be viewed in a retroactive light: what happens afterward makes you understand what went before.

We shall never encounter God in the moment when that encounter takes place. It's always afterward that we can say, with astonishment: "So that strange situation, that impression, that unexplainable event was God." And such statements are never gratuitous, because God acts, however it may appear to us, in coherence and continuity. It is by understanding his past actions that we can grasp what he is doing in the present. But the reverse of this is just as indispensable:

working backward from the apocalypse, that is, from the end
of history as revealed to us in Scripture (but this end *is* the
Kingdom of God), we can read and understand the past
record of God's actions.

Anamnesis shows us the fidelity of the Lord. But the
movement of faith is unceasing, because no explanation it
offers is ever finished. We never completely grasp what God's
work was all about, any more than we can write finis to the
apocalypse. Every new situation we find ourselves in, every
event, every crisis, every conflict, every adventure in ordinary life evokes for faith a new anamnesis and a new understanding of the last times that have been laid down in the
secret of the Lord.

There must be no stopping, no concluding, no thinking
that we have finally understood the strategy and tactics of the
omnipotent God or that we have a grip on the meaning and
motive power of history. That would be the heresy that the
theologians and the churches are forever bringing back. The
past is not made up of superimposed layers of dead sedi-
ments, so that one need only bore down into it and extract a
"core" to know what its component parts are. Nor, by the
same token, is the future written in the stars or in any apocalypse. That would be a return to belief in unchanging fate.
Everything is always in motion and subject to renewal, because, to repeat, the God of Abraham and of Jesus Christ is
the God of beginnings. He is continually laying the groundwork for a new beginning, one that is collective and historical
as well as individual and for each one of us, if only we turn
toward him and our faith asks for the wiping out of the burdens crushing us (forgiveness for sin, in pious terms) and a
fresh start on new foundations (to be born again). And in
turn the final act of the apocalypse is just another new beginning.

Thus the movement of faith, when faith is not narrowly

defined as attending dreary cultural ceremonies or believing in lifeless abstract truths, is a constant struggle against the amnesia of the group we live in and against the dead weight of destiny, which in our eyes inevitably determines our future. Christians (if they *are* Christians) must be the memory of society. But it's not enough to recall what God or Christ have done: that has to be integrated into the history of all people, into their communal and collective history. The two cannot be sundered.

In other words, Christians must have an exact memory for the entire history of their group, their society, their milieu, their class. They must serve to orient the men and women who are lost, with no past or landmarks to plot their course. I don't mean that all Christians have to be historians (though they do, to a small extent!), but rather the ones who harvest, store up, and protect the results of everything their generation has attempted and experienced, so that they can teach it to generation after generation, to prevent moderns from being tossed about by every wind of doctrine.

Can others besides Christians do all this? Quite obviously they can—Christians haven't cornered the market. But in these times of trouble I see few people actually doing the job, and Christians have a powerful motive for accomplishing it. But they have to be prudent about it, because they mustn't alter the collective memory, bending and falsifying it in their insistence on bringing into it some action by God, which they can then contemplate. All they have to do is let things speak for themselves and beside that—but without sermonizing— beside that, to witness to the presence of their God. In the same way among the flock of lost sheep following the path of fate they have to recreate the certainty that they have been given the possibility of acting and of finding themselves once again master of the ship (after God, and through God's repeated gift of grace).

Christians must make everyone realize that if people do nothing, the force of circumstances will inevitably grow stronger. If people refuse the freedom offered them, they will act by means of some sociological or psychological mechanism. They will reduce themselves (and the fault will be all theirs) to slavery, alienation, objectification. One wonders if the situation today is harsher and more difficult than it ever was before. Let's just say that people are more conscious of being dogged by a concrete rather than metaphysical fate. Hence the Christian must reaffirm the possibility of creating a real future, because the *eschaton* (time of Last Things) is headed our way. The last times, the horizon against which we can recognize our freedom, have arrived. The Kingdom of heaven is in our midst, secretly, mysteriously at work. Shake off your chains (I mean the slavery of technology, of the state, of bureaucracy, positivism, money, parties, dictatorships, etc.), and you will be astonished to see that in fact they are crumbling into dust. A single man like Solzhenitsyn stands up and the whole system is on trial.

Once again the future is wide open, a future is possible. I return to my earlier question: Can people other than Christians do the job and say what has to be said? But, to repeat: I see few people actually doing it, and Christians have a powerful motive to get going. They are doubly guilty if they don't. This is the urgent task facing Christians and the churches, to reconnect people in all societies with their past, which explains where they are today, and to promise them in truth the possibility of an open-ended future. This will take great sacrifices, just as every appearance of God on the scene requires people to sacrifice their idols. Here is where the break occurs—the times when people wish they could have their old slavery back, with their ever-available gods, and so they prefer the slavery of tomorrow, submission to destiny. But faith inevitably places people before the radical choice of

God versus slavery, while it is never mistaken about the choices the Christian makes. It knows that people must be helped to recover their identity.

When faced with the rising tide of misery in our time we absolutely must acknowledge the limits of faith. We cannot by some miracle put to flight the horrors of war, starvation, torture and prison camps, unjust distribution of wealth, the arms build-up, the exploitation of the weak. Faith can do nothing directly about these catastrophes, nor, taking them as a whole, can any individual or system. There is no solution, either political, economic, or global.

But, despite everything, faith is not impotent or hollow. Even apart from the way it can inspire useful activities such as Amnesty International or the Cimade, the attempted assassination of Hitler and a whole host of other political initiatives —why not? All this is quite valuable, provided one keeps it in the proper perspective, seeing that such action is always ambiguous, relative, an emergency measure that after a certain amount of time becomes distorted and ultimately part of the process of fate. We must do such things and know when to stop: they will not block the advance of the monsters threatening us.

But faith operates at other levels. First of all it leads us to remake humanity, to fashion a people without fear, a people rooted in a true past, a free people, capable of standing up under fire because they are profoundly motivated, those, as Paul says, always beaten and never discouraged, those who are confident of the future and practice the spirit of prophecy. The material conditions can be identical to those they once lived under, but when these new people come into being, they dominate circumstances, however lethal they might be. And wherever they exist, the group they belong to benefits from it. They become, not charismatic leaders, but those who let others show what they can do.

Anyone who has lived in a tragic situation knows how much the presence of such people assures the survival of others. I'm not talking about an elite, in the sociological sense of a permanent, hereditary body, but about the sort of people who amid downfall and defeat prevent brutish excesses simply by being there. Remember that Hitler positively backed down before Martin Niemöller, that Martin Luther King, Jr., through his presence and his policy of nonviolence, achieved more than all the Black Panthers and Black Muslims combined. They were an expression of destiny; they were the incarnation of true men. It's a matter of being men like these for others. "Be men," said Isaiah and Paul—there we have what is nowadays an essential job for faith.

But we mustn't stop there. There are other tasks, located on two contradictory levels. One requirement of faith will consist in tracing the calamities that plague us back to their actual origins—past ideologies, partisan conflicts, methodologies, sociological theories and behaviors, past psychoanalysis and politics. This won't take us all the way back to the things hidden since the beginning of the world, but to those historical moments when a society goes off in the wrong direction, charging off toward derailment. Science cannot of itself bring us to that point; neither can historical precision or intelligence. We need spiritual lucidity (along with everything else) and a courage both intellectual and psychic. The shock of awareness is painful.

That is why I think faith in the Lord of history is almost indispensable. In other words, we are engaged in a kind of voluntary feedback: going back to the origin of the crisis to see if we can start off in a different direction. This implies both the conviction that there is no preestablished fate and the confidence that because God is the God of beginnings (and, as he shows all throughout the Old Testament, the God of new beginnings), we have been given, in him and by him, faith's perennial possibility of starting anew. But, in fact, I think we can hardly manage this without faith. And once we have, we are not to derive a program or grand plan from that beginning, but to intervene on a specific, point by point basis. The idea is to get the maximum result in a precisely delineated case without claiming to change the whole situation. We must act in a fragmentary, detailed fashion, all the more so since the interpretive return to the origins is more all-encompassing and productive of meaning.

We are ultimately brought to exodus and exile. Faith inevitably brings us to live out the exodus and to place ourselves in exile. Elsewhere I have spoken at length of an incognito existence, in the context of hope. Here the last word that can bear witness to faith is the one sending us back to the exodus.[53] If we are incapable of going on the exodus of repentance, the exodus from our old ways of living and thinking, then we must hear the call to the exodus that lies outside of our time and this book. This is not the exodus of death to be imposed on all of us, where faith has nothing to do because death is the triumph of destiny, nor the exodus of overwhelming defeat, where we are swept away by the tide of panic and do nothing but follow a stampeding mass of people, stricken with irrational fear. Nor is it exile. We are exiles already.

As Christians we must be completely aware of this. We are in this world, not of it. As God's faithful children, we have been exiled in what is the source of hatred of God. We don't come from this place; we aren't at home here. Our land, our world, our milieu, our professions are not our homeland. ". . . They are seeking a homeland. If they had been thinking of that land from which they had gone out, they would have had opportunity to return. But as it is, they desire a better country, that is, a heavenly one. Therefore God is not

---

53. I refer readers to Jean Sulivan's admirable book, the last one he wrote, *L'Exode*.

ashamed to be called their God" (Heb. 11:14–16). The last and most essential testimony to faith is to acknowledge that we are exiles, and that we must live on this earth as strangers and sojourners. The author of the Letter to the Hebrews ties this in closely with faith. "These all died in faith, not having received what was promised, but having seen it and greeted it from afar, and having acknowledged [by faith] that they were strangers and exiles on the earth" (Heb. 11:13).

Contrary to all the modern theologians, we do not have to settle down; we do not have to busy ourselves before all else with organizing our surroundings, our class, our political system, our economy; we do not have to become wise stewards of the goods entrusted to us. The first and last act of faith is to acknowledge that we are strangers and exiles, and that perhaps we also have to take an interest, by accident as it were, in what's happening in this temporary place called the world. But no more than that. The faithful have no choice but to be exiles. They have to recognize themselves as such, and sometimes they actually have to pull up stakes and leave. One immediately thinks of Abraham and his faith in God (our God) that makes him abandon everything and set off. Moses too leaves behind country, wife, and occupation to enter upon that incredible adventure of faith.

All those whom God summoned to faith broke with the world, which always leads us astray into beliefs. They did not withdraw to some Thebaid; their exodus was rather of a kind that led them into mortal combat with this world. Exile and exodus are the two faces of the same reality for the people of faith, who are exiled because the world hates them. "If the world hates you, know that it has hated me before it hated you" (John 15:18). As long as we are wonderfully adapted to this world, accepted by it, integrated into its activities—including the resistance movements—we are of the world and, whatever our feelings, we have nothing to do with faith.

Even as the break occurs exiles must for their part undertake the exodus. "Shake off the dust from your feet as you leave that house or town" (Matt. 10:14), says Jesus to his disciples when he sends them off to proclaim the Gospel. When that house or city or workplace or country will not receive the word of faith, leave them. Pay no more attention to them. Follow the one who is in actual fact a stranger and exile, "Foxes have holes, and birds of the air have nests; but the Son of man has nowhere to lay his head" (Matt. 8:20).

When we claim to be following him, while at the same time keeping a tight grip on our professional functions, our careers and activities, leading the normal, comfortable lives of hard-working, conscientious, efficient citizens, what does that have to do with faith? We always run into the same question, the same demand that drives us into a corner, You, come and "follow me." And Levi rises, abandons everything, his publican's cash box, his office, his pride; he doesn't even go to tell his family about it. He leaves. If you wish to fulfill the most normal religious obligations, you are told, "leave the dead to bury their own dead" (Matt. 8:22).

This is a radical exodus. "And what will become of us, Lord, who have left everything to follow you?" "What does that matter to you?" (John 21:21–22, paraphrase). Faith is gauged by this exacting demand, this sublime indifference. Let the world roll on to its catastrophic end, since it refuses to listen, you, regardless of that, follow me. But we . . . with all our fine speeches and preoccupations and political concerns and pseudo-thirst for justice (which has nothing in common with the justice of the Beatitudes) by means of politics and revolution, we have left nothing behind. We claim that we're always ready to do it, while keeping a little nest egg, some insurance, a margin of comfort, on the side.

We simply let things leave *us* behind, because we can't do

otherwise. And we shed tears of regret over the energy we had when we were young, over our vanished wealth, our lost days of happiness, instead of weeping in repentance for our failure to go out on the exodus. Faith asks to have the courage of Jesus, on the far frontier even beyond Abraham, when in the middle of his last conversation with his disciples, as he reveals to them the core of his message, while at the other end of the city the soldiers march out to arrest him, he stops and tells them, "but I do as the Father has commanded me, so that the world may know that I love the Father. Rise, let us go hence."

This is the final exodus. When Abraham arises and goes on his way, that is the exodus of the promise, the road to conquest of a new land and a whole line of descendants. When Moses arises and goes on his way, that is the exodus of freedom for the people. When Jesus at this moment arises and goes on his way, that is the exodus of the banishment of death, bearing witness that by despoiling himself and enduring the loss of all power, he has followed the commandment of faith up to the point where it seems to be negated, up to radical failure.

The hour of decision has come, and it can only come once. Faith calls upon us to leave this world, this age, and its works. If we let old age and death do the job of separating us from them, if we merely submit to our lives' fading away, to the decline of our powers and the objectification of fate, we shall have thrown away our chances. We shall have simply demonstrated that we are objects in the hands of Chronos, instead of having chosen the moment of our departure, of our break with the past, that is, instead of having given to time and our world a meaningful center, through a decision announcing that the moment has come. The *kairos*, the event is here.

History as we know it, restless, troubled, topsy-turvy, is a dismal platitude without a single event, *eventus*, a coming from outside. But, thanks to faith's decision to enter upon the exodus, we can break that restless monotony with something essentially new, as seen in the way we break off old ties. Faith calls upon us to leave behind a whole world, of social classes, people, states, with all the varieties of politics, technology, and science, *not* under the mistaken notion that they are evil, condemned, incorrigible, as if we had to save ourselves from them, like Noah when the Flood came. This is not what the exodus is about.

We must break off and leave them, so that they can hear that strange word of God which cannot be uttered except both at the center and from an infinite distance. The point is not to break off the dialog or to retire to the desert, but the word of God can be proclaimed only by someone who places himself outside "the world," while staying at the very heart of the questioning that goes on within it.

Jonah fled before God's command, but that was not his exodus. On the contrary, for him the exodus of faith was his entrance into Nineveh. This was a journey beyond the safety of the past, a far cry from Tarshish, that appealing, anonymous commercial city, the city where he would be in peace (except that he never managed to get there). This was dropping all his set speeches and self-justifications, as he came in from the outside and proclaimed God's message, stranger though he was. He came out of seclusion to put himself at the heart of that world. In Nineveh at the entrance to the king's palace—it was there that this stranger, coming so absolutely from another world, setting himself down after that exodus in the heart of the world he had invaded, it was there—at the center and far, far away—that he was able to pronounce the radical word. And in this world, in these times we have nothing else to say, faith has nothing further to say, than "Yet forty days . . ." And now, men and women of faith, of faith as weak as mine, prepare yourselves for the exodus, for the time is coming.

Index